Ancient Battle
Formations

Ancient Battle Formations

Justin Swanton

Pen & Sword
MILITARY

First published in Great Britain in 2020 by
Pen & Sword Military
An imprint of
Pen & Sword Books Ltd
Yorkshire – Philadelphia

Copyright © Justin Swanton 2020

ISBN 978 1 52674 006 9

A CIP catalogue record for this book is
available from the British Library.

Typeset by Mac Style
Printed and bound in the UK by TJ International Ltd,
Padstow, Cornwall.

Pen & Sword Books Limited incorporates the imprints of Atlas,
Archaeology, Aviation, Discovery, Family History, Fiction, History,
Maritime, Military, Military Classics, Politics, Select, Transport,
True Crime, Air World, Frontline Publishing, Leo Cooper, Remember
When, Seaforth Publishing, The Praetorian Press, Wharncliffe
Local History, Wharncliffe Transport, Wharncliffe True Crime
and White Owl.

For a complete list of Pen & Sword titles please contact

PEN & SWORD BOOKS LIMITED
47 Church Street, Barnsley, South Yorkshire, S70 2AS, England
E-mail: enquiries@pen-and-sword.co.uk
Website: www.pen-and-sword.co.uk

Or

PEN AND SWORD BOOKS
1950 Lawrence Rd, Havertown, PA 19083, USA
E-mail: Uspen-and-sword@casematepublishers.com
Website: www.penandswordbooks.com

Contents

Foreword

by Paul Bardunias

Interest in ancient warfare stems from a wide variety of sources. Many scholars will look for much needed context for examinations of ancient cultural development, while others will seek to understand the human experience of warfare itself. So much of the material culture that has survived from lost cultures involves depictions or possessions of warriors and warfare, that interpretation demands an understanding of how they were used. Outside of academia, there are those who seek to broaden their understanding of ancient warfare as recreational wargamers, live action role players, and reenactors. The study of ancient cultures may now draw upon the diverse pool of talents that those interest groups possess. Alongside the traditional philologists and archaeologists, we see contributions from wargamers like Phil Sabin and, as reenactors have morphed into experimental archaeologists, input from those who have worn plausible recreations of panoply and marched in formation with others, like Christopher Matthew and myself. Ancient Battle Formations seeks to synthesize the understandings of warfare seen through different viewpoints in a way that allows the development of testable hypotheses.

Most ancient authors were warriors themselves or immersed in the warrior culture of their day and expected their audience to bring the knowledge of a similar experience to the understanding of their works. No living student of history can meet this requirement.

Understanding the military of lost eras requires a reconstruction of warfare in its original context, but most scholars have no military experience and those that do earned it in the context of early modern and modern warfare, at a time when huge conscript armies required extensive drill based on dehumanization and need for discipline as much as the tactical requirements of a battlefield. We can work to build context through analogy with cultures of similar technological levels for whom we have better records of warfare. Hans Van Wees' focus on warriors of the New Guinea highlands as analogy for Homeric combatants challenged a paradigm of massed warfare in early Greek hoplites, while a focus on Renaissance arms manuals has shown a wealth of information on the handling of spears and pikes.

Regardless of the source of information, be it first-hand experience in modern warfare or analogies from other warrior cultures, a means of filtering what is plausible from what is not is needed. Much of the fine detail in our understanding of the physics and mechanics of weapons use and the movement of large masses of men has been based on what authors find intuitively plausible. The scientific process is designed to test the veracity of intuition, to falsify notions that seem reasonable until tested. Experiments, simulations, and the analysis of the physical properties and limitations of weapons and armor provide data that can be used to falsify hypotheses put forward and establish an accurate view of warfare in the ancient world. Experimental archaeology and historical martial artist recreation are a source for learning the limits of period-accurate technology and determining how a human body makes use of weapons and how masses of warriors coordinate movement. While we can never prove with surety that we have an accurate view, we can winnow away views that demonstrably fall short of what is possible for human physiology and groups of humans.

This book aims to take the surviving manuals on battle formations, as laid down by ancient tacticians like Asklepiodotus, Aelian, Arrian, and Vegetius, and test them against the descriptions of ancient battles, as well as modern experimentation in order to create context for a more accurate translation and understanding of the terms and tactics presented. By applying these concepts to a broad sample of cultures in the ancient world, we can see within this volume the evolution of tactics over time. This approach also compares different tactical systems in a manner that allows us to build analogies between them and broaden the base of our primary information about warfare in ancient societies. Novel experiments, as well as those of previous authors, are used to form a new understanding of the tactics brought to the field by ancient armies. Crucially, many original ideas are presented as hypotheses that can be tested and falsified. Each question is analyzed with the intention of bringing as many fields of study to bear on the topic as possible. This "combined arms" approach promises to provide insight into the battlefields of the past that has thus far eluded us.

Introduction

1. Method

It's surprising how little hard data we really have on the military history of Antiquity. Everything we know from the primary sources about the functioning of the famous Roman *Triplex Acies* for example can be printed on half a sheet of paper. Everything we know about the details of the second Persian campaign into Greece comes from a single author, Herodotus.

Archaeology and numismatics adds something to the primary sources, but not much. We are not even sure of what the spearhead and butt (or sauroter) of a sarissa looked like and archaeology tells us nothing about how the sarissa was wielded in battle. Most of what we know about the events of those times, as opposed to the art, architecture or burial practices, comes from written sources. And the written sources can sometimes be terribly sparse.

This is especially true of battle formations. With the exception of the authors of the three Hellenistic military manuals from Antiquity that have survived – Arrian, Aelian and Asklepiodotus – plus the author of the Roman manual, Vegetius, most writers in that period did not pay that much attention to the fine points of the structure of an army (the Hellenistic manuals, frustratingly, deal only with the Seleucid army and Imperial Roman cavalry, whilst Vegetius limits himself to the Roman army, which to a large extent is his idealised conception of what it should be rather than what it actually was). Diodorus, who gives the most detailed description of the Battle of Chaeronea, does not even make it clear whether Alexander attacked the Theban Sacred Band on horse or on foot. Livy is the only author who spares a few paragraphs to describe how the famous line relief system of the Roman legion worked – he is the only one and this was the key component of the Roman army for six centuries!

To the sparsity of the primary sources is added the question of the reliability of those sources. This doubt proceeds from the scientific method of experimental investigation, which keeps an open mind on a hypothesis until repeated and verifiable experiments validate or refute it. Side by side with experimentation goes observation: using strictly controlled methods to add to the pile of raw data that can be experimented on. So we know more about the composition of Martian soil thanks to the Viking probes and their successors that went to Mars and collected samples (observation) which were then tested (experimentation).

The scientific method gradually increases our knowledge of the subject under investigation, and with that increase of knowledge comes an increased certitude about its nature and characteristics.

This works fine for chemistry, biology or physics, but with history there's a catch: the great bulk of raw data – the written record – is never going to increase. Most of what we know about the past comes from those written records and it's pretty much out of the question that we will discover a substantial cache of books from the past that fill in all the details we want filled. So collecting new data is effectively out.

But it gets worse. These written records, and this is important, *cannot be subjected to scientific experimentation*. We're dealing with human testimonies, hence we can never, ever, acquire scientific certitude about whether Greek hoplites practised *othismos*. We take the authors on trust, a trust not built on scientific verification, but on a human assessment of their reliability. Are they internally consistent? Does what they say look objective or does it smack of propaganda? Do they agree with other sources we deem reliable, especially if these sources are independent? Is what they affirm physically impossible? And (occasionally) does what they affirm correspond with the archaeological and numismatic record?

Is there any other context in which we form our judgments this way? There is one: a trial. Law courts allow the testimony of witnesses, sometimes even hostile witnesses, as evidence that may tip the final verdict. The witnesses are cross-examined to see if what they say is consistent or contradictory and their testimony is compared to that of other witnesses and any hard evidence the court might have. But very often the verdict is determined substantially on the word of witnesses from which the judge or jury form a *moral certitude*, i.e., a certitude free of reasonable doubt. And this certitude is enough to sentence a man to life imprisonment or death.

Moral certitude is an important concept and it will play a large part in this book. Along with moral certitude goes the concept of *probability*. Probability means we can't be morally certain about something, but we can form a conclusion about it which is more likely than other explanations and – in the absence of conclusive proof – the one most worth holding. Finally there is *plausibility*, which means an explanation that isn't the most likely since no other explanations are available, but which makes good sense in the context of what we know. Through this book I will present conclusions based on proofs that will fall into the category of morally certain, probable or plausible. It will be up to the reader to decide how convincing these arguments are.

Separating scientific certitude from moral certitude has one other consequence in my approach to the primary sources. The scientific method considers any affirmation as not proven until established beyond doubt by observation and experimentation. A scientist approaches his subject matter with a preliminary agnosticism: he forms a working hypothesis to give direction to his research but a hypothesis by its nature is not certitude.

In a court of law it works a bit differently. The testimony of a witness is accepted as trustworthy unless it can be discredited by internal inconsistencies or contradictory evidence. If what a witness says is coherent and doesn't contradict other known facts it will be taken as true. There are of course cases in which such testimony is in fact wrong and can lead to the innocent being convicted, but these occurrences are generally rare exceptions in a functioning legal system that is designed precisely to prevent this from happening.

When examining the primary sources I will take the same approach. I start by accepting what they say as true and then test their affirmations for internal consistency, agreement with other primary sources and whether they accord with factual data from archaeology and other disciplines. If what they say holds up, I will accept it. This will evidently make for something of a controversial book.

One final – and crucial – point about the sources: it is essential, given how little the ancient authors actually treat the topics covered in this book, to understand exactly what they are saying. This introduces the problem of translations. The art of translation is to find the nice balance between transliterating a primary source author word-for-word from the Greek or Latin into English, which can make him difficult or impossible to understand, and paraphrasing him in an English that is good but does not accurately convey his meaning. The latter problem is made worse if the translator does not grasp what the writer is trying to say. Ancient authors, like contemporary authors, often assume their readers will understand the terms they use and leave out clarifications they take for granted their readers already know. If translators in a distant, post-apocalyptic technology-free age read that 'John pressed the light switch and it gave him a shock', how would they interpret it? That John was surprised by the light switch? When reading the ancient texts it is crucial to come to an accurate understanding of every word in them. Get one critical word wrong and the whole comprehension of a passage can be substantially skewed – something which in fact has happened several times. I will be giving examples of this throughout the book.

2. An Overview of Battle Formations

Warfare in Antiquity was completely unlike modern warfare. The most conspicuous difference being that in time of war soldiers in the ancient world hardly ever fought. A full-blown modern war is an ongoing business: there is a front line that can be shelled, bombed and assaulted from one day to the next. Troops are repeatedly subject to fire and in constant danger of being killed. There is little they can do about it except hunker down in their trenches or fortifications and pray it will pass and leave them alive. Most soldiers manage to cope, more-or-less, though a significant percentage may be affected by shell-shock or PTSD. But this kind of psychological trauma does not, by and large, stop them from functioning as soldiers. At the outset of World War I shell-shock affected as much as 10 per cent of British officers and 4 per cent of the British army's rank and file, but by 1917, after working out that a few days' rest was the most effective way of treating incipient shell shock, figures were down to 1 per cent, and three quarters of those returned to active service. After several months of attacking and being attacked, if a soldier hasn't already cracked there is not much that can mentally push him over the edge.

Modern soldiers also never see more than a fraction of the enemy. Each side's forces are spread out over a front hundreds of miles wide. Local fighting is small-scale: one company attacks another; both have some artillery and perhaps air support, but the individual soldier never feels he is confronting the entire enemy army.

Two thousand years or more ago it was a very different story. In time of war a soldier might serve in the army without ever experiencing a battle, or experience only one, two or maybe three. And when he marched forward with his unit on to the battlefield he could see the totality of the enemy arrayed before him in a line sometimes kilometres long. Such a spectacle, combined with his inexperience, could inspire only one emotion in him: sheer terror.

The business of his own army was to counteract that terror and the business of the enemy was to take advantage of it. Battle formations and their corresponding tactics had two purposes: give each constituent soldier the conviction his formation could protect him, and convince the other side that their formation could not protect them.

Plutarch describes how Phocion led an Athenian army against a Macedonian force that had landed on the Athenian coast at Rhamnus and had occupied the adjacent territory. Once the two armies had formed up for battle one of Phocion's infantrymen got a little too sure of himself.

> After he had drawn up his men-at-arms, one of them went out far in advance of the rest, and then was stricken with fear when an enemy advanced to meet him, and went back again to his post. 'Shame on you, young man,' said Phocion, 'for having abandoned two posts, the one which was given you by the general, and the one which you gave yourself' – *Life of Phocion*: 25

The reckless soldier runs ahead and then loses his nerve when an opposing soldier comes forward to meet him in single combat. But once back in line he is prepared to fight (with a good dose of healthy shame to egg him on).

How does a formation give confidence to the individual who is part of it? By assuring him that he has only **one** opponent to worry about – the single enemy soldier in the opposing formation that will actually be in front of him when the two battlelines meet. A typical soldier could handle a one-on-one fight, that is, he could handle it if it was conducted in a way that was not too much for him. This brings up another aspect of ancient warfare. Unlike the popular portrayals in movies like Braveheart, 300 and the like, foot melee combat was not a wild, free-for-all affair. Infantry fights could sometimes go on for hours, which necessarily implied moments of sparring followed by periods of breaking off to rest, as no man can hack away at his adversary with a sword or jab furiously at him with a spear for hours without respite. The actual fighting part of melee combat was in short bursts, in which each soldier fought one opponent, from behind the cover of a shield and protected on his flanks and rear by his formation that kept its line intact. His resolve was further stiffened by the fact that with at least seven ranks (often more) of fellow soldiers behind him, he could not cut and run if the mood took him. If his formation looked like it could stand firm, he would stand firm.

On average, so long as a formation held together during a fight, it lost surprisingly few soldiers, about 5 per cent or so. This represents less than half the men in the front rank only of a typical infantry line 8 ranks deep. A formation was not beaten by sheer attrition – unlike modern warfare – but by the men losing confidence in its ability to defeat the enemy. Battlefields in Antiquity were confused places: dust, noise and the close-packed ranks and files made it impossible for any individual soldier to know the big picture. He was aware only of his immediate surroundings: his own situation and that of the men next to him.[1] Nonetheless he could pick up signs that things weren't going well: a sudden sound of fighting at the flank or rear of the line where there shouldn't be any fighting; the perception that his companions around him (and possibly he himself), could not cope with the enemy; or simply a surprising event – an unexpected noise, the appearance of fresh enemy troops to his front, or something similar, that rattled his sense of what was expected and hence what his unit could handle.

As Napoleon put it:

In all battles a moment comes when the bravest troops, after having made the greatest efforts, feel inclined to run… Two armies are two bodies that meet and endeavour to frighten each other; a moment of panic occurs, and that moment must be turned to advantage. When a man has been present in many actions, he distinguishes that moment without difficulty.

This loss of confidence was practically instantaneous. It worked like a telegraph, spreading through the ranks like lightning. The moment the men lost trust in their formation it dissolved and fled. It was at this point that the real killing started. Infantry or cavalry in pursuit would cut down the fleeing troops, inflicting losses up to 15 per cent, 20 per cent of the enemy army, or even more. If the enemy was surrounded it could be cut down to the last man. But, barring an encirclement (where the encircled army had no choice but to fight), the battle was always decided by the first side that lost its nerve.

The most effective formations in the ancient world were those that gave their soldiers the most confidence in their ability to successfully resist enemy attacks and inflict morale-shattering blows on the enemy in their turn. This raises the subject of troop types. The equipment of a soldier determined how he was to fight, and that often determined the kind of enemy soldier he was best suited to take on. As a broad rule, troop types in Antiquity could be divided as follows:

Lightly-armed skirmisher foot
These used weapons like bows, javelins or slings for ranged combat, and were not intended to engage in hand-to-hand combat. If charged by enemy foot, they were expected to be able to outrun them. They were vulnerable in the open when facing more mobile enemy cavalry.

Lightly armed medium foot
These were peltasts, essentially equipped to fight like skirmisher foot but capable of hand-to-hand combat at a pinch, especially against cavalry.

Massed archer infantry
These specialised in ranged combat like skirmisher foot, but were generally expected to be able to engage in hand-to-hand combat if necessary.

Melee infantry

These may have been equipped with ranged weapons like javelins, but were essentially meant to fight hand-to-hand against enemy troops. They usually carried shields and had some kind of protective body armour.

Lightly-armed skirmisher cavalry

These worked like skirmisher foot, but the additional speed of their horses meant they could operate against more heavily equipped enemy cavalry and still keep their distance from them.

Shock cavalry

These were cavalry who were expected to charge enemy formations, mounted or foot, but were not usually expected to stand and fight enemy infantry in hand-to-hand combat as the mounted rider would then be at the mercy of surrounding infantrymen. If a charge did not succeed, they needed to break off quickly to avoid annihilation.

In addition to these general troop types, there were a few specialist types, among the better known of which are *cataphracts*, *chariots* and *elephants*. Cataphracts were mounted troops of which both the horse and the rider were well-armoured, enabling them to both charge and fight enemy infantry when immobile in hand-to-hand combat.

Chariots came in two kinds: light chariots, for example Gallic chariots which were the means of transport of Gaulish nobles. Lightly-constructed, they were used as a missile platform and a speedy means of getting the noble warrior to and from the battlefield. They were not generally meant to charge into enemy troops though they could do so.

Chariots of the Fertile Crescent, used by the Sumerians and other armies of that region up to the Achaemenids, were generally more heavily built. They served both as missile platforms and shock weapons, charging into enemy formations to break and scatter them. Some, like the Achaemenid chariots, were equipped with scythes on the axles to inflict more damage when ploughing into the ranks of enemy infantry.

Elephants were the ultimate shock weapon of the ancient world. Meant to terrorise and break up enemy infantry, and disperse enemy cavalry by terrifying the horses, they were effective provided the elephants themselves were not driven into a panic, something which Roman armies in particular became very adept at doing.

Not every army possessed all these troop types and a formation was usually not expected to be able to stand against all of them, but those it habitually encountered it did have to be able to engage or at least avoid if it was to survive on the battlefield.

A specific troop type could be good at fighting one kind of enemy troop type and bad at a fighting another. A general worth his salt played a game of scissors-paper-stone with the enemy, matching each type against a suitable opponent and doing all he could to ensure that a unit's weakness was not exploited by an enemy unit capable of taking advantage of it. A general who ignored this rule paid the price.

In 391 BC a Spartan army moved into Corinthian territory and occupied the Corinthian port of Lechaeum. Leaving a garrison of infantry in the port, the Spartan commander Agesilaus marched on with the rest of his army. Part of the garrison at the port consisted of men from the city of Amyclae, who asked to return home to take part in a religious festival. The garrison commander decided to escort the Amyclaeans home with a force of Spartan hoplites, passing close by the walls of Corinth. He wasn't concerned by the Corinthian and allied force in the city, convinced they were thoroughly cowed.

Corinth was allied to Athens who had sent an Athenian force to Corinth under Iphicrates and Callias. The two Athenian generals saw the Spartan *mora* of 600 men march past the city unprotected either by cavalry or skirmisher foot. Iphicrates led his peltasts out of the city and shadowed the Spartan column, showering them with javelins. The Spartans charged the peltasts but without success: the more lightly armed and armoured peltasts were easily able to outrun the Spartan hoplites. Eventually the Spartans withdrew to the sea and, when they saw Callias' Athenian hoplites approaching from the city, they ran into the waves to the boats sent from Lechaeum to rescue them. In all, the Spartans lost 250 men killed for no recorded loss by the peltasts. Stripped of the protection supplied by skirmisher foot or cavalry, the Spartan infantry were helpless.

Less important than matching appropriate troop-types was the effect of terrain. By and large terrain did not play a decisive part in most battles of this period for the simple reason that an army usually was able to engage its enemy only on terrain both sides felt suitable, and that generally meant flat and open ground. An army could always refuse battle and march away since deploying into lines for battle from a march column or a campsite took time, more than enough time for the enemy to decamp and get clear. Only occasionally was an army able to use ground that gave it a crucial advantage, as did Leonidas at Thermopylae, where a Greek force of 7,000 hoplites successfully held off a far larger Persian army for three days, thanks to a pass only 50 yards wide at its narrowest point, with steep mountain slopes on one side and the sea on the other. The Persians, unable to make proper use of their numbers, were forced to send their troops forward in 50-yard wide groups against a foe whose arms, defensive armour and tactical formation made them the unequalled masters of close-quarter combat in that age. The hoplites worked their way through the Persians like a meat grinder, only finally losing when they were outflanked by a Persian force that used a goat track round the mountain.

But this was rare. Battles by and large depended on the general arranging his different categories of troops into formations that made the best use of their inherent strengths whilst ensuring those formations were matched against enemy units they could manage, keeping them away from enemy units they were ill-equipped to handle and protecting them from modes of attack they could not cope with.

In this book I will start with an overview of the structure and performance of the formations described in the Hellenistic manuals and then use that data to examine those formations that proved the most successful in Antiquity and mastered the battlefields of their time – a mastery which lasted for centuries. Summing up everything written above, these formations were outstandingly good at fulfilling one or more of the following needs:

• make the individual soldiers feel well protected from the outset by their unit,
• ensure each individual soldier clearly understood his place and function within the formation, minimising confusion and disorder,
• ensure the soldiers did not lose confidence in their unit's ability to withstand and eventually overcome the enemy,
• inflict an effective blow against the enemy unit guaranteed to demoralise and rout it.

The period covered by this book ranges from the second Persian invasion of Greece to the end of the Principate in the 2nd century AD. This was the time when the appearance of new formations and military doctrine had the most dramatic impact on warfare. One can argue that from the 3rd century AD, armies did not consist of anything significantly new until the invention of gunpowder, and just refined or remixed what had already existed for centuries. In any case to cover the late Imperial period onwards would really need another book (or books).

I will look at the three formations, all of them infantry, that ruled the battlefield in this era:

- the Greek hoplite phalanx
- the Macedonian phalangite phalanx
- the Roman *Triplex Acies*

I had considered including one other formation that for a brief period played a decisive role in winning battles – the Macedonian cavalry wedge. Its prominence on the battlefield however lasted only during the campaigns of Alexander the Great, and the heavy cavalry of the Successor states proved much less crucial to the outcome of a battle, which now depended by and large on the performance of the pike phalanx. Understanding just how Alexander's lance-armed Companions were so effective is difficult as there is simply too little material in the primary sources to be able to formulate more than a best-fit hypothesis, and the purpose of this book is to prove how the outstanding formations of Antiquity worked, not how they might have worked.

The formations dealt with here of course cover only a small percentage of all the formations used in this period, but these were the battle-winners. Not that they always won their battles; generalship, troop quality and unexpected factors like ambushes all helped to make the battlefield an uncertain place for even the best organised and equipped army. But, all things being equal, these formations dominated the others of their era and their success led to widespread imitation.

Note

1. 'By day certainly the combatants have a clearer notion, though even then by no means of all that takes place, no one knowing much of anything that does not go on in his own immediate neighbourhood' – Thucydides: *The Peloponnesian War*: 7.44.1.

Chapter 1

The Fundamentals of a Formation

1. Introduction

The point and purpose of a formation is twofold: to induce and permit a collection of individuals to operate as a unit of soldiers and to allow each man to make an effective contribution for minimal outlay of energy. A formation achieves this by conferring orientation, familiarity and security on its component individuals and by maximising the damage-producing front presented to the enemy while minimising the damage-vulnerable aspect of each individual.

Essential qualities of the formation are: 1) the ability of its men to move together without haste, delay or confusion; 2) the effective concentration of a unit's weaponry on its forward aspect; 3) maximising the effective protection of its men; and 4) providing sufficient basis for confidence to keep the men facing the enemy and fighting.

Practically the only detailed information we have on the military formations of Antiquity comes from four sources: the Hellenistic tactical manuals of Asklepiodotus, Aelian and Arrian, and the Roman manual of Vegetius (the *Arthaśāstra* of Kauṭilya gives useful additional information on chariots).

Asklepiodotus is the earliest of the three Hellenists. It is generally supposed that he was a pupil of the philosopher Poseidonios (Ca. 135–50 BC), whom he used as the source for his manual. Poseidonios was a Macedonian who lived in the Seleucid Empire, and Asklepiodotus' *Ars Tactica* describes the Seleucid military system, itself an amalgam of Macedonian and Persian military doctrine, evident from the reference to elephants and chariots along with detailed descriptions of the structure of the Macedonian phalanx.

Next in order of time is Aelian. His tactical manual was dedicated to the Emperor Hadrian (117–138 AD) though initially begun for Trajan. Aelian gives a list of sources he used to compile his manual among which the name of Asklepiodotus is conspicuous by its absence. The similarities between the two manuals makes it evident Aelian drew from Asklepiodotus, but since Asklepiodotus himself drew from Poseidonios whom Aelian cites as a source, it is possible Aelian viewed Asklepiodotus' manual as essentially Poseidonios' own work.

Arrian, probably born in Nicomedia between 85 and 92 AD, was a contemporary of Aelian. He had a brilliant military and political career as *legatus Augusti pro praetore* of Cappadocia. In 135 AD he had the responsibility of repulsing a threat by Sarmatian Alans and prepared a plan for his army of which the text survives, but there is no proof a battle actually took place. The following year he wrote his manual, probably to commemorate the 20th year anniversary of Hadrian's reign. His work reproduces and paraphrases parts of Aelian's *Tactics*.

These three authors are not copies of each other, but together give a clear and fairly coherent picture of how infantry and cavalry units were organised and structured, and how they adopted different formations best suited to different situations and needs. Strictly speaking they apply to the Seleucid and to a lesser extent the Roman army, but the principles they contain were equally relevant to any organised army that preceded the invention of gunpowder – and even, in many respects, to armies for centuries afterwards. The three tacticians divide an army into the following categories:

1. **Infantry**, which subdivides into heavy infantry, light skirmisher foot and peltasts. Heavy infantry is infantry that is equipped essentially for hand-to-hand fighting. Light skirmisher infantry usually had no shields or protective armour, and was equipped with ranged weapons like slings, javelins and bows. They were meant to engage enemy from a distance, and flee if charged. Peltasts were an intermediate type, equipped with javelins as their primary weapon but also possessing swords and a shield but no body armour. They could engage light and intermediate cavalry and could outfight light foot. Against heavy foot they limited themselves to ranged missile attacks, fleeing if charged.

2. **Cavalry**, which subdivides into armoured heavy cavalry, light skirmisher cavalry, and lance- or javelin-armed intermediate

cavalry. Armoured heavy cavalry were cataphracts, with both horse and rider covered in protective armour, and capable of engaging heavy infantry in hand-to-hand combat. Light skirmisher cavalry were unarmoured and used ranged weapons like javelins and bows as their primary weapon. They would limit themselves to ranged combat, evading if charged. Intermediate cavalry came in different kinds, and could be armed with javelins and lances, capable of both ranged combat and charging into contact with enemy, but not meant to fight heavy infantry in a static melee.

3. **Elephants** used for war were of two kinds, the Indian, distinguishable by its smaller ears and different head configuration, and the African. While a few African savannah elephants were fielded by the Ptolemaic army at Raphia in 217 BC, the bulk of African elephants were those of a smaller breed more easily obtained, trained and transported. The relative docility and tractability of this smaller species was important for transportation by sea, often a major consideration for Ptolemies and Carthaginians alike.

   The typical war elephant took years to train, and was trained to seize, tusk and trample opponents. Indian elephants were also taught to throw a man seized by the trunk, but Hellenistic armies considered this to be superfluous.

   Elephants were very hard to kill. Alexander's army at the Hydaspes fought against Porus' elephants for much of the day, seriously wounded many of them, but there is no indication that they managed to kill a single one until the battle was effectively over.[1] Similarly, there is no mention of elephants being killed at Zama in 202 BC, and in battles like the Metaurus, where the Carthaginian army was wiped out, about half the elephants survived, those slain having been killed by their drivers when they stampeded. Elephants could nevertheless be wounded and the pain of wounds could send them into an uncontrollable frenzy. One rampaging elephant sufficed to put a stop to Pyrrhus' pursuit of the Romans at Heraclea in 280 BC. In order to protect elephants against being wounded, they were often given protective drapes and housings and sometimes full metal armour. Armoured or otherwise, they were always most vulnerable from the rear, and for this reason were often accompanied by light infantry whose task was to support them and to prevent opponents working round to the elephants' more vulnerable sides and back.

Elephants carried a fighting crew of two to four men (sometimes more), often housed in a tower or howdah carried on the elephant's back. These would be armed with bows and/or javelins; in Hellenistic armies one crewman might carry a pike as a final means of discouraging enemies who were attempting to hamstring the elephant or stab its sensitive rear area. In combat, the elephant would do most of the killing, trampling down opponents by main force while seizing occasional men with its trunk or trying to put a tusk through them. Elephants were also useful for breaking down gates of fortified camps and cities.

4. **Chariots** were predominantly of the two-wheeled, two- to four-horse variety. The chariot was the premier weapon of the biblical era, a kingdom's strength often being measured in chariots. Chariot crews were the most highly-trained of their nation's armed forces, and were usually kept on permanent establishment.

All chariots had a driver, and although it was possible to be a driver-warrior, some Pharaohs being depicted crewing their chariot alone, with the reins about their waist for managing the horses and thus leaving their arms free to use a bow, the typical chariot had a fighting crewman who was usually a javelinman or an archer, while some had an additional shieldbearer or shieldbearers.

Chariots, like elephants, were intended primarily as formation-breakers, but unlike elephants, which tended to apply themselves to the periphery of the opposing formation and gradually break their way through it, chariots customarily undertook to break the enemy formation with a single decisive charge. The charge would be decisive only if the enemy being charged lacked sufficient resilience and depth to stand against the chariotry, so chariots were reliant upon their foes being either apprehensive or demoralised. Chariotry was customarily used in massed formations.

Following these categories, I will use the Hellenistic manuals as a guideline in understanding the fundamental characteristics of a formation, be it foot, mounted or elephant. Vegetius will be used to round out the picture. Let me start with heavy infantry.

2. Heavy Infantry – Organisation

The list of formations given above contains diverse troop types that worked in very different ways, nevertheless it is possible to pick out general principles that governed how a formation moved and fought and in consequence how it was structured.

When a body of men come together to fight hand-to-hand – which was the proper mode of combat for heavy foot – the two groups tend to flatten out into two lines with little or no intermingling. One sees this in battles between Russian football supporters (where the police are often conspicuous by their absence). A good example can be seen here: https://www.youtube.com/watch?v=g-GplRfIq6A

This is natural. A human being who fights another human being fights in one direction – to his front – and as part of a crowd he will want his two sides and rear protected, which is best achieved by forming a line. He will also want to fight at odds no worse than one-to-one, also taken care of by forming a line.

The file

A line is hardly a formation as such, just the natural result of two groups of men who collide in combat. What is characteristic of infantry formations and square mounted formations is the use of **files** to form a line. Files were initially the smallest combat units on the battlefield and are described in some detail in the manuals. They generally varied in size from eight to sixteen men:

> It is necessary, first of all, to divide the phalanx, that is, to break it up into files. Now a file is a number of men dividing the phalanx into symmetrical units, and by 'symmetrical' I mean those which do not interfere with the fighting efficiency of the phalanx. Accordingly some have formed the file of eight men, others of ten, others of twelve, and yet others of sixteen men – Asklepiodotus: 2 (cf. Aelian: 4)

> Some make the number of the file ten, others add two to the ten, some even make it sixteen. Let our deepest one be at sixteen. The latter is proportionate to the formation's length, the phalanx's depth, both for shooting arrows and for throwing spears from the

lightly armed of those standing in formation. If it is necessary to double the depth to thirty-two men, the formation will [still] be proportionate. If the length is set at eight in front, the phalanx will not be entirely depthless. But if you wish to extend the phalanx at eight to four, it becomes depthless. – Arrian, *Tactics*: 5

Each file was composed of a file leader (*lochagos* in Asklepiodotus[2]) who was the first man in the file and the one who did the actual fighting. Behind came the other members of the file with the file-closer (*ouragos*) – the file leader's second in command – at the end, whose job was to ensure the file remained straight and prevent any of the troops in the file from taking the option of early military retirement (see Diagram 1).

Diagram 1: The file, showing the *lochagos* and the *ouragos*.

Each individual soldier of a file was also either a 'front-man' (*protostates* in Asklepiodotus) or a 'back-man' (*epistates*).[3] The file leader would be the first front-man, the man behind him a back-man, the third man in the file a front-man, the fourth man a back-man, and so on, to the last man of the file, the file-closer, who was always a back-man.

Initially a file was the most basic unit in an infantry formation, but later on it was split into half-files (*hemilochion* or *dimoiria*) and finally quarter-files (*enomotia*).[4] These half and quarter divisions were necessary to enable the formation to perform the manoeuvre known as doubling (see below) and, possibly, to facilitate marching in column.

The Line

Files were placed side-by-side to create a complete line with uniform depth, the file leaders adjacent to each other to form a continuous front:

Now when one file is placed beside another, so that file-leader stands beside file-leader, file-closer beside file-closer, and the men in between beside their comrades-in-rank [*homozygoi*], such an

arrangement will be a formation by file [*syllochismos*], and the men
of the files forming the same rank, front rank men, and rear rank
men, will be called comrades-in-rank because they stand side by
side. – Asklepiodotus: 2.4

According to the manuals a complete line of heavy infantry consisted of
1,024 files each with 16 men forming the three tacticians' ideal phalanx
of 16,384 men.[5] 1024 is chosen as the number of files because it is
divisible by 2 all the way down to 1. Each half-division was a distinct
sub-formation with a separate name and a separate commander, at least
in theory. This enabled the general to create a unit of any size composed
of an appropriate number of sub-formations, or, if he preferred, to
choose, for ease of control, the sub-formation that most suited his needs.

    Why a line 1,024 files wide? Wider lines were possible and indeed
used on occasion, but one sees here an interesting correlation between
Macedonian and Roman infantry lines. The Republican Roman
Consular army of four legions arranged in three lines of Hastati,
Principes and Triarii had a similar width. Each legion deployed
200 yards wide giving a total frontage of 800 yards.

    The only intact Roman version we have of a military manual in
Antiquity is *De Re Militari*, composed at the end of the 4th century AD
or early in the 5th. Its author, Publius Flavius Vegetius Renatus, appeals
for a reform of the Roman army along the lines of its excellence – or
as Vegetius imagined its excellence – in the early imperial period. His
book has a number of anachronisms, for example attributing the use of
plumbati to Republican infantry, nonetheless his elements of Roman
army organisation, tactics and weaponry are accurate enough once put
in the right chronological place.

    For Vegetius, a line of infantry should be no wider than 1,656 yards
wide with one yard per file:

One thousand paces contain a single rank of one thousand six
hundred and fifty-six foot soldiers, each man being allowed three
feet. Six ranks drawn up on the same extent of ground will require
nine thousand nine hundred and ninety-six men. To form only
three ranks of the same number will take up two thousand paces,

but it is much better to increase the number of ranks than to make your front too extensive. – *De Re Militari*: 3

A Roman pace was about 1.48 metres or 4 feet 10 inches (the Roman foot being slightly shorter than an English foot). Each file would then have slightly less than three feet but near enough as no matter. For Vegetius, a frontage of 1,656 yards was preferable for an army of 10,000, 20,000 or 30,000 men, the larger army deploying in greater depth rather than in too wide a frontage:

> But if the field of battle is not spacious enough or your troops are very numerous, you may form them into nine ranks or even more, for it is more advantageous to engage in close order than to extend your line too much. An army that takes up too much ground in front and too little in depth, is quickly penetrated by the enemy's first onset. After this there is no remedy. – *Ibid.*

This is a description of a late Roman army deployed in a single line. It would seem that this was about the limit that infantry could deploy and still manoeuvre as a single body under the control of the general, probably because visual or vocal commands could not be perceived at a greater distance. An order to advance would be understood by one section of the army but not by the other that was too far away, resulting in part of the infantry moving forwards whilst part remained in place, creating a gap in the line the enemy could exploit. At the Battle of Cannae the Romans fielded two double Consular armies for a total strength of 80,000 heavy infantry, but rather than deploy twice or four times as wide the Roman general Varrus chose to deploy in much greater depth, allowing Hannibal to stretch his outnumbered infantry and overlap the Roman line with his African veterans.[6] Command limitations were the single most important factor in how wide infantry could deploy (Hannibal, with a better-trained and more battle-experienced infantry, could not only deploy wider but also execute envelopment manoeuvres that were beyond the raw Roman recruits).

There was another reason for fixing the number of files at between 800 and 1,600. Trained professional armies of this period rarely exceeded 30,000 men, for the simple reason that this was about as large as an army could be and cover a reasonable distance from campsite to campsite in a single day. It was for this reason that Napoleon split his Grand Armee into corps of 20,000–30,000 men on average that marched separately and united to fight a battle. Presuming half a 25,000 man army was line infantry, if deployed 1,200 yards wide it would form a line about 10 ranks deep which generally was as deep as it needed to be – capable of absorbing an enemy attack whilst most of the ranks kept order and morale intact.

It is commonly assumed that armies in Antiquity kept to roads or tracks and marched in columns as wide as the road or track available to them. The Roman Empire built an extensive network of roads for military use. Most authors affirm that the Roman infantry marched 6 abreast,[7] however many Roman roads were wide enough only for a column 4 abreast to march at a comfortable spacing of three feet per file. And where there were no roads usually the best an army could hope for would be tracks wide enough for a cart, allowing the infantry to march two abreast only. The minimum spacing between ranks of a column to allow the soldiers to march without obstructing each other is about 4 feet. At two men per rank, the infantry file alone would stretch for nearly 15km, which would more than double if the cavalry, support personnel and baggage were added. This is impossibly long.

Gary Brueggeman, in his online study of the Roman marching column, calculated the baggage train for a single legion to be at least 2km long.[8] A Consular army of 4 legions (over 20,000 infantry plus cavalry and support personnel) would have a baggage train more than 11km long. Brueggeman estimates that such an army, marching in a single column at 2.76mph or 4.44km/h, could cover 16km in a day, with 8 hours between the departure of the vanguard from the original campsite to the arrival of the rearguard at the new campsite, leaving them time to care for the pack animals, repair equipment, cook meals, scout the area, forage for food, firewood, restock water supplies, drill and relax.

This however assumes that the infantry march 6 abreast. If, as was often the case, they had only a track allowing them to march 2 abreast, then the distance the army could cover in a day would be reduced to 6–8 km. Clearly something is wrong here.

The tacticians give the answer. None of them affirm that an army necessarily kept to the road it was travelling along, quite the opposite:

> The transportation of the baggage is a matter of the utmost importance and requires the responsibility of a special officer. Baggage is conveyed in five various ways: it may move ahead of the army; it may follow behind the army; it may proceed **on one flank or the other**; or it can proceed in the centre, **surrounded by troops**. – Aelian: 50

Asklepiodotus gives a variety of formations the army could adopt whilst marching: advancing in lines, oblique lines, curves, squares, half-squares, and multiple columns.[9] When his phalanx marched in column the files now formed the ranks, i.e. creating a column 16 men wide – far wider than the widest road. The Macedonian and Seleucid infantry at least were accustomed to marching off-road, sometimes in highly structured battle formations.

Vegetius confirms the need to march off-road in order to protect the baggage:

> The flanks of the baggage, exposed to frequent ambuscades, must also be covered with a sufficient guard to secure them. – *De Re Militari*: 3

The baggage itself remained a single unit, most probably keeping to the track or road as wheeled vehicles would have difficulty in advancing cross-country. Hence it was the baggage, with the addition of a vanguard and rearguard that determined the minimum length of an army on the march.

A baggage train 11km long, with perhaps an extra kilometre for van- and rear-guards, advancing at 4.44km/h,[10] could cover 35.52km or 22 miles in 8 hours.

Vegetius describes how far Roman infantry were expected to march in a given time period:

> The first thing the soldiers are to be taught is the military step, which can only be acquired by constant practice of marching quick

and together. Nor is anything of more consequence either on the march or in the line than that they should keep their ranks with the greatest exactness. For troops who march in an irregular and disorderly manner are always in great danger of being defeated. They should march with the common military step twenty miles [30km] in five summer-hours, and with the full step, which is quicker, twenty-four miles [35.5km] in the same number of hours.
– *De Re Militari*: 1

This distance had to be covered in full kit and the infantry practised it regularly:

It was a constant custom among the old Romans, confirmed by the Ordinances of Augustus and Hadrian, to exercise both cavalry and infantry three times in a month by marches of a certain length. The foot were obliged to march completely armed the distance of ten miles from the camp and return, in the most exact order and with the military step which they changed and quickened on some part of the march. – *Ibid*.

These marches were not confined to roads but took place cross-country, in good and bad terrain:

They made these marches not in plain and even ground only, but both cavalry and infantry were ordered into difficult and uneven places and to ascend or descend mountains, to prepare them for all kinds of accidents and familiarize them with the different manoeuvres that the various situations of a country may require.

Leaping is another very necessary exercise, to enable them to pass ditches or embarrassing eminences of any kind without trouble or difficulty. – *Ibid*.

Notice that these are one-day training marches, without the baggage accompanying the infantry and at an optimal speed of 6km/h, but the distances accord nicely with how far an army of about 30,000 individuals could march in a single day at a slower speed to match that of the baggage and to prevent excessive fatigue when on a long campaign march that included setting up camp and other duties.

If Roman infantry were habituated to marching off-road why then the Roman roads? Three reasons. Firstly the baggage would be able to move at maximum speed without being held up by muddy tracks or difficult terrain.

Secondly, a smaller force could keep both its troops and baggage on the road and advance at maximum speed, covering a reasonable distance each day without unduly fatiguing the troops. This would be useful for a rapid redeployment of forces within Roman territory where there was no need for flank guards to protect the baggage.

Thirdly, the Roman roads were all wide enough to accommodate a wagon-wide baggage train whilst leaving at least half the road free for cavalry or messengers to move rapidly along the column. This would be necessary if an enemy was near, enabling the general to send orders quickly to the different segments of his column and move cavalry with speed to threatened points.

The larger the army, the longer the baggage train and the shorter the distance the army could cover in a day. This is because the tail end of a longer baggage train would leave the camp only much later in the day and hence have less time to cover ground before having to stop for the night.

An army of 60,000 men with the vanguard, baggage and rear guard forming a hypothetical column about 25 km long would be able to cover about 10 km in one day, presuming the baggage advances along a road or track in a single column. A problem arises when considering very large armies, such as the enormous hosts of the Achaemenid Persian Empire. Most modern authors reject the numbers given by the primary sources, nonetheless their own figures often remain very large. Modern estimates of the Persian army at Gaugamela go up to 120,000 men. Such an army would not be able to travel more than about 5km in a day. One wonders how it would manage to cover any significant distance during the campaign season and not strip the countryside to keep itself fed. Without going into detail which is beyond the scope of this book, if such an army advanced across a broad front, over terrain that had been cleared in advance of obstacles that would obstruct the progress of troops and baggage, it could cover as much distance per day as a smaller army.

Returning to the organisation of an infantry line, the arrangement into files lined up side-by-side served a number of purposes which we will look at now.

One thing an individual needs when in close-quarter combat is **fighting space**: this means width but also depth.

The fighting man needed enough width to be able to use his weapons freely, but not so much width that he could be attacked simultaneously by several enemy troops more closely-arrayed than him.

In 371 BC a Spartan army of 10,000 infantry and 1,000 cavalry under the command of the Spartan king Cleombrotus invaded the territory of the Boeotian League. The Spartans had the best hoplite troops in Greece and the Boeotian general Epaminondas resorted to a new tactic to overcome them.

Greek armies habitually deployed their elite troops on the right of their line to take advantage of a Greek phalanx's natural tendency to drift to the right. The elite troops, i.e. the best-trained troops, facing fresh air, would be able to execute a left wheel and envelope the left of the enemy line, routing it. Regular citizen hoplites lacked the training to execute this left wheel.

Epaminondas anticipated this and deployed his best infantry and cavalry on the *left* of his line, with the added provision that his Theban troops deployed unusually deep. This part of the line was to advance towards the Spartan elite which faced them and smash it, whilst the rest of the line hung back, waiting to engage only once the mass of Theban hoplites had rattled the enemy by seeing off their best troops.

As the Boeotian line advanced towards the Spartans, the Spartan general Cleombrotus realised what they intended to do and ordered the Spartan right to extend its line rightwards, with the intention of enveloping the Thebans – whose depth meant their formation was not very wide – and smash them. To the left of the Thebans however (or possibly behind them) was the elite unit of Thebes, the 300-man Sacred Band, put there precisely to prevent this from happening. According to the manuals, an infantry line would widen itself by the files increasing the space between themselves, and then having half of each file composed of followers move into the newly vacated space to take its place alongside the half of the file composed of leaders, a process known as doubling:

> The width of the phalanx is doubled by number when the frontage of the formation, consisting of 1,024 files, is changed to 2,048 files, by moving a proper number of 'back-men' [*epistates*] into the intervals between the files. – Aelian: 28

The commander of the Sacred Band, Pelopidas, saw the Spartans commence this manoeuvre and ordered an immediate charge. The Sacred Band ran towards the Spartans and caught them in mid-manoeuvre, files widening but with the newly-opened gaps between the files not yet wide enough to accommodate the followers. The Sacred Band, able to fight the Spartans in the front rank at nearly 2 to 1 odds, wreaked havoc among them:

> In the battle, while Epaminondas was drawing his phalanx obliquely towards the left, in order that the right wing of the Spartans might be separated as far as possible from the rest of the Greeks, and that he might thrust back Cleombrotus by a fierce charge in column with all his men-at-arms, the enemy understood what he was doing and began to change their formation; they were opening up their right wing and making an encircling movement, in order to surround Epaminondas and envelop him with their numbers. But at this point Pelopidas darted forth from his position, and with his band of three hundred on the run, came up before Cleombrotus had either extended his wing or brought it back again into its old position and closed up his line of battle, so that the Lacedaemonians were not standing in array, but moving confusedly about among each other when his onset reached them. – Plutarch, *Pelopidas*: 23

Files were an easy way of regulating space, since the entire spacing of the line depended on the spacing the file leaders adopted, i.e. files kept the spacing in a line uniform, a necessary feature for several reasons which will be seen below.

Generally, the space allotted to each file corresponded fairly closely to the width of a shield. This enabled the soldiers to combine their shields into a solid wall of protection, giving enemy weapons no access to them except over the top of the shield rims.

As important as width was depth. One sees this need for depth in all forms of melee weapon duelling.

Have a look the following examples:

Fencing:
https://www.youtube.com/watch?v=fqZJtCLLFdk

Rapier fighting:
https://www.youtube.com/watch?v=W2q40nsbXZE

Sabre fighting:
https://www.youtube.com/watch?v=n5w2Mh6CyXo

Longsword fighting:
https://www.youtube.com/watch?v=5zueF4Mu2uM

Polearm fighting:
https://www.youtube.com/watch?v=GSJgPVQJGyk

Polish spear fighting:
https://www.youtube.com/watch?v=mYf6FHbA04M

Masai spear fighting:
https://www.youtube.com/watch?v=HGz8uhuHmRc

Quarterstaff fighting:
https://www.youtube.com/watch?v=TMjsHE5p2vs

The common denominator of all these contests involving different weapons used in very different ways is the duellists' need to be able to give ground when necessary, especially when receiving an attack by their opponents' weapon. A duellist who cannot move backwards is at an immediate and serious disadvantage.

A typical file had about three feet between the centre point of each man of the file which allowed the front man a certain amount of give when fighting his opponent:

Now, a Roman soldier in full armour also requires a space of three square feet. But as their method of fighting admits of individual motion for each man – because he defends his body with a shield, which he moves about to any point from which a blow is coming, and because he uses his sword both for cutting and stabbing – it is evident that each man must have a clear space, and an interval of at least three feet both on flank and rear, if he is to do his duty with any effect. – Polybios, *Histories*: 18.30

Note that Polybios' three feet is measured from the centre point of a legionary to the centre point of each legionary beside him and the legionary behind him, which gives the spacing shown in Diagram 2.

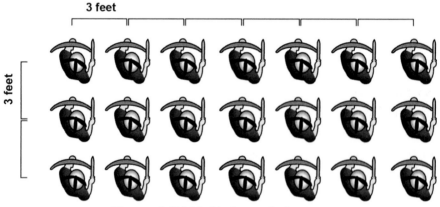

Diagram 2: Polybios' legionary deployment.

It is often assumed that Polybios's legionaries each occupied a width of 6 feet since he affirms that one legionary faced two phalangites in battle and each phalangite occupied a space of 3 feet. This however arises from a misunderstanding of *Histories*: 18.29 which is commonly rendered as follows:

Many considerations may easily convince us that, if only the phalanx has its proper formation and strength, nothing can resist it face to face or withstand its charge. For as a man in close order of battle occupies a space of three feet; and as the length of the sarissae is sixteen cubits according to the original design, which has been reduced in practice to fourteen; and as of these fourteen four must be deducted, to allow for the distance between the two hands holding it, and to balance the weight in front; it follows clearly that each hoplite will have ten cubits of his sarissae projecting beyond his body, when he lowers it with both hands, as he advances against the enemy: hence, too, though the men of the second, third, and fourth rank will have their sarissae projecting farther beyond the front rank than the men of the fifth, yet even these last will have two cubits of their sarissae beyond the front rank; if only the phalanx is properly formed and the men close up properly both flank and rear

And then a little later:

The result of this will be that each Roman soldier will face two of the front rank of a phalanx.

So three feet plus three feet equals six feet. The phrase 'three feet of space' is interpreted as three feet of width, which means that for Polybios a close-order phalanx corresponds to the intermediate order of the tacticians, clearly a contradiction.

But what exactly is Polybios saying? The phrase 'space of three feet' translates the Greek: ἐν τρισὶ ποσὶ – *en trisi posi* – literally 'in three feet'. What do the three feet refer to? The answer lies in the passage that follows this phrase. After establishing the three feet distance, Polybios goes on to do some maths. A sarissa is 14 cubits (21 feet) long – a cubit being about 1½ feet. Of the 14 cubits, only 10 project in front of the phalangite's grip. This allows one to calculate how many ranks would have their sarissa project past the front rank. The answer is 5 ranks, with the sarissa of the 5th rank projecting 2 cubits past the front rank men.

But something is missing from the equation: the distance between each rank. Without that factor it is impossible to calculate how many ranks can bring their sarissas to bear beyond the front of the phalanx. Polybios gives that distance. Where? When he states that a phalangite in close order occupied three feet (or 2 cubits), that is, three feet of *depth*. With that figure the maths is easy: 10 cubits minus 2 cubits (4th rank) minus 2 cubits (3rd rank) minus 2 cubits (2nd rank) minus 2 cubits (front rank) = 2 cubits of sarissa projecting ahead.

Polybios indicates the width occupied by the phalangite file when he mentions that the phalanx is in 'close order'. Each file of a close order phalanx occupies a frontage of one cubit, or about 1½ feet, as described by the tacticians. Hence a Roman soldier occupying a space three feet wide will face two phalangites in close order and ten sarissa-points along with them.

Does Polybios affirm that Roman soldiers occupied a frontage six feet wide? To reproduce the passage from Livy quoted above:

> Now, a Roman soldier in full armour also requires a space of three square feet. But as their method of fighting admits of individual motion for each man – because he defends his body with a shield, which he moves about to any point from which a blow is coming, and because he uses his sword both for cutting and stabbing – it is evident that each man must have a clear space, and an interval of at least three feet both on flank and rear, if he is to do his duty with any effect. – *Histories*: 18.30

The phrase 'a Roman soldier in full armour also requires a space of three square feet' translates the Greek: ἵστανται μὲν οὖν ἐν τρισὶ ποσὶ μετὰ τῶν ὅπλων καὶ Ῥωμαῖοι – *istantai men oun en trisi posi meta ton hoplon kai Romaioi*. Word for word: 'they stand so then in three feet with arms also the Romans'. Or in better English: 'So the Romans also occupy three feet when in arms.' The 'also' refers back to the three feet of depth occupied by the phalangites, hence the meaning is that Romans ranks, like phalangite ranks, are three feet apart.

'It is evident that each man must have a clear space, and an interval of at least three feet both on flank and rear' translates the Greek: προφανὲς ὅτι χάλασμα καὶ διάστασιν ἀλλήλων ἔχειν δεήσει τοὺς ἄνδρας ἐλάχιστον τρεῖς πόδας κατ᾽ ἐπιστάτην καὶ κατὰ παραστάτην, – *prophanes hoti chalasma kai diastasin allelon echein deesei tous andras elachiston treis podas kat' epistaten kai kata parastaten*. Literally: 'Clear that looseness [i.e. not to be too tightly packed] and standing-apartness from each other need to have the men at least three feet in respect of those behind and those on the side.' In better English: 'Clearly the men need to be loosely arrayed and have space between each other – at least three feet to the men behind and the men on either side.'

One measures the three feet from which point to which point? There can be only two points that apply in all cases: from the midpoint of one file to the midpoint of an adjacent file, or from the midpoint of a rank to the midpoint of the rank behind it. This means in fact that each man occupies a space measuring three by three feet.

Getting back to the subject of fighting space, if the file leader gave way, the men behind him had no trouble falling back in unison, unlike a disorganised mob in which the front men would find themselves blocked by a mass of men behind them who would not know if they were supposed to give way or not with one front-rank fighter surging forwards and another seeking to recoil. This in fact is why surrounded infantry were invariably slaughtered. Pressed back against each other into a dense mob in which the spacing between files collapsed and the files themselves were no longer able to recoil, the file leaders were obliged to fight exactly where they stood. Their inability to yield ground against enemy strikes whilst the enemy could fall back against their own blows was a deadly handicap for which they had no remedy.

This ability to recoil by file gave an additional advantage to the file leader. If he fell back and his opponent advanced to meet him, the latter would find himself facing hostile enemies on three sides and would be quickly cut down. The formation supplied a refuge for a front rank fighter who was momentary outfought, enabling him to recover himself and get back into the fray without being overwhelmed by his adversary. There was however a limit to this kind of protection. If too many file leaders fell back, adjacent file leaders would become exposed in turn to attacks by neighbouring enemy files and would be obliged to give way themselves. This could precipitate a falling-back of the entire formation, which was often a prelude to panic as the men got the idea that their file leaders (supposedly the best fighters of their formation) could not cope with the enemy.

Quintus Sertorius was a successful Roman general and Governor of Spain. In the civil war between Marius and Sulla he sided with Marius and when Sulla gained the ascendancy Sertorius retired to Spain, which he held for several years against Pompey, Sulla's protégé. At the Battle of Sucro Sertorius defeated and nearly killed Pompey:

> When the fighting was at close quarters, it happened that Sertorius was not himself engaged with Pompey at first, but with Afranius, who commanded Pompey's left, while Sertorius himself was stationed on the right. Hearing, however, that those of his men who were engaged with Pompey **were yielding before his onset and being worsted**, he put his right wing in command of other generals, and hastened himself to the help of the wing that was suffering defeat.
>
> Those of his men who were already in retreat he rallied, those who were still keeping their ranks he encouraged, then charged anew upon Pompey, who was pursuing, and put his men to a great rout, in which Pompey also came near being killed, was actually wounded, and had a marvellous escape. – Plutarch, *Life of Sertorius*: 19.3–4

A line giving way before enemy was usually a precursor to defeat. A file leader might fall back briefly, but he would have to come back into the fight as quickly as possible to cover the men on his flanks. One point about the above example: Roman lines, of which there were habitually three, were meant to fall back one behind the other if they were being outfought by the enemy. In this case however something else was happening: the legion lines as a whole were giving way and the inability of any segment of those legions to hold the enemy in place was clearly a signal the legions were losing the fight. Sertorius had to do something.

Files also made it easy for the front rankers to be replaced the moment they were incapacitated, by the second man in the file simply stepping forward to replace the man in front making the protective line uniform once more.

File Spacings

According to the tacticians there were three spacings for infantry files: open order, intermediate order and close order:

> The needs of warfare have brought forth three systems of intervals: the most open order, in which the men are spaced both in length

and depth four cubits [about 2 yards] apart, the most compact, in which with locked shields each man is a cubit distant on all sides from his comrades, and the intermediate, also called a 'compact formation,' in which they are distant two cubits from one another on all sides – Asklepiodotus: 4.1

We will now examine the space allocated to the infantry in terms of both width and depth as there are three different proportions. In the first instance, the men are sometimes arranged in an open order when the situation calls for such a deployment. When so drawn up, each man occupies a space of 4 cubits. When arranged in an intermediate order, each man occupies 2 cubits and, when arranged in a close order, he occupies a space of 1 cubit. – Aelian: 11.

Here is a diagram (Diagram 3) of the different spacings: close order at the top, intermediate order below it and open order at the bottom (shield widths for the close and open orders correspond to Macedonian phalangites, and for intermediate order to Greek hoplites).

Diagram 3: Close, intermediate and open order spacing.

The open order is a natural disposition without a particular name. The other two orders are found only in a disciplined military context:

The interval of four cubits seems to be the natural one and has, therefore, no special name; the one of two cubits and especially that of one cubit are forced formations. – Asklepiodotus: 4.3

In an article published in the *Journal of Cross-Cultural Psychology*,[11] 8,943 people from various nationalities were tested to determine what distance they would be comfortable with when encountering strangers, acquaintances and family and close friends. The results were then plotted on graphs and showed a range of about 80–150cm for strangers with an average of 115cm. A man's average shoulder width is about 45cm. Add that to 115cm and you get 1.6m or 3.3 cubits. This tallies well with the 'natural' spacing of 4 cubits per file for an open order file, with the men in each file perhaps knowing each other but not being terribly familiar with the men in adjacent files.

It is also possible to establish an approximate open order by each soldier of the front rank stretching out arms such that his fingertips touch those of the man beside him. The width of a human arm span is approximately equal to his height, and since a man of that period had an average height of around 170cm, that would give a close enough approximation to 4 cubits (192cm) breadth.

A marching formation could advance in open order, two yards per file, the natural spacing of a crowd of men on the move, and which permitted the men to move around obstacles in their path. On the battlefield however, open order served another purpose: it enabled one unit to pass through another, or one unit to insert itself in the other, making use of the file-wide gaps in both cases. Asklepiodotus distinguishes between heavy infantry files inserted between heavy infantry files – *parembole* – and light infantry files inserted between heavy infantry files – *parentaxis*.[12] As seen earlier, a formation could widen itself by expanding its files laterally from intermediate order to open order and then having half of one file occupy the spaces between the files. This could be done either by the back half of a file moving up alongside the front half, or every other man of a file stepping sideways to form a new file. The latter enabled the new file to be formed alongside the old one very quickly. This is important as will be seen later.

Intermediate order, or one yard per file, was the standard disposition for battle. It corresponded to the width of the 3-feet-wide aspis, or heavy infantry shield, which was the gauge used by Greek hoplites to establish this width: when shields touched edge-to-edge the spacing was right (although Greek phalanxes contracted during their advance towards the enemy, ending up with their shields overlapping each other just before contact with the enemy). This spacing also worked for Roman Republican and Imperial infantry, whose oval or rectangular shields were about 2½ feet wide, leaving a slight gap between one shield and the next which allowed a legionary to move freely in combat.

There is a final interval of file spacing: close order. The only formation which adopted this order was the Macedonian phalanx and its successors, in which each file occupied a breadth of only one cubit or 48cm,[13] a little more than the average shoulder width of a man. This compression was possible only because the Macedonian phalangite used a smaller shield with a diameter between 64 and 76cm, with his elbow inserted in a central *ochanon* and his arm on the right side, making it possible for shields to overlap substantially on the left side.[14] In this formation two phalangites could fight one enemy soldier in intermediate order with predictable results. Provided it preserved its formation, there was nothing that could frontally beat a close-order phalanx except another close-order phalanx. It had to be outflanked or broken up by bad terrain first.

These three intervals also applied to the file's depth, or the spacing between ranks. A file that had adopted open order in depth had about two yards between the centre point of one man of the file and the centre point of the man in front of and behind him. This enabled men of another file to insert themselves in the spaces between the men of the first file to create a new file with twice as many men. It also allowed skirmisher troops space to use their weapons.

A file with an intermediate depth had about a yard between the centre point of each man of the file, which was sufficient to allow the men to use their melee weapons freely. The third spacing, close order, effectively meant the men of a file were so close together the shield of one man was pressed against the back of the man in front of him. This disposition was adopted following – or rather was the natural result of – the infantry tactic known as *othismos*, when the men of a file pushed against each other in an attempt to force the enemy back and break the cohesion of his formation.[15]

3. Heavy Infantry – Manoeuvres

The files with their intermediate and open order spacings permitted the infantry formation to execute a variety of manoeuvres. The manuals divide them into four categories: changing the formation's facing, countermarching, doubling, and insertion or interjection.

Changing the formation's facing

This was the means by which a formation was able to change the direction it faced by 90° increments, so as to face to its left, right or to its rear. There were two ways of doing this. The first way was simply for each individual soldier to turn toward his right: 'turn to the spear', or towards his left: 'turn to the shield.' The formation as a whole did not move or change shape. The kind of change of facing was easy and quick to execute, and was used in the heat of battle to counter an enemy attack against one's flank, or to attack the flank of an enemy formation oneself.

> Right- or left-facing, then, is the movement of the individual men, 'by spear' to the right, and 'by shield' – called in the cavalry 'by rein' – to the left; this takes place when the enemy falls upon the flanks and we wish either to counter-attack, or else to envelop his wing, i.e., overlap the wing of the enemy. – Asklepiodotus: 10.2

The second means was for the formation to wheel as a group around its left or right front corner so as to end up facing towards its left or right. When executing a wheel, the formation would close up first:

> It is a quarter-turn, when we close up the entire syntagma by file and rank in the compact formation and move it like the body of one man in such a manner that the entire force swings on the first file-leader as on a pivot, if to the right on the right file-leader, and if to the left on the left file-leader, and at the same time takes a position in advance and faces 'by spear' if pivoting right and 'by shield' if pivoting left. – Asklepiodotus: 10.4

Note the term 'syntagma' which Asklepiodotus uses to describe a unit composed of 16 files. The syntagma is the basic unit of manoeuvre since its width was equal to its length (the standard size of a Macedonian phalanx file being 16 men). The entire phalanx line could not wheel as a single entity. It had to do it by syntagmas where each probably used the other as a reference point, as shown in diagrams 4–9.

Diagram 4: Syntagma in line.

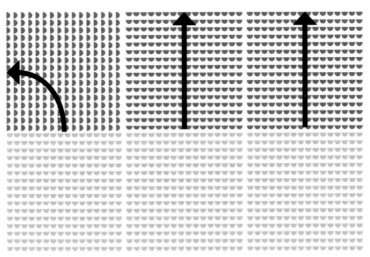

Diagram 5: The first Syntagma wheels left.

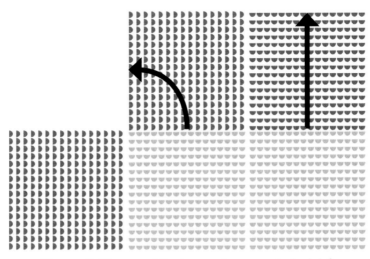

Diagram 6: The second Syntagma advances and wheels left.

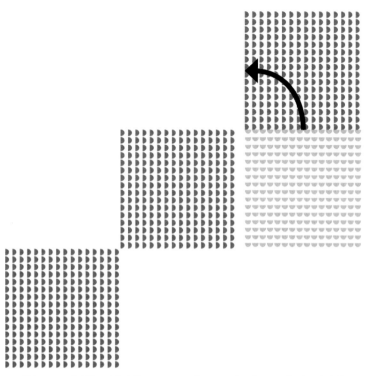

Diagram 7: The third Syntagma advances further and wheels left.

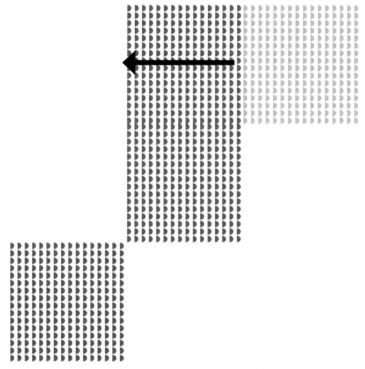

Diagram 8: The third Syntagma aligns with the second.

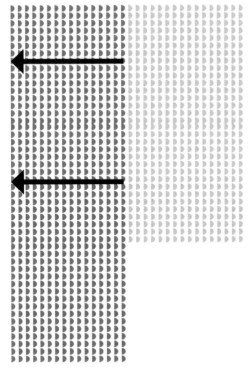

Diagram 9: The second and third Syntagma align with the first.

As is evident, changing the facing of an infantry line was a complex affair, and could be done only by well-trained regulars. Most Greek hoplite infantry were incapable of it and, in battle after battle, if one wing routed its opponents, it would simply pursue them straight ahead rather than wheel and roll up the rest of the enemy line.

A syntagma could execute a double-wheel to end up facing its rear or a triple-wheel to end up facing its flank: right if it wheeled left or left if it wheeled right. A triple-wheel to the right would leave it on the same line with its original position as opposed to a simple 90° wheel to the right, which would leave it further forward from its original position. This might be an important difference if the syntagma was looking to occupy the best terrain.

Countermarching
Countermarching was a manoeuvre that enabled a formation to change its facing by 180° whilst preserving the same order of men in each file,

i.e. the file leaders end up remaining in the front of each file whilst the file closers remain in the rear. This is different from each individual man turning about: in that case each file closer would now be in the front of a file whilst the file leader would be at the back – and the file leader was the best fighter in the file.

Countermarching required that the formation be in open order, with each file occupying a frontage of two yards, leaving a gap between one file and the next. There were three ways of executing the manoeuvre.[16]

Macedonian countermarch
Each file leader turns 180° to face towards his rear. The rest of the file then marches past him and takes up position behind him, ending up with the file facing the same direction as the file leader and in the same order behind him as it was originally (see Diagram 10).

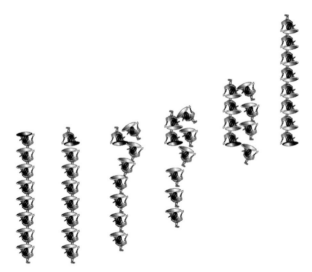

Diagram 10: The Macedonian countermarch.

There was one problem with the Macedonian countermarch. Countermarching was done, among other reasons, to enable a phalanx formation to face an enemy approaching it from the rear. When countermarching in this fashion, it gave the impression that the phalanx was retreating from the enemy, and impressions are everything in ancient warfare. This might hearten the enemy and convince them to attack with greater *élan*.

Laconian countermarch

To offset this, a formation could try the Laconian countermarch. With this method, each man in the file first turned 180° to face towards his rear. The file leader now found himself at the rear of the file whilst the file closer was now at the front. The file leader then marched down the gap between his file and the adjacent file, passed the file closer, and took up a position in front of him at the same distance he had occupied in the rear. The rest of the file followed the file leader and took up its new position behind him. When the manoeuvre was complete, the file closer now found himself at the rear of the file (see Diagram 11).

Diagram 11: The Laconian countermarch.

Choral/Cretan/Persian countermarch

There was a third option if the phalanx wanted to stay on the same ground it already occupied, and that was the Coral or Cretan or Persian countermarch. In this manoeuvre, the file leader marches down the side of the file. The second man in the file meanwhile advances until he stands on the spot originally occupied by the file leader. The rest of the file move up behind the second man. The file leader reaches the spot originally occupied by the file closer and stops, facing 180° away from the rest of the file. The second man in the file marches down the side of the file whilst the third man followed by the rest of the file moves up to occupy the position vacated by him. The second man takes his place behind the file leader and the third man marches down the side of the file, and so on until the file closer reaches the spot originally occupied by the file leader. He turns round and now the entire file is facing 180° from its original orientation whilst still occupying the same ground as before (see Diagram 12).

Diagram 12: The Choral/Cretan/Persian countermarch.

Countermarching could also be done by rank, i.e. swopping positions of the men at the wings with the men in the centre of the phalanx by moving them along the spacing between one rank and the next, with the ranks naturally in the open order spacing. This however took time, as the width of a phalanx was many times greater than its depth (about a kilometre in width for the ideal phalanx of 16,384 men envisaged by the manuals, as opposed to about 16 metres in depth). Which made it unwise to attempt it in proximity to the enemy who, seeing the switch taking place, could charge the formation before the manoeuvre was complete, catching the phalanx in a state of confusion before files were properly reformed.

Doubling

Doubling comes in two kinds, of which each kind has two further subdivisions, giving four kinds of doubling in total.

In the first kind the width and depth of the phalanx remain unchanged, but the files or ranks are doubled in number. Files are doubled in number by every even-numbered man (the 'back-man' or *epistates* in a file) stepping sideways into the space between the files to form a new file. This condenses open order files into intermediate order files, or intermediate order files into close order files. The spacing between the ranks is increased. The ranks could then close up to restore the previous spacing between them (see Diagram 13).[17]

Diagram 13: Doubling: the first method.

Aelian in describing this process does not recommend it:

> However, there are some who disapprove of doubling in this manner, especially when an enemy is close at hand, and choose rather to place the light-armed troops and the cavalry on the wings, so as to give the appearance of the phalanx being doubled, when, in fact, the phalanx remains as it was in its usual order. – *Tactics*: 28

The reason for this reticence is clear: the front-rank man of the newly-formed second file is neither a file leader nor as good a fighter as the file leader. Furthermore the original file will lose its file-closer – the man responsible for good order and fighting commitment of the file – as he moves across to form the last man of the new file. Both files' fighting ability is thus compromised.

There is however an advantage to this method of doubling. First, it can be done very quickly and secondly, it enables phalangites in intermediate order to form close order files whilst keeping their shields in front of them – an impossibility if rearward files were obliged to march down the spaces between intermediate-order frontward files. Doubling in this manner is useful then as an emergency manoeuvre in the heat of combat.

Rather than doubling files to form a close-order phalanx, Aelian recommends something different: the phalanx closes up its files, reducing its width.[18] Light troops and cavalry occupy the space on its flanks to compensate for the narrower frontage.

The manuals curiously enough do not mention doubling files by the rear half-files marching up alongside the front half-files, even though the existence of half-files as separate units with their own officers would suggest that this happened (see Diagram 14).

Diagram 14: Doubling by moving up rear half-files.

Aelian however does describe the reverse process: even-numbered files countermarching to the rear and taking up position behind odd-numbered files, which suggests this technique was also used to double the number of files.[19]

Ranks can also be doubled in number by a reverse process: one file joins another file next to it to become a new file with double the number of men of each original file. This is accomplished by men of one file inserting themselves between the men of another, effectively becoming *epistates* or the even-numbered men of the file. It requires that there be initially at least an intermediate spacing between the ranks of one yard per rank to permit the men to fit (see Diagram 15).[20]

Diagram 15: Doubling ranks.

The second kind of doubling increases the width or depth of the phalanx. Doubling by width happens when the files spread out laterally, from intermediate to open order or from close to intermediate order. This kind of doubling is often followed by a doubling of the number of files as described above, to bring the phalanx from open order back to intermediate order.

This doubling can also be achieved by the even numbered ranks countermarching to the flank (see Diagram 16).[21]

Diagram 16: Doubling by width.

Doubling by depth happens when the even-numbered files countermarch to the rear and take up station behind the odd-numbered files, creating new files with double the number of men and also double the original length (see Diagram 17).[22]

Diagram 17: Doubling by depth.

Insertion and interjection

Insertion (*parentaxis*) and interjection (*parembole*) are essentially the same thing. In the case of insertion, the files of a phalanx are in open order, and the spaces between the hoplite files are occupied by files of light troops: peltasts or skirmisher foot. You thus have a formation in which half the files are heavy infantry and half are light troops. Since light troops are half the number of heavy troops their files will have half as many men.[23]

Interjection is the same as insertion with the difference that heavy infantry files occupy the spaces between the files of a phalanx. In other words the phalanx consists of two heavy infantry formations intermeshed together.[24]

Only the best trained troops were capable of all these formation changes and manoeuvres. The average Greek citizen hoplite, for example, could form a line with files in intermediate order – shield rims touching – but could do little else. Only full-time professionals like the Spartans, the Theban Sacred Band, and the Macedonian and Roman infantry could execute wheels, countermarches and doublings. But the ability or inability to adapt one's formation to the needs of the battlefield and perform manoeuvres at crucial moments of the battle became increasingly important at time went by, eventually resulting in the massive and poorly-trained irregular armies of Spain, Gaul and the Fertile Crescent giving way to the much smaller professional forces of Macedonia and Rome.

4. Cavalry

Cavalry formations were all about shape. Unlike infantry, cavalry did not necessarily form up in files and ranks. They could form files without ranks, ranks without files, or have neither ranks nor files. Cavalry vs cavalry engagements were usually straightforward frontal affairs, but against infantry more care was needed. A cavalryman needed to keep moving when attacking foot soldiers as he was extremely vulnerable if his horse was brought to a standstill. Immobile in a body of infantry he would not last long as he was in an exposed position on his horse, surrounded by enemy on all sides and locally outnumbered. The one exception to this was cataphract cavalry. Both horse and rider were armoured and the horses were obliged to keep close together, presenting a solidly-protected front against enemy foot.

Cavalry formations came in three fundamental shapes: the rhomboid, the wedge and the square. Cavalry were mobile entities, meant to manoeuvre around infantry formations and either harass them from a distance or attack them in their vulnerable flanks or rears. But they were also capable of assaulting infantry frontally. Depending on how cavalry was intended to operate on the battlefield, it adopted the shape that best suited its purposes.

Square formation

The cavalry square was used by the Persians and Sicilians and, in a modified form, by the Greeks. The square has a number of advantages, the first being that it is easy to keep in alignment as it is composed of ranks and files, like the infantry. The riders simply had to keep behind the men in front of them in their file and stay alongside the men in adjacent files.

> The Persians, Sicilians, and Greeks regularly used the square formation since it can hold the squadrons in both rank and file. – Asklepiodotus: 7.4

> The Persians, the Sicilians and, generally speaking, the Greeks used square formations, being of the opinion that they were more easily formed and better suited to the easy preservation of the formation and general use. – Aelian: 18.5

There were other advantages to a square. In a charge, the best riders of the formation, the file leaders, would all contact the enemy at the same time, applying maximum shock effect:

> Additionally, in this form only, the experienced officers have the ability to charge the enemy simultaneously. – Aelian: 5.

> And alone of all these formations, all the leaders fall on the foes together. – Arrian: 16.

Another bonus was the ability of a square formation to break off easily from the enemy. Polybios in his *Histories*, when describing the frontage of the Greek cavalry at the Battle of Issus, gives each file a width of

2 yards, in other words, a cavalry file corresponds to an open order infantry file in terms of lateral space:

> At the most cavalry in a regular engagement is drawn up eight deep, and in the midst of [μεταξύ – *metaxu*] each of the squadrons there is need for a space equal to the fronts [of the squadrons] inasmuch as it is equivalent to [squadrons] wheeling [left/right] and caters for [squadrons] wheeling about [to their rear]. Therefore eight hundred will cover a stade [200 yards] of front; eight thousand, ten stades; three thousand two hundred, four stades; and so eleven thousand two hundred would cover the whole of fourteen stades [of the Greek cavalry]. – Polybios, *Histories*: 12.18.

It is worthwhile taking a little time to examine this passage. Generally it is interpreted as a line of cavalry that is split into separate squadrons with squadron-wide gaps between them, rather like the popular conception of the punctuated chequerboard lines of the Republican legion. The gaps allow the squadrons to wheel 180 degrees and retire through the spaces to their rear.

This interpretation means that each squadron with 100 horses in the front rank is only 100 yards wide with a gap also 100 yards wide to its right and left. This consequently means that each file of horses is only 1 yard wide – horses in adjacent files will be a only few inches from each other.

This poses all sorts of problems.

First, the horses, a foot or less apart, will be unable to turn individually in place, something which Asklepiodotus affirms they can do:

> Right- or left-facing, then, is the movement of the individual men, 'by spear' to the right, and 'by shield' – **called in the cavalry 'by rein'** – to the left; this takes place when the enemy falls upon the flanks and we wish either to counter-attack, or else to envelop his wing, i.e., overlap the wing of the enemy. – *Tactics*: 10.2.

Secondly, an entire mounted formation, the rhombus, becomes impossible as it is built around the ability of the horses to turn individually in place and face one of its four corners, enabling rapid changes of direction and movement.

Thirdly the squadrons will have exposed and vulnerable flanks, inviting an enemy to pour through the gaps and hit each squadron on three sides, a sure recipe for disaster.

Fourthly there is the difficulty of maintaining a continuous line of squadrons separated by large gaps that must be kept at the correct width at all times to enable the squadrons to wheel around into them if necessary.

What then to make of Polybios?

The key to understanding this passage is the word μεταξύ – *metaxu*, best rendered as 'in the midst of', with the possible meanings of 'between' or 'among', depending on the context. So taking another look at the passage:

> … and in *the midst of* [μεταξύ] each of the squadrons there is need for a space equal to the fronts [of the squadrons] inasmuch as it is equivalent to [squadrons] wheeling [left/right] and caters for [squadrons] wheeling about [to their rear].

There is need for *one* space in the midst of *each* of the squadrons. The implication is that the space is within the squadron. 'Space' translates διάστημα – *diastema*, which means a stretch or extension that may or may not be occupied by something. The three dimensions of an object – length, breadth and height – are signified by διάστημα.

This space is 'equivalent to' – δύνασθαι – *dunasthai* – the squadron 'wheeling to the right or left' – ἐπιστροφαῖς – *epistropsais*. δύνασθαι can also mean 'to be able to' but that does not fit this context as no formation needs space either within or next to it to be able to execute a 90 degree wheel. Furthermore using *dunasthai* in the sense of 'to be able to' comes out as 'the [squadrons] wheeling left/right to be able to' – do what? The Greek does not say and the clause is left hanging in mid-air.

Asklepiodotus affirms that when a formation executes a wheel it first contracts to close order:

It is a quarter-turn [*epistrophe*], when we close up the entire battalion
by file and rank in the compact formation and move it like the body
of one man in such a manner that the entire force swings on the
first file-leader as on a pivot, if to the right on the right file-leader,
and if to the left on the left file-leader, and at the same time takes
a position in advance and faces 'by spear' if pivoting right and 'by
shield' if pivoting left. – *Tactics*: 10.4

Closing up from open to intermediate or from intermediate to close
order halves the frontage of a formation. From this perspective, the space
required is equivalent to the wheeling squadron, not to the squadron
originally in line, and hence is half the width of the squadron before it
wheels. If there was no difference in width between a wheeling and a
stationary squadron Polybios would have had no reason for applying the
space specifically to the wheeling squadron.

So what Polybios in effect is saying is that when squadrons with 100
horses per rank are in line they are one stade (200 yards) wide. Within
that width there is enough space that when the squadron closes up to
a width of 100 yards this leaves a space next to it of the same width,
100 yards, that 'caters for [squadrons] wheeling about [to their rear]',
i.e. enables squadrons to wheel around and retire without bumping
into adjacent squadrons as would happen if they kept to their original
spacing (see Diagram 18).

The problem is solved if the horse files compact together before
wheeling, as in Diagram 19.

In conclusion, a cavalry force of 800 men deployed 8 deep with 100
cavalrymen in front rank will spread across the entire stade – 200 yards
– with each man occupying a frontage of two yards, or six feet. A horse
from nose to tail measures about 7 feet. The spacing will look as in
Diagram 20.

This is much looser than an infantry formation. Each horse that has
charged enemy can easily wheel and retire down the gaps between the
files, or the entire unit can face about simultaneously and break off.
When turning around, the horses will have a lateral space of 6 feet,
which is enough to avoid colliding with the horses in adjacent files (the
horses raise their heads when turning to shorten their body length). The

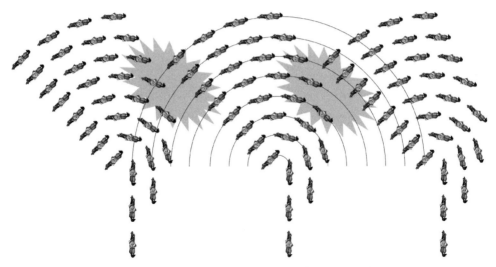

Diagram 18: Squadrons wheeling left in regular order.

Diagram 19: Squadrons closing up before wheeling

Diagram 20: Cavalry spacing.

square can remain in movement: charging infantry, breaking off and then facing about to charge again. The infantry never get the chance to grapple with individual horsemen.

> Indeed this formation is more easily deployed than any other, in that the riders, being deployed by row and column, it provides easier **attacks and retreats**. – Arrian: 16.

Besides wheeling as described above, breaking off can be done in one of two ways, by each horseman wheeling, generally to the right[25] so as to be covered by his shield, and moving back through the gaps between the files – effectively countermarching. This would especially suit a ranged missile attack, each rank coming within range of enemy infantry, throwing its javelins, then breaking off to allow the next rank to throw its javelins in turn (see Diagram 21).

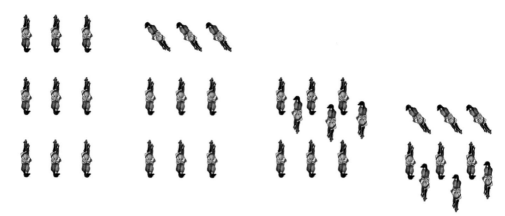

Diagram 21: Breaking off by countermarching.

Breaking off can also be done by all the horsemen turning about in place and the entire formation moving off. This would be appropriate for a charge that had not succeeded in penetrating or routing enemy infantry or cavalry (see Diagram 22).

Diagram 22: Breaking off by turning.

This raises a question: if a square cavalry formation can execute a 180 degree change of direction simply by countermarching to its rear then why does Polybios describe cavalry doing 180 wheels by squadron as described above? Wheeling is a much slower and more vulnerable procedure: a line of squadrons that retires by countermarching will be facing the enemy at all times whilst executing the manoeuvre. Wheeling squadrons need more time to complete the manoeuvre and present vulnerable flanks to the enemy whilst in the wheel.

One possible answer is that wheeling by squadron is a much more natural process for horses that tend to follow each other in the same direction, whilst countermarching involves horses moving in a direction opposite to the facing of adjacent horses, which goes against their grain. Hence countermarching requires better-trained horses than wheeling and cavalry may not always have that degree of training.

Squares came in two kinds. For the first kind the number of ranks matched the number of files, which in fact produced an oblong rectangle that was much deeper than it was wide given the length-to-width ratio of a horse (see Diagram 23).

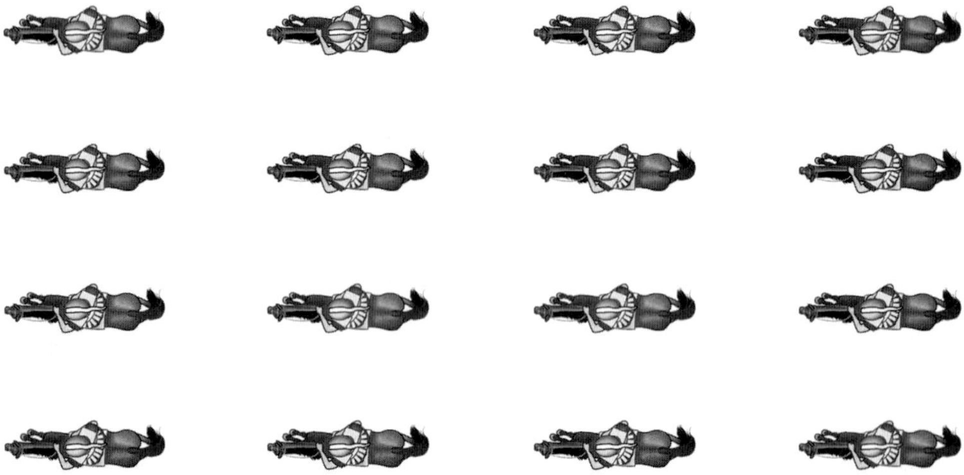

Diagram 23: Cavalry in 'square' with as many files as ranks.

The second kind was square in shape, which was accomplished by having more files than ranks: twice as many files as ranks or even three times as many files as ranks.

> … the Greeks modified the squadron formation by making it an oblong in mass, while giving it to the eye the appearance of a square. For they drew up the riders with a front of sixteen and a depth of eight, but they doubled the interval between the riders because of the length of the horses. And some made the number of men in length three times that of the depth and then tripled the interval in depth, so that it again appeared to be a square… − Asklepiodotus: 7.4

Diagram 24 shows a square with twice as many files as ranks. The distance between the riders in rank is twice that of the riders in file:

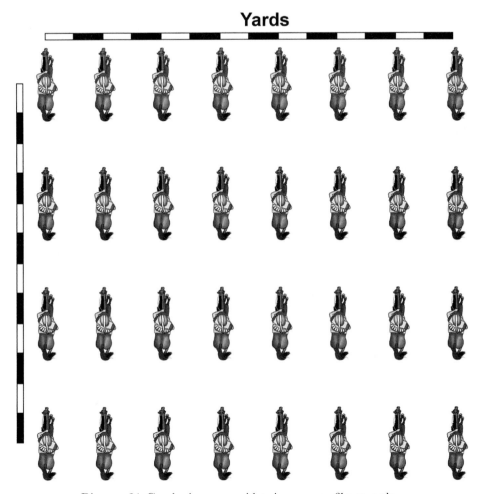

Diagram 24: Cavalry in square with twice as many files as ranks.

Diagram 25 shows a square with three times as many files and ranks, and with the rank spacings triple those of the file spacings. Notice that the distance between each rank allows for one rank to break off from the enemy whilst leaving enough distance for the next rank to get up the speed to charge into contact:

Yards

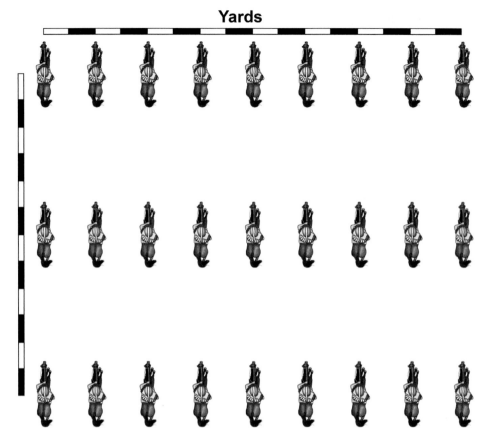

Diagram 25: Cavalry in square with three times as many files as ranks.

In this passage doubling the interval between the riders means that the riders themselves (not their horses) were twice as far from the men behind and in front of them as they were from the men in either side of them. This meant that in the doubling option, there were 4 yards between the bodies of each rider in a file, which meant about 2 yards between the nose of a horse and the tail of the horse in front of him. For the tripling process, the riders in a file were 6 yards and the horses 4 yards apart. This ensured the horses never came too close together. Unlike infantry, cavalrymen in rear ranks gave no support to cavalrymen further forward in the line. If the horses came in contact with each other it was likely to disrupt the formation:

Those following in the rear ranks in no way support the leaders as happens in infantry formation. The rear ranks do not contribute to how well and enemy charge is resisted, nor do they increase the momentum of those before them, nor close up with them, nor, holding on to each other, make a solid mass. If the leading files are pressed forward from the rear, the horses become annoyed, create disorder and are more likely to do harm to themselves than to the enemy. – Aelian: 18

The maximum recommended depth for a cavalry square that intended to engage in hand-to-hand combat with the enemy was 8 horses, though cavalry that engaged in ranged missile combat could deploy deeper, with more ranks to deliver a succession of javelins or arrows to the enemy.

Rhombus Formation

The rhombus, or diamond-shape, was originally used by Thessalian cavalry and later incorporated into the Macedonian army. Each corner of the diamond was occupied by an officer who could lead the entire squadron if its men faced left, right or to the rear. This meant the rhombus could change facing immediately and head off in a new direction by the simple expedient of each man turning his horse. This made the rhombus very agile on the battlefield, able to turn right or left or to its rear and, still in formation, attack enemy immediately. It was impossible to attack a rhombus in the flank since it could turn to meet a flank charge in a second or two.

It appears that the Thessalians were the first to use the rhomboid formation for their squadrons in cavalry fighting, and this with great success both in retreat and in attack, that they might not be thrown into disorder, since they were able to wheel in any direction; for they placed their crack troopers on the sides and the very best of these at the angles; and they called the man at the fore angle a squadron-commander [*ilarches*], the one at the rear angle a squadron-closer [*uragos*], and those on the right and left angles flank-guards [*plagiophylakes*]. – Asklepiodotus: 7.2.

The formation comes in four variants: a) with files and ranks, b) with files but without ranks, c) with ranks but without files, d) with neither files nor ranks.[26]

The first variant, with ranks and files, is shown in Diagram 26.

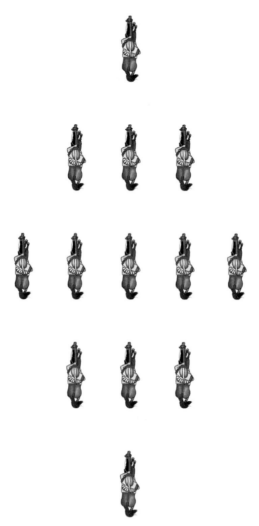

Diagram 26: Cavalry in rhombus with files and ranks.

Like the square, it had the advantage of being easy to maintain: the men in a file simply had to keep in line with the men in front of them and remain abreast of the men in adjacent files. When the rhombus turned right or left, the new files would need to increase in length to separate the horses from each other and also contract together to recreate the original shape (see Diagrams 26–29).

Diagram 27: The cavalry begin the turn.

Diagram 28: The turn is complete.

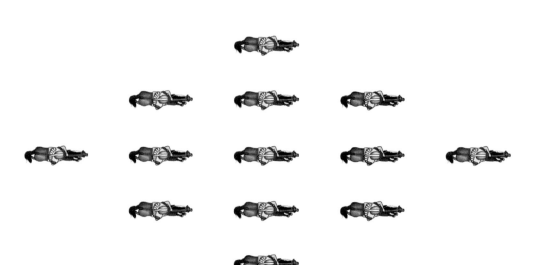

Diagram 29: The files contract and the ranks open out to resume original spacing.

The second variant, with files but without ranks, is shown in Diagram 30.

Diagram 30: Cavalry in rhombus, files but no ranks.

The flattened angle of the leading edge of the rhombus is due to the horses on either side of the lead horseman reaching to the shoulders of his horse, as described by Aelian:

When the leader of the troop [*ilarch*] is placed at the head of the formation, the next succeeding horsemen, on either side of him, ought not to form a rank behind the leader, but should be positioned so that the heads of their horses reach to the shoulders of the horse upon which the leader is mounted. To allow the men to preserve the due distance from each other, those that are posted on the right and left, and those positioned to the rear, should avoid the disorder that can arise in the case of the horses coming into close contact with each other; for some horses, vicious by nature, are apt to do harm to the soldiers and horses around it by bucking and rearing and turning about (due to its long shape) and by lashing out with its feet at the horses upon which the soldiers are mounted. – Aelian 19

Trying to create a perfectly shaped rhombus with this arrangement would leave the horses dangerously close to each other, as shown in Diagram 31.

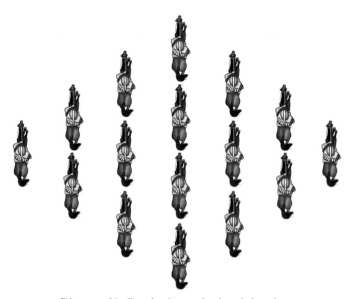

Diagram 31: Cavalry in overly closed rhombus.

When turning right or left, the horsemen would need to take a little care in reforming the files correctly before resuming the front-flattened diamond shape again (see Diagrams 30–35).

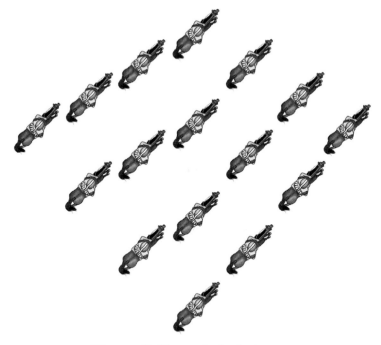

Diagram 32: The cavalry begin the turn.

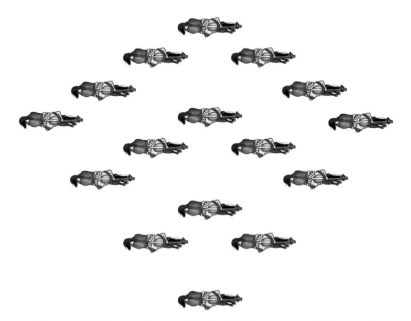

Diagram 33: The turn is complete, but the files are out of alignment.

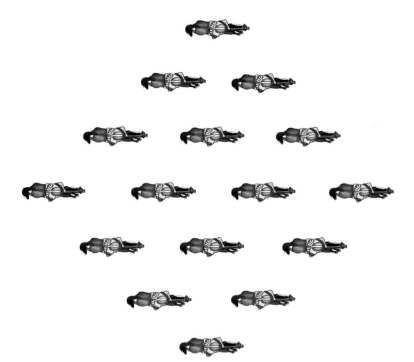

Diagram 34: Correcting the files.

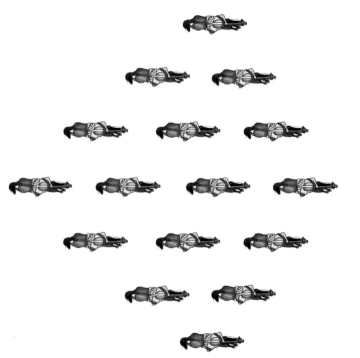

Diagram 35: The manoeuvre is complete.

This variant enabled the rhombus to charge an enemy unit with nearly the same simultaneous impact as a cavalry square.

The third variant, with ranks but without files, is shown in Diagram 36.

Diagram 36: Cavalry in rhombus, ranks but no files.

This rhombus was very narrow which gave it several advantages. The first was the ability to slip through tight gaps, either in terrain or in an enemy line. The second advantage was to convince the enemy the cavalry formation was smaller than its actual size and precipitate them into making a foolhardy attack:

[this rhomboid] narrowest along the forehead would be most useful if it were necessary to conceal the horsemen's depth so as to summon the foes out into disadvantageous boldness. – Arrian: 17.

The fourth variant had neither ranks nor files and looked as in Diagram 37.

This was the most flexible of the four variants. The horses have plenty of space for turning and the rhombus, virtually square in shape, needs very little adjustment once the cavalrymen have turned right or left.

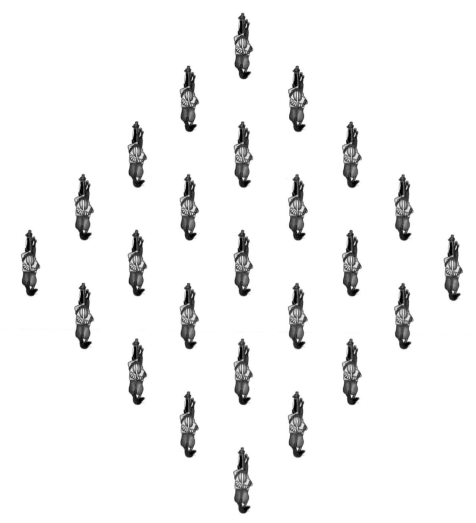

Diagram 37: Cavalry in rhombus, no ranks or files.

Wedge Formation

A wedge is effectively the front half of a rhombus. None of the manuals specify whether there were different kinds of wedges as there were rhombuses, but as they were based on the rhombus it is probable they varied in structure (see Diagrams 38–41).

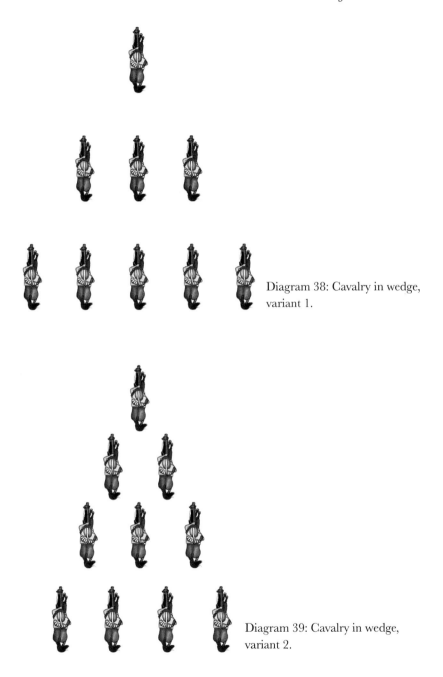

Diagram 38: Cavalry in wedge, variant 1.

Diagram 39: Cavalry in wedge, variant 2.

Diagram 40: Cavalry in wedge, variant 3.

Diagram 41: Cavalry in wedge, variant 4.

The principal advantage of a wedge is that it is the best configuration for breaking through an enemy formation:

It is said that the Scythians and Thracians invented the wedge formation, and that later the Macedonians used it, since they considered it more practical than the square formation; for the front of the wedge formation is narrow, as in the rhomboid, and the wedge is only half the size, and this made it easiest for them to break through, as well as brought the leaders in front of the rest, while wheeling was thus easier than in the square formation, since all have their eyes fixed on the single squadron-commander, as is the case also in the flight of cranes. – Asklepiodotus: 7.3

We hear that the Scyths especially have used wedges and, having learned from the Scyths, the Thracians. Even Philip the Macedonian trained the Macedonians to use this formation. The same formation also seems useful because its leaders are close together and its sharply broken off 'forehead' easily provides the means to cut through every enemy formation. – Arrian: 16

Why exactly is a wedge so apt for slicing through enemy units? To attempt to answer the question fully is beyond the scope of this book. One thing to notice for now is that, unlike a rhombus where the best riders (and fighters) were spread along all four sides of the formation, in the wedge they were concentrated on the two leading edges on either side of the front point, giving the wedge more effective combat-power when it hit the enemy.

Wedges do not change direction right or left like rhombuses, but wheel as an entire unit following the wedge leader. A wedge however is quite capable of countermarching in order to execute a 180 degree change of direction (see Diagrams 42–47).

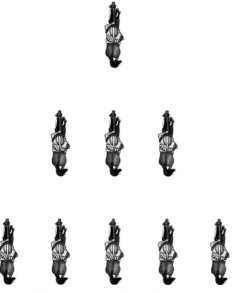

Diagram 42: Cavalry wedge, advancing.

Diagram 43: Cavalry wedge, the leader begins the countermarch.

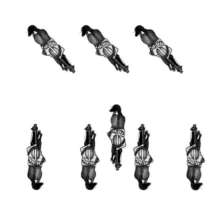

Diagram 44: Cavalry wedge, the second rank begin the countermarch.

Diagram 45: Cavalry wedge, the countermarching troops pass through the rear ranks.

Diagram 46: Cavalry wedge, the rear ranks begin to turn.

Diagram 47: Cavalry wedge, the countermarch is complete.

Mixed Cavalry/Skirmisher Foot Formation

One last configuration that proved effective especially against enemy cavalry was the mixed formation. This consisted of inserting light, missile armed infantry within the cavalry files, possible since there was a space of about 4 feet between one file and the next. This would have doubled the amount of missiles the formation could loose at the enemy, and further augmented its efficacy since a man on foot can cast a javelin or loose and arrow or slingstone harder and further than a mounted man in a sitting position. Furthermore, in melee combat a horseman in an all-cavalry unit would find himself confronting two opponents in a mixed formation – a cavalryman and a skirmisher foot, the latter ideally placed to kill or otherwise incapacitate his horse whilst he was kept occupied by his mounted opponent.

> The cavalry on the side of his opponents were disposed like an ordinary phalanx of heavy infantry, regular in depth and unsupported by foot-soldiers interspersed among the horses. Epaminondas again differed in strengthening the attacking point of his cavalry, besides which he interspersed footmen amongst their lines in the belief that, when he had once cut through the cavalry, he would have wrested victory from the antagonist along his whole line. – Xenophon: *Hellenica*: 7.12.

The ploy worked:

> At first they engaged in a cavalry battle on the flanks … as the Athenian horse attacked the Theban they suffered defeat not so much because of the quality of their mounts nor yet on the score of the riders' courage or experience in horsemanship … but it was in the numbers and equipment of the light-armed troops and in their tactical skill that they were far inferior to their opponents. – *Ibid*.

The mixed formation may have looked like Diagram 48, in which the skirmisher foot are safe from a charge by enemy cavalry and have plenty of space to wield their weapons.

Yards

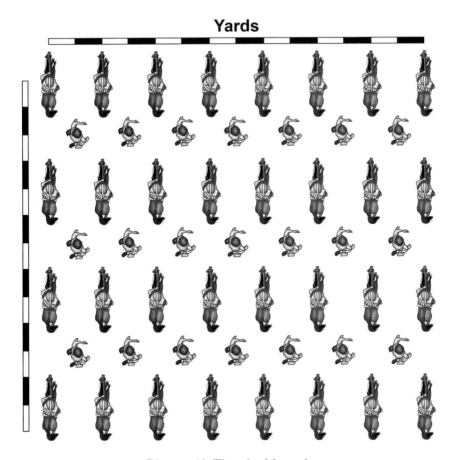

Diagram 48: The mixed formation.

Countermarching by cavalry is still possible since the skirmisher foot are able to insert themselves into the cavalry files, clearing the file gaps for the countermarching horses to pass, after which the skirmisher foot return to their original position and allow the horses behind them to move up. It would require co-ordination and training to accomplish.

5. Skirmisher Infantry

According to the Hellenistic manuals the light troops were ideally half as numerous as the heavy foot. They were organised much like the heavy infantry, having as many files, but with half the number of men per file. They were always positioned with heavy infantry, either before, behind or even within a heavy foot formation. When positioned before or behind the heavy foot they matched them file for file:

> The name and size of the various units of light troops are as follows [then a description of the various light infantry units] 8,192 men arranged in 1,024 files. – Aelian: 16

> Now these light infantry will also have 1,024 files, if they are to stand behind the phalanx of the hoplites and extend the same distance, without, however, a depth of sixteen men – for they are only one half as strong – but obviously of eight men. – Asklepiodotus: 6.2

> The light infantry and peltasts will be stationed by the general as the situation demands, sometimes before the line of battle, sometimes behind it, and on other occasions now on the right flank and again on the left; the first is called van-position [*protaxis*], the second rear-position [*hypotaxis*], and the third flank-position [*prosentaxis*]. Sometimes they are incorporated in the phalanx and stationed one beside each man; and this is called insert-position [*parentaxis*], because there is an insertion of different branches of the service, e.g., light infantry with hoplites – Asklepiodotus: 6.1

> Sometimes the psiloi will be positioned in the front of the line, while at other times they will be positioned behind the line, depending upon the tactical requirements of each situation. They may, for example, be formed in this manner: arranged into 1,024 files (the same number of files as are in the phalanx itself) they will, however, be positioned so that the first file of psiloi is directly behind the first file of the phalanx, the second file of light troops behind the second file of the phalanx, and so on. The files of the light infantry ought not to be sixteen men deep, but only half that number, namely eight deep. Thus, 1,024 files of light troops will contain 8,192 men – Aelian: 15

Protaxis [πρόταξις] describes the positioning of the light-armed troops in front of the armed infantry who make up the phalanx.

The repositioned light troops then assume the role of file-leaders, or *protostatae*. – Aelian: 30.

Why were light troops half as numerous as the heavies?

Two reasons. First, all the three types of skirmishers – javelinmen, archers and slingers – need plenty of depth to use their weapons. An archer at full draw has a depth of about four feet and so would require about six feet to remain clear of the men in front of and behind him. This also applies to a slinger and a javelinman. For Vegetius, all Roman infantry were trained to use javelins:

> Besides the aforementioned exercise of the recruits at the post, they were furnished with javelins of greater weight than common, which they were taught to throw at the same post. – *De Re Militari*: 1

The distance between ranks of Vegetius' infantry was 6 feet. This distance, double that of Polybios who described the intervals of Roman infantry when using their swords, gives the soldier the space to cast his javelin.

Secondly, great depth did not serve any purpose for skirmisher troops and, at least in the case of javelinmen, could dangerously limit the range of their weapons. A line of javelin 8 men deep at two yards per rank would be 16 yards deep. A line of 16 ranks would be 32 yards deep.

How far did ancient javelineers throw their javelins? In a study[27] by Steven Ross Murray, William A. Sands and Douglas A. O'Roark of the Colorado Mesa University, a test was made of the range of an ancient Greek javelin. Two highly trained collegiate throwers, using a run-up and proper throwing technique, threw a facsimile of an ancient Greek javelin with and without the use of an *ankyle* (ancient leather throwing strap). Without the ankyle throws ranged between 33.2 and 49.5 yards. With an ankyle they ranged between 56.5 and 66.2 yards.

Presuming that ancient javelineers were more experienced with the ankyle and could throw further, their maximum range would probably not on average exceed about 70–80 yards. In this context, a difference of 16 yards matters. The javelineers, throwing from in front of a heavy infantry line, could not allow the enemy to get too close: they had to be able to retire through the heavy infantry files leaving enough time after they had passed for the heavy infantry to double their files from open to intermediate formation and be ready for the onset of the enemy foot. The shallower the javelin line the better.

For slingers and archers, lines that are too deep posed a different problem. Vegetius states that slingers cast their stones overhead and that slingers and archers trained to hit a target 200 yards away:

> The archers and slingers set up bundles of twigs or straw for marks, and generally strike them with arrows and with stones from the fustiablus at the distance of six hundred feet. They acquired coolness and exactness in action from familiar custom and exercise in the field. The slingers should be taught to whirl the sling but once about the head before they cast the stone. – *De Re Militari*: 2.

200 yards is little below the extreme distance a skirmisher bow could shoot. Slingers could cast a little further than a bowshot, but in round numbers 200 yards is a convenient marker of a bow and sling's maximum range. To ensure that a skirmisher formation could as a whole more accurately hit this extreme range target, weaker shooters could be placed in the front ranks and stronger shooters at the back. If the entire formation deployed in files of 8 men with 2 yards per rank (see below), the rear rankers would be 16 yards further away from the target than the front rankers, enough to significantly cancel out their different shooting ranges.

It is important to understand that it was not aiming that mattered for a skirmisher, but an accurate estimate of range. His opponent was an enemy line that was impossible to miss if his shot veered off right or left, however the line was relative thin: his arrow or bullet could easily overshoot or fall short.

One also needs to keep in mind that skirmisher troops were designed to shoot at a target that was approaching them and which they would eventually have to evade (the one exception was when they were used to stop a cavalry advance by shooting at the horses). They had limited time to loose their missiles and the distance between them and the enemy line was constantly shortening. This imposed a particular restriction on their style of fighting. If slingers or archers used massed fire – all shooting together over the heads of their comrades without most being able to see the target – then they could only do it accurately at maximum range unless they were highly skilled. This seems counterintuitive, but in fact it is much easier to fire an arrow or sling a bullet to the same point at extreme range than to a much closer point. This is because at extreme range the elevation of a bow or the angle at which a slinger looses his bullet may vary without much variation in the distance his missile travels. At shorter ranges a slight change in elevation or loosing angle results in a significant change to how far the missile goes. Hence a typical archer or slinger could shoot constantly to his maximum range without having to see his target, but he needed to sight anything nearer in order to be sure of hitting it.

In consequence a skirmisher line could reliably use massed fire only whilst the enemy was at extreme range (Balearic slingers, armed with three different kinds of sling, could employ massed fire three times during an enemy's advance). Once the enemy line had advanced within the extreme range window, only the skirmishers in the two or three front rows could continue shooting at their opponents with a reasonable hope of hitting them.

There were two hypothetical ways all the skirmishers could continue shooting. The first is to rotate the ranks, with two front ranks moving down between the files to the rear after having shot, allowing the ranks behind them to shoot, and eventually returning to the front to shoot again.

This system would chime with Vegetius's remark that 'the slingers should be taught to whirl the sling but once about the head before they cast the stone.' For this conveyor belt method of shooting to work to maximum effect each shooter needs to loose his missile as quickly as possible and get out of the way of the next man in the file. The skirmishers have to bombard the enemy line with as many missiles as they could before being obliged to retire through their heavy troops. There is no leisure for time-consuming techniques (see Diagrams 49–52).

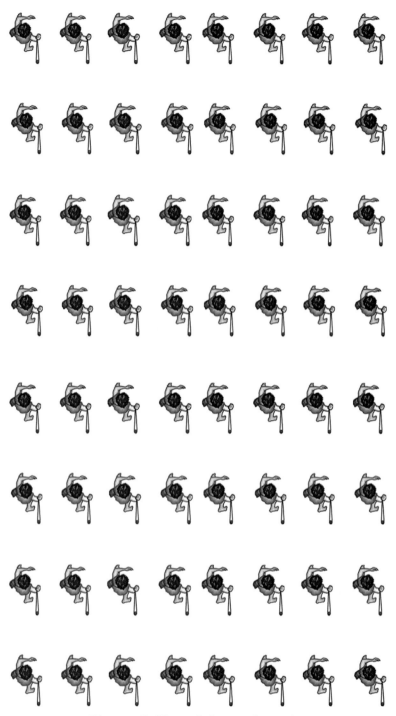

Diagram 49: Slingers in intermediate order.

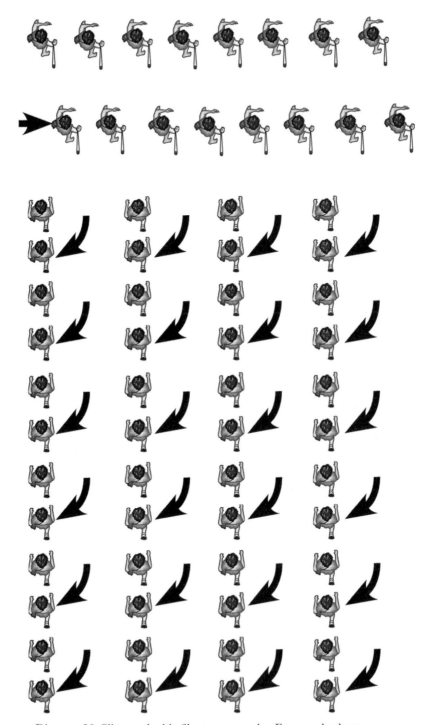

Diagram 50: Slingers double files to open order. Front ranks shoot.

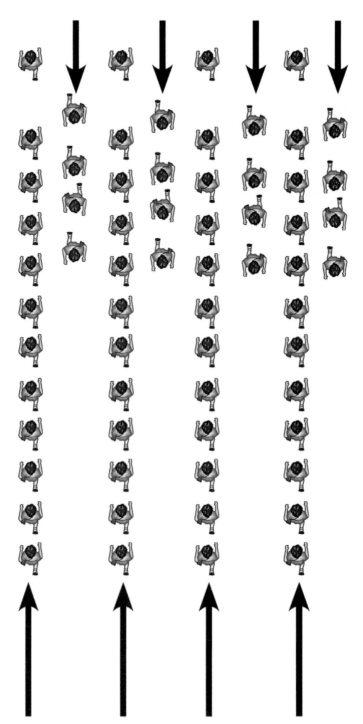

Diagram 51: The front-ranks countermarch to the rear.

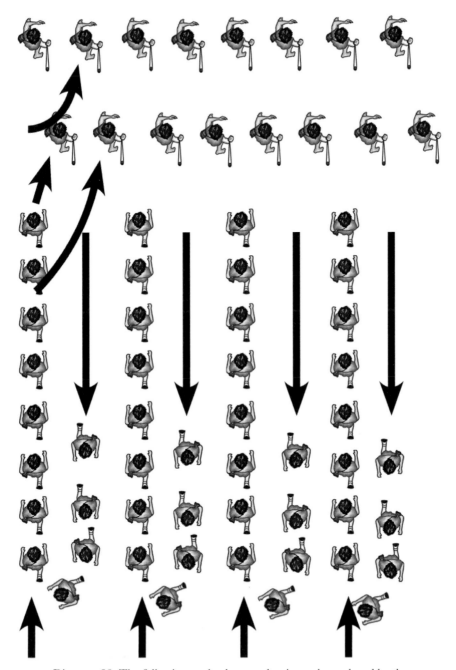

Diagram 52: The following ranks shoot and retire, to be replaced by the ranks behind them. The cycle continues indefinitely.

The second way is simpler and easier. The front rank shoots then kneels down. The second rank shoots over the heads of the first rank and kneels down. The third rank then shoots over the front two ranks, and so on. When the last rank has shot, all the skirmishers stand, reload their weapons, and recommence the process. This system would also make sense of Vegetius's injunction that slingers needed to shoot quickly. Each rank had to loose its missile promptly and kneel to allow the next rank to fire, keeping up a rapid and continuous barrage against the approaching enemy.

There are historical examples of archers firing over kneeling front rank troops. Charles the Bold's 1473 Burgundian Ordnance[28] specified that: 'The pikemen must be made to advance in close formation in front of the said archers, kneel at a sign from them, holding their pikes lowered to the level of a horse's back so that the archers can fire over the pikemen as if over a wall'.

The Roman infantry used this tactic in 389 BC against a Gallic army:

> Gaius Sulpicius, the dictator, marched against them, and is said to have used the following stratagem. He commanded those who were in the front line to discharge their javelins, and immediately crouch low; then the second, third, and fourth lines to discharge theirs, each crouching in turn so that they should not be struck by the spears thrown from the rear; then when the last line had hurled their javelins, all were to rush forward suddenly with a shout and join battle at close quarters. – Appian, *Gallic History*: 1.1.

The problem however is that there is nothing in the sources that suggest these techniques were in general use by skirmishers. It is quite possible and, using Occam's Razor, probable, that skirmisher foot did not usually go in for this kind of sophistication, being content simply to use all their troops for massed fire at extreme range, then just their front two or three ranks for direct shooting at shorter ranges before retiring through the heavy infantry.

Either way, having many ranks of skirmisher foot did not confer any advantage. Massed fire at extreme range would have the same disruptive effect with eight missiles per file as with sixteen, and the area beaten by a massed volley would be about the same for sixteen as for eight ranks. At close range of course the extra rearward ranks of skirmishers would be pointless as shooting remains limited to the frontmost ranks. In terms of overall effect having extra ranks of shooters is a waste of manpower, unless one has many more ranks – fifty or a hundred say – in which case the beaten area of massed fire is much deeper, allowing the shooters to disrupt the advancing enemy for a longer period of time. This of course implies much larger armies than those conceived by the manuals.

One last disadvantage of too-deep skirmisher lines was the danger of the skirmishers getting charged by the enemy in front of their heavy infantry before they had had the time to retire through them. The fewer men there were that had to pass between the heavy foot files, the quicker the retirement could be completed and the more time the heavies would have to double from open to intermediate spacing before their opponents reached them. This also gave the skirmishers more time to pepper the enemy before falling back, leaving the enemy disorganised at the moment the two heavy infantry lines clashed. Deep lines would have to fall back earlier, allowing the enemy time to recover from the effects of missile fire.

Once behind the enemy line skirmishers could continue to shoot indirectly at the enemy line. Javelinmen would simply throw any javelins they had left over the heads of their own troops into the enemy ranks – they would have enough skill to miss friendly soldiers 16 yards away and hit enemy foot 20 or 30 yards away. Archers and slingers would need to fall back to extreme range to be sure of hitting enemy rather than friend. Archers were probably more accurate at extreme range than slingers – support fire by archers is attested in the sources but no mention is made of slingers in this role.

One final question remains. Asklepiodotus affirms that light troops were sometimes placed within formations of heavy infantry:

Sometimes they are incorporated in the phalanx and stationed one beside each man; and this is called insert-position [*parentaxis*], because there is an insertion of different branches of the service, e.g., light infantry with hoplites – *Tactics*: 6.1.

This is repeated by Aelian:

> Entaxis occurs when it is considered appropriate to insert the light armed infantry into the intervals between each man of the phalanx. – *Tactics*: 30.

Why insert the lights between the heavies? There are two possible reasons for this. The first is that the light troops can shoot approaching enemy for a longer period of time before retiring, allowing the heavy infantry to double files at the last moment to receive the enemy attack. This would be effective if the approaching enemy did not have light troops of its own capable of targeting the heavy infantry the skirmishers are placed among.

The second reason is ease of battlefield manoeuvring. If lights are to deploy in front of the heavy troops they need to preserve the same frontage as the heavies and ensure their files correspond in positioning to those of the heavies and facilitate a rapid retirement to the rear of the heavy foot. The easiest way to achieve this is for the lights to march with their files inserted between those of the heavy foot. When the heavy formation stops the light troops can continue their advance, stop a short distance ahead of the heavy line, and commence skirmishing. Retiring simply involves the lights turning 180 degrees and moving straight back between the heavy files. Under battlefield conditions the simpler a manoeuvre is to execute the better.

6. Peltasts

Peltasts were a halfway house between light and heavy foot, leaning more to the light side.

> The peltasts wear the style of armour known as 'argilos', which is similar to Macedonian armour only lighter. This type of soldier carries a *pelta* shield, and his spear is much shorter than the Macedonian pike. As such, his armour is in between that of the 'heavy infantry' and that of the 'light infantry' (being lighter than that of the hoplite but heavier than that of the psiloi) and this has

often caused the peltasts to be confused with the 'light infantry' – Aelian: 2.

> The corps of the peltasts stands in a sense between these two [heavy infantry and skirmisher infantry], for the *pelta* is a kind of small, light shield, and their spears are much shorter than those of the hoplites. – Asklepiodotus: 1.2.

Earlier versions of the peltast carried javelins only in addition to their pelta shield. A sword, spear, helmet and body armour were added but with the exception of the shield not every peltast had all of these.

The principal difference between peltasts and skirmisher foot was the ability of peltasts to engage in hand-to-hand combat with cavalry, though on one occasion – at the Trebia – Hannibal's *Lonchophoroi* also seem to have engaged the Roman infantry on the flanks and rear.

In 401 BC Cyrus, the younger brother of the ruling Persian king Artaxerxes, raised an army in Anatolia and marched on the Persian capital. The two armies met at Cunaxa on the bank of the Euphrates near modern day Baghdad. In addition to his Persian troops Cyrus had gained the support of 10,400 Greek hoplites and 2,500 peltasts. His Persians numbered 100,000 men. Artaxerxes, according to Zenophon, had assembled a much larger force:

> The enemy's forces were reported to number one million two hundred thousand, with two hundred scythed-chariots, besides which he had six thousand cavalry under Artagerses. These formed the immediate vanguard of the king himself. The royal army was marshalled by four generals or field-marshals, each in command of three hundred thousand men. Their names were Abrocomas, Tissaphernes, Gobryas, and Arbaces. (But of this total not more than nine hundred thousand were engaged in the battle, with one hundred and fifty scythed-chariots; since Abrocomas, on his march from Phoenicia, arrived five days too late for the battle.) Such was the information brought to Cyrus by deserters who came in from the king's army before the battle, and it was corroborated after the battle by those of the enemy who were taken prisoners. – Xenophon, Anabasis: 7

These numbers are discounted by contemporary writers. Wikipedia gives an indeterminate number for Cyrus' Persian infantry – but limited to the tens of thousands – plus 1,600 cavalry and 20 chariots, whilst Artaxerxes is assigned 40,000 men in all. Whether Xenophon's figures should be discounted in favour of these much smaller estimates is an entire subject in itself and beyond the scope of this book.

After passing over a defensive trench abandoned by Artaxerxes Cyrus was surprised by his brother's army whilst marching south along the Euphrates in column. He quickly formed his troops into line. The hoplites held the right wing near the Euphrates with 1,000 cavalry plus the 2,500 peltasts between their right flank and the river. The Persians formed up on the left of the Hoplites. Cyrus, with 600 cavalry in the centre between the Greeks and the Persian infantry, was positioned opposite Artaxerxes who likewise took up position in the centre of his own line. Artaxerxes kept most of his 6,000 cavalry with himself, but placed a strong force of horse to the left of his infantry next to the river, opposite the peltasts.

As the hoplites charged and scattered the Persian cavalry before them, Tissaphernes, leading a body of Persian horse, attacked the peltast flank guard. The peltasts however were ready for them:

> The latter [Tissaphernes] had not fled in the first shock of the encounter; he had charged parallel to the line of the Euphrates into the Greek peltasts, and through them. But charge as he might, he did not lay low a single man. On the contrary, the Hellenes separated to let them through, hacking them with their swords and hurling their javelins as they passed. – *Anabasis*: 10.

Choosing from the repertoire of manoeuvres available in the manuals, the Peltasts could either have doubled files from intermediate to open order, leaving a 4-foot gap between one file and the next,[29] or simply bunched the files of their subunits together, leaving wide gaps between them. Horses, naturally reluctant to charge straight into human bodies unless they have to, made for the gaps, passing harmlessly between the peltasts whilst these stabbed at their riders. Persian cavalry were habitually armed with javelins against which the peltasts' shields were adequate protection.

Against heavy foot peltasts limited themselves, like light foot, to skirmishing from a distance and retiring out of range if charged. There is no case of peltasts ever voluntarily engaging in frontal melee combat against heavy infantry.

7. Elephants

As formations go elephants had only one – the line. The elephants' job was to see off cavalry or disrupt an infantry line, killing a number of foot in the process but more importantly convincing the remainder of the vulnerability of their own formation and its inability to protect them. Elephants were not generally meant to defeat enemy infantry single-handed since, in the armies covered here, there were usually not enough of them for the job. In this case they worked best in conjunction with their own infantry.

At the Battle of the Hydaspes the Indian commander Porus deployed 85 of his elephants in front of his infantry with the remainder in reserve.[30] The elephants each occupied a frontage of 30 yards, stretching in a line about 2.5km long, behind which 30,000 infantry deployed in a line that extended beyond the flanks of the elephants. The elephants looked like they could be bypassed through the wide gaps between them but this in fact was a trap:

> First he placed the elephants in the front, each animal being not less than a plethrum [30 yards] apart, so that they might be extended in the front before the whole of the phalanx of infantry, and produce terror everywhere among Alexander's cavalry. Besides he thought that none of the enemy would have the audacity to push themselves into the spaces between the elephants, the cavalry being deterred by the fright of their horses; and still less would the infantry do so, it being likely they would be kept off in front by the heavy-armed soldiers falling upon them, and trampled down by the elephants wheeling round against them. – Arrian, *The Anabasis of Alexander*. 5.15.

Alexander avoided the trap by engaging and defeating Porus' cavalry.

There were one or two exceptions to this rule. If elephants were numerous enough they could be packed virtually shoulder to shoulder and used to crush the enemy infantry single-handed. In 255 BC during the First Punic War a Roman army under the command of Regulus landed in North Africa and beat a Carthaginian army near Adys. The panicked Carthaginians hired Xanthippus, a Spartan general, who arrived with 2,000 Greek mercenaries. Xanthippus laid his hands on every elephant he could find – nearly 100 – and at the battle of Bagradas he deployed them against Regulus in front of a force of Carthaginian citizen spearmen and his mercenaries whilst his cavalry, which far outnumbered the Roman horse, took up position on the flanks.[31]

To counter the elephants Regulus deployed his infantry much deeper than usual. As will be seen in Chapter 4, a Republican legion typically occupied a frontage of about 200 yards in three lines, each one maniple deep, fronted by velite skirmishers. Here, the Romans deployed 'many maniples deep', implying a doubling from one maniple per line to two. This would have halved the frontage of the legion. Since Regulus's foot numbered 15,000 men, this suggests he had a standard Consular army of two Roman and two Allied legions (usually making up an infantry complement of 20,000 men but his army had suffered losses in the previous battle). With four legions each now occupying 100 yards the Roman foot would have deployed 400 yards wide. According to Polybios the elephants fronted the 10,000 Carthaginian spearmen but not the 2,000 mercenaries next to them, which suggests the elephants covered 5/6 of the Roman line, or about 333 yards – about 3½ yards per elephant, or 10½ feet (see Diagram 53).

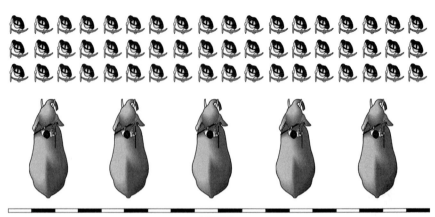

YARDS

Diagram 53: The deployment of the Carthaginian elephants at Bagradas.

An African forest elephant is about 5 feet wide at its widest point which meant there was about five feet or so between one elephant and the next, sufficient for the animals to move and turn in place (a forest elephant is about 4 yards in length), but not close enough to prevent some Roman legionaries from passing between the elephants where they were promptly dispatched by the Carthaginian spearmen. The Romans facing the Greek mercenaries defeated them and were able to leave the battlefield as the only survivors.

In most other battles elephants deployed with a frontage of 10 to 50 yards per elephant. Skirmishers accompanied them to prevent enemy missile troops from targeting them, but it is still a mystery as to why the enemy heavy foot could not simply surround each elephant and hamstring or kill it. It is possible they tried exactly this, with the elephants turning right and left in rage to keep them at bay, killing several in the process. It is also possible that enemy infantry had no choice but to keep their ranks when attacked by elephants, as breaking formation to surround the beasts would leave them disrupted and vulnerable to an attack by enemy foot. One can hypothesise that elephants were used against enemy infantry to achieve precisely this effect.

8. Chariots

Of all the troop types, the manuals have the least to say about chariot formations, merely giving their unit breakdown without any description of how they were organised and used in battle. Pictorial representations of chariots in battle from Egyptian reliefs are problematic as the images are stylised and two-dimensional, giving little idea of depth and hence the distance between chariots, but the relief of the Battle of Kadesh on the north wall the Great Temple of Abou seems to show the chariots of each opposing army organised into a loose line with some distance between one chariot and the next. It is highly unlikely that opposing chariots physically ploughed into each other as horses will not normally charge into contact with other horses, hence chariot vs chariot combat probably consisted of the two opposing chariot lines stopping a short distance from each other whilst their crews shot arrows, threw javelins or even dismounted to engage enemy charioteers in hand-to-hand combat, this kind of fighting continuing until one side eventually broke. The space between chariots would enable a charioteer to turn his vehicle[32] without colliding with his neighbours and withdraw from the engagement.

Chariots however were not meant just to engage other chariots. The *Arthaśāstra* of Kauṭilya, an Indian treatise on statecraft, economic policy and military strategy, composed between the 3rd and 2nd centuries BC, lists the uses of chariots. These are heavy chariots with 5 horses to each car, but what is said about them probably applies to similar chariots of the Fertile Crescent.

> Protection of the army; repelling the attack made by all the four constituents of the enemy's army [infantry, cavalry, elephants, chariots]; seizing and abandoning [positions] during the time of battle; gathering a dispersed army; breaking the compact array of the enemy's army; frightening it; magnificence; and fearful noise – these constitute the work of chariots. – *Arthaśāstra*: 10.4.
>
> Running against; running round; running beyond; running back; disturbing the enemy's halt; gathering the troops; curving, circling, miscellaneous operations; removal of the rear; pursuit of the line from the front, flanks and rear; protection of the broken army; and falling upon the broken army – these are the forms of waging war with horses.
>
> The same varieties with the exception of [what is called] miscellaneous operations; the destruction of the four constituents of the army, either single or combined; the dispersion of the flanks, wings and front trampling down; and attacking the army when it is asleep – these are the varieties of waging war with elephants.
>
> The same varieties with the exception of disturbing the enemy's halt; running against; running back; and fighting from where it stands on its own ground – these are the varieties of waging war with chariots. – *Arthaśāstra*: 10.5.

So besides manoeuvring on the battlefield, exerting psychological intimidation, pursuing broken enemies and rounding up their own forces, chariots were also expected to engage all troop types and break 'the compact array of the enemy's army'. To this end the *Arthaśāstra* recommends deploying chariots in several lines each as compact as possible.

> The infantry should be arrayed such that the space between any two men is a sama [about 28cm, in between intermediate and close order]; cavalry with three samas; chariots with four samas [i.e. roughly a yard] – *Arthaśāstra*: 10.5.

This is as close as chariots in a line can get without fouling each other. The space between one line and the next however is quite generous.

> A bow means five aratnis [= 240cm]. Archers should be stationed at the distance of five bows [from one line to another]; the cavalry at the distance of three bows; and chariots or elephants at the distance of five bows [about 12m] – *Ibid*.

Chariots in lines this compact cannot wheel without hitting their neighbours, and once committed must move forwards. They were thus meant to plough straight into enemy infantry, to which the 'compact array' implicitly refers. Could they do this? Will horses charge directly into a solid line of foot?

The answer is most certainly yes.[33]

A galloping horse has tremendous kinetic energy and is quite capable of knocking down several adjacent men in succession.[34] Without experimentation (with possibly fatal results for the participants) it is impossible to know just how many men a horse at full gallop *can* knock flat, but there is an equation that gives some idea of the forces involved.

How much energy is needed to knock over a standing man? Assume a man weighing 70kg is hit around his midriff, about a metre above the ground, and that the man is standing with his feet a yard apart. The equation is:

mgl = Fh
where **m** is the mass of the man (70 kg);
g is a constant: 9.8;

l is the distance from the man's tipping point to his centre of gravity, assumed to be half the width of his spread feet or 0.45m;
F is the force in Newtons;
h is the height at which the man is hit.

The equation becomes:

70 x 9.8 x 0.45 = **F** x **l**
F = 308.7 Newtons.

The next question is to determine how much force is needed to stop a charging horse.

A horse in Antiquity was smaller than a horse today. Horses in Roman times were 11–12 hands high, weighed in the region of 250kg and could probably get up a speed of 40km/h.

First we need to work out how much kinetic energy is in a galloping horse. The equation is:

$$\begin{aligned}
\text{Kinetic Energy} &= 0 \cdot 5 \text{ x } 250\text{kg x velocity}^2 \\
&= 0 \cdot 5 \text{ x } 250 \text{ x } 40\text{km/h}^2 \\
&= 0 \cdot 5 \text{ x } 250 \text{ x } 11.11\text{m/s}^2 \\
&= 0 \cdot 5 \text{ x } 250 \text{ x } 123.45 \\
&= 15{,}432 \text{ Joules}
\end{aligned}$$

Next, and this is the tricky part, we need to factor in the distance the horse must traverse whilst hitting the men, as the more time the horse spends ploughing through infantry the less force is required to bring it to a halt. Presuming that each rank occupies a depth of one yard, the equation is as follows:

$J = Fm^2$
J is the kinetic energy in Joules;
F is the force in Newtons;
m is the number of ranks, each a yard in depth.

Which gives:

$$15,432 = 308.7 \text{ x } \mathbf{m^2}$$
$$15,432 \text{ / } 308.7 = \mathbf{m^2}$$
$$49.99 = \text{m}^2$$
$$7.07 = \mathbf{m}$$

The horse will plough through seven ranks of infantry before being brought to a halt.

This is probably far too conservative an estimate as it assumes that the infantryman's body will be slowing down the horse for the full distance of a yard, unlikely as the man is knocked down almost immediately and no longer exerts any drag on the horse's progress. It does however give an idea of the impressive power of a charging horse and explains how Roman cavalry could pierce right through a line of enemy infantry in all likelihood at least eight ranks deep and probably more. It also suggests why infantry lines were rarely less than eight men deep.

Packing the horses together into a single compact unit – the chariot – made them even more potent against infantry. Unlike cavalry, horses harnessed to a chariot cannot shy away from an obstacle in front of them. Two horses yoked together would tend to go in opposite directions, cancelling each other out, and in a four-horse arrangement the two central horses would not be able to change direction at all.

The chariot then was the ultimate infantry battering ram and ruled the Ancient battlefield for centuries, only losing its supremacy as infantry gradually learned how to neutralise its fearsome inertia by deploying deep, by compacting ranks together to make the individual men harder to knock over, by opening gaps to let the chariots through, and finally by digging trenches before the infantry lines as the Romans did against Mithridates. When horse breeds became larger cavalry grew in importance, able to plough through unprepared infantry in the same ways chariots did and capable of traversing terrain unsuitable for chariot wheels. By the time the legions ruled the Mediterranean the day of the chariot was done.

Notes

1. Curtius, *History of Alexander*: 8.14.40.
2. Asklepiodotus: 2.2; Aelian: 5.
3. Asklepiodotus:2.3; Aelian: 5.
4. Asklepiodotus:2.3; Aelian: 5.
5. Asklepiodotus: 2.7; Aelian: 8.
6. Polybios, *Histories*: 3.113.2.
7. https://romanarmy.info/march2_basics/march_basics.html
8. https://romanarmy.info/march4_baggage/march_baggage.html
9. Asklepiodotus: 9.12.
10. https://romanarmy.info/march7_days/march_days.html
11. Journal of Cross-Cultural Psychology 2017, Vol. 48(4) 577–592.
12. Asklepiodotus: 5.1.
13. See discussion on the length of a cubit in Chapter 3: 3. *The Phalangite's Panoply*.
14. See discussion on the phalangite shield in Chapter 3: 3. *The Phalangite's Panoply*.
15. See discussion on othismos in Chapter 2: 7. *The Phalanx in Combat*.
16. Asklepiodotus: 10.13–15; Arrian: 23; Aelian: 26.
17. Aelian: 28; Arrian: 25.
18. Asklepiodotus: 12.9: *If the centre must assume the compact position, we shall command the right wing to left face and the left wing to right face, then to advance to the navel of the phalanx, to face to the front, and to advance the rear ranks, and we shall have the desired formation.*
19. Aelian: 28.
20. Aelian: 28; Arrian: 25
21. Asklepiodotus: 10.18.
22. Aelian: 28.
23. Asklepiodotus: 6.1; Aelian: 30; Arrian: 26.
24. Asklepiodotus: 6.1.
25. Arrian: 36, 39, 40.
26. Asklepiodotus: 7.5; Aelian: 19.
27. 'Recreating the Ancient Greek Javelin Throw: How Far Was the Javelin Thrown?' by Steven Ross Murray, William A. Sands, and Douglas A. O'Roark, *Nikephoros*, Volume 25.
28. *Charles the Bold: The Last Valois Duke of Burgundy*, by Richard Vaughan. Page 210
29. Closing up their syntagmas to form close-order blocks with gaps between each block for the horses to pass would probably have left them too cramped to effectively employ their weapons.
30. According to Arrian Porus led 200 elephants against Alexander and deployed them in a single line with each elephant 30 yards apart (*Anabasis*: 5.15.4). His 30,000 infantry deployed behind the elephants in a 'dense

phalanx' (*Anabasis*: 5.16.2) that extended beyond the flanks of the elephant line. If all 200 elephants had deployed in this manner, their line would be 6km long and the infantry line longer. The infantry would be at best 5 ranks deep if in intermediate order, which hardly corresponds to the 'dense phalanx' [πυκνός φάλαγξ] described by Arrian. Curtius affirms that Porus initially deployed at the Hydaspes with 85 elephants in front of 30,000 infantry (*History of Alexander*: 8.3.6). Presuming he duplicated this deployment after Alexander had crossed the river (Arrian affirms Porus had the same number of infantry at the main battle), the elephant line would be 2.5km long and the infantry line behind it would be about 12 men deep. This was still a very long line and Curtius describes Porus losing control of his 'scattered forces' (*History of Alexander*: 8.14.22). The best way to resolve these accounts seems to be to accept that Porus kept most of his elephants in reserve during the battle, deploying as many as could create a line of manageable length.

31. Polybios, *Histories*: 1.32–33.
32. A really tight turn by a chariot could be achieved by a side pass movement of the horse, combined with the horse turning towards the direction it is moving. This would enable the chariot to wheel virtually on a dime. It would require well-trained horses. Wheels of chariots found in Tutankamen's tomb rotate independently of each other, facilitating tight turns of this nature.
33. Republican Roman cavalry routinely charged through formed enemy heavy infantry: Livy, *Histories*: 3.70; 8.30.6.
34. Several examples of this:
   https://www.youtube.com/watch?v=rvSS9MaVWlg
   https://www.youtube.com/watch?v=_PbVIl7DRDo
   https://www.youtube.com/watch?v=D-0vzjTvesw

Chapter 2

The Hoplite Phalanx

1. The Battle of Thermopylae, 480 BC

It was day three of the battle between a coalition of Greek city states under the leadership of the Spartan king Leonidas and the Persian Empire under Xerxes. The Persians had spent four years preparing for their invasion of Greece and had brought an enormous army to Greece. Leonidas had a large army by Greek standards – 7,000 hoplites – but he was outnumbered dozens to one by the Persians.

He had however chosen the perfect battlefield. The Middle Gate of the pass at Thermopylae was 50 yards wide at its narrowest point between mountain slopes and the sea. The Persians could not outflank the Greeks by sailing past them and landing an army behind them, as the Athenian navy guarded the narrow straits between the long island of Euboea and mainland Greece. Nor could they march above the Greek line and outflank it by land, as the pass at that point was bordered by steep cliffs. Xerxes' only choice was a frontal assault.

This he had tried on day one and day two. On the first day he sent in his Median troops followed by the finest troops in the Persian army, his crack Immortals. The battle lasted the entire day without the Greeks giving an inch. On the second day Xerxes chose the best fighters out of every contingent of his army and then promised them riches if they overcame the Greeks, and death if they retreated. With that incentive, the attack against the Greeks was conducted with reckless fury but was no more successful than the combats of the previous day.

Fortune now smiled on Xerxes. A Malian Greek, Epialtes, revealed the existence of a track around Mount Callidrome to the Greek rear. Greeks in the Persian camp defected and brought news to Leonidas that his position was fatally compromised. He ordered the bulk of his army to retreat, keeping only his Spartans along with the Thespians and Thebans, less than 1,400 men all told.

With time against him Leonidas resolved on an all-out attack on the Persians. Until then the Greek army had remained at the Middle Gate, defending a stretch of shoreline 50 yards wide. This meant that the infantry line, deployed as compactly as possible, was no more than about 70–80 files wide. If the hoplites deployed 12 deep at the most, then Leonidas needed to commit only about 900 men at any one time, leaving the rest of his force in reserve. He was fighting a slow battle of attrition with time on his side: the enormous Persian army could not sit forever around the Malian Gulf.

But time had now run out. Advancing from the Middle Gate the Greeks assaulted the Persian host in a do-or-die attack that initially was successful. As passable land beyond the Middle Gate widened to about 100 yards or so Leonidas deployed all his men in a phalanx line 9 men deep or less. Many of his men's spears were already broken from the previous two days' fighting and they were reduced to fighting with swords and, ultimately, teeth.

But it was enough to drive the Persians back. Two of Xerxes' brothers and two half-brothers were killed. Leonidas himself was slain but his men were able to retrieve his body and keep up the pressure on the Persians. It was only when the flanking force of Immortals appeared in the Greek rear that the attack was halted. The survivors retreated to a small nearby hill where they were cut down, not by hand-to-hand fighting, but by an endless rain of arrows. The defenders of Thermopylae were dead to the last man but the supremacy of the Greek phalanx had been branded forever in the minds of Persian kings. In subsequent campaigns the best troops in the Persian infantry would be mercenary hoplites.

Their reputation as the best fighting men in the Eastern Mediterranean and more than a match for any kind of soldier the Persian Empire could pit against them would last another 152 years until the Greek hoplite as supreme infantryman gave way to the Macedonian phalangite. What exactly made him so good?

2. The Origins of the Hoplite Phalanx

The earliest detailed record of Greek combat is the *Iliad*. Written by Homer sometime between the late-8th or early-7th century BC, it focuses on the closing period of the ten-year Trojan War. Some scholars debate the historicity of the war as well as the authorship of the epic poem by Homer, but it is generally agreed that the account gives an accurate picture of the equipment and fighting methods of Greek warfare two hundred years before Thermopylae, with some details that belong to the earlier age of the Trojan War in the 13th century BC.

Homer's well-equipped Greek fighting man would be armed with a bronze cuirass (actually iron by the time of Homer – bronze was a deliberate Homeric anachronism), bronze greaves, a helmet made of bronze or, occasionally, of leather. In one case a helmet was made of boar's tusks which heralds back to the Mycenaean Greece of the 13th century BC. He carried a shield made of four to seven layers of ox-hide with sometimes a thin covering of bronze, possibly all attached to a wickerwork frame (as the mock-woven pattern embossed on the bronze rim of later shields probably attests), a sword, and two spears.

Depictions of hoplites on vases show one spear to be shorter than the other. The shorter spear was clearly a javelin and was thrown in combat; the larger spear could either be thrown or used in hand-to-hand combat. In the cases where each combatant has two spears or sometimes only one, the larger spear is used as a missile weapon about as often as a melee weapon. The use of both spears for throwing is confirmed by the Chigi vase. This is a Proto-Corinthian *ople*, or pitcher, found in an Etruscan tomb at Monte Aguzzo, near Veio, and dated between 650–640 BC. Not far from its handle is the depiction of two spears of different lengths, both with an ankyle or leather throwing thong, leaning against a shield. To the left of these is another partial depiction of two other spears, also of different lengths and equipped with ankyles.

The sword is an auxiliary weapon and is employed when a spear is thrown, broken or in rare cases is unsuitable for the kind of combat taking place. It is often used to finish off an opponent who has already been wounded by the spear.

A fully-armoured warrior had virtually no exposed area of his body an enemy weapon could penetrate. His shield covered him from his neck to his knees. His greaves protected his lower legs. His helmet covered his skull, most of his face and a large part of his neck. In consequence

Homer's combatants usually did not try to insert a spearpoint or sword blade in the few, tiny chinks of his opponent's armour, but attempted, by brute force, to drive a spear or javelin straight through the armour into the opponent's body. Over half of the fatal wounds described in the *Iliad* are caused by spears penetrating the shield and cuirass. Many other mortal injuries were caused by the spear penetrating the helmet. Only occasionally do warriors die from wounds to exposed parts of the body like the arm or leg.

Shields and cuirass however offer good protection. Spears thrown or thrust at shields generally do not penetrate them but either glance off the bronze covering or are stopped by the layers of hide. The spear needed great force to penetrate the armour which required that the warrior have considerable physical strength.

This need for strength in the arm and shoulder muscles is reflected in the high regard for physical fitness that was an important part of Greek culture. Of the nine different kinds of contests held at the Olympic games (traditionally first held in 776 BC) – running, discus, jumping, javelin, boxing, wrestling, *pankration* (wrestling and boxing combined), chariot racing and horse racing – six required strong arm and shoulder muscles. Even jumping involved throwing back a jumping weight to increase distance. The strong, well-muscled Greek became an ideal in Greek art, but he represented a necessity on the battlefield. A physically weak soldier was all but useless.

Combat in the Homeric period often consisted of fights between champions, the result of which could prompt the losing side to become disheartened and flee. The mere presence of a champion with a great reputation for martial prowess was sometimes enough to cause his opponents to give way.

There are examples however of combat between two bodies of soldiers with or without individual contests by champions.

The Trojans fight the Achaeans near their ships:

The Trojans advanced in a dense body, with Hector at their head pressing right on as a rock that comes thundering down the side of some mountain from whose brow the winter torrents have torn it….but the closely serried battalions stayed him when he reached them, for the sons of the Achaeans thrust at him with swords and spears pointed at both ends. – *Iliad*: 13.

This combat between groups of warriors involved fighting with spears and contact between opposing shields. The Danaans fight the Trojans in a well-ordered phalanx:

Shield clashed with shield and spear with spear in the rage of battle. The bossed shields beat one upon another, and there was a tramp as of a great multitude. – *Iliad*: 4.

The Achaeans fight the Trojans outside Troy's gates:

When they were got together in one place, shield clashed with shield, and spear with spear, in the conflict of mail-clad men. Mighty was the din as the bossed shields pressed hard on one another – death – cry and shout of triumph of slain and slayers, and the earth ran red with blood. – *Iliad*: 7.

It could also involve sword-play:

… but meanwhile the hosts were fighting and killing one another, and the hard bronze rattled on their bodies, as they thrust at one another with their swords and spears. – *Iliad*: 14.

Even so the Achaeans were still charging on in a body, using their swords and spears pointed at both ends, but when they saw Hector going about among his men they were afraid, and their hearts fell down into their feet. – *Iliad*: 15.

Since a spear outreaches a sword but cannot be used once an opponent had advanced into close contact with its wielder, combats involving both weapons would imply either that the swords were used to hack off the spearpoints or, more likely, that once warriors had advanced to shield contact, they discarded their spears – now useless – and used their swords instead.

Bodies of fighters in a phalanx could form up with ranks and files compressed together, virtually shoulder-to-shoulder, shields overlapping and helmet crests in different ranks touching each other:

> With these words he put heart and soul into them all, and they serried their companies yet more closely when they heard the words of their king. As the stones which a builder sets in the wall of some high house which is to give shelter from the winds – even so closely were the helmets and bossed shields set against one another. Shield pressed on shield, helm on helm, and man on man; so close were they that the horse-hair plumes on the gleaming ridges of their helmets touched each other as they bent their heads. – *Iliad*: 16.

The main ingredients of the Greek phalanx that fought at Thermopylae were already in place in the age of Homer. All that was required were a few final refinements.

3. The Hoplite's Panoply

The Spear

Its Construction

The most significant change in equipment between the Homeric warrior and the hoplite of classical Greece was in the spear. Gone were the two spears of the Archaic period, both of which could be used as missile weapons. In their place was a single spear designed uniquely for melee combat. A red figure amphorae in the Vatican museum, attributed to the 'Achilles painter' is one of the earliest artistic representations of this new weapon. It shows a hoplite holding an upright spear that is about half as long again as his height. The spear has three components: the spearhead, the shaft, which tapers towards the spearhead, and the sauroter (also known as the *styrax* or *ouriachos*) fixed to the base of the shaft. In addition, a handle grip can be seen about a quarter of the way up the shaft from the sauroter.

Spearheads consisted of an iron or bronze leaf-shaped blade and a hollow metal socket. Their length varied from 93mm to 290mm, but generally averaged around 279mm in length, with a maximum blade width of 31mm, a blade length of 202mm, a socket length of 77mm, and an average weight of 153g. the hollow inner tube of the socket was on average 18mm wide.

The sauroter was variable in shape and size. They could be from 160mm to 300mm in length, and weigh from 237g to 689g. Every sauroter had a hollow socket at one end, with a width of 19mm to 25mm. On average, the common bronze 'long-point' sauroter was 259mm long and weighed 329g. An additional metal ring was sometimes added to a sauroter to increase its weight.

The Greek poet Tyrtaeus[1] and Homer[2] both describe spear shafts as being made of ash wood (Cornelian Cherry was also sometimes used), though an army on the field would fashion replacement shafts out of any wood available. The shaft could be tapered from 25mm (the width that best gives strength whilst keeping weight to a minimum) at the point of balance to the width necessary to fit in the sockets of the spearhead and sauroter, but that would have been done only by a skilled craftsman. In the field less skilled men would have had to fashion untapered shafts about 25mm in diameter, paring down the width of both ends to fit into the sockets of the spearhead and sauroter.

It is difficult to know exactly how long a shaft was since wood rarely survives in the archaeological record. The only extant example of a shaft are fragments discovered in a grave at Vergina, Greece. It was found with the spearhead and a small *styrakion*, or mini-sauroter, *in situ*. The length of the shaft was calculated at 188.2cm, whilst the spearhead was 275mm long and the styrakion 63mm long. The small size of the styrakion would have put the point of balance of the spear forward of its midpoint, which means this weapon was most probably a javelin.[3]

Vase paintings show spears about one and a half times longer than the height of a hoplite. Since the average height of a Greek in Antiquity was about 170cm, that gives a spear length of between 230cm to 280cm. Add to that the weight of an average spearhead and sauroter and the total spear would come in at about 1.332kg. Spearheads and sauroters were attached to the shaft either with pitch or a nail driven through the shaft tube.

What was unique about the spear was its point of balance. Holding any shafted weapon at this point puts the least strain on the wrist as muscles are needed only to hold the weapon aloft, with little effort required to keep it horizontal. If the grip is too far away from the point of balance the wrist must make a constant effort to keep the spear level. Furthermore, a spear with most of its weight on one side of the place where it is gripped is more difficult to wield, having more inertia in the heavy end if one tries to rotate it. For this reason javelins and spears are always held at or near their point of balance, with an equal weight on either side of the place where the spear is gripped.

Christopher Matthew gives a formula for calculating the point of balance of a classical Hoplite's spear.[4] Using this formula, the point of balance of an average spear 255cm long would be 89 cm from the end of the sauroter, or about 1/3 the way up the weapon, which corresponds approximately with the placing of the spear grip in the Achilles painter vase. This made the spear an ideal melee weapon, as most of its length projected in front of the hoplite, maximising his reach against opponents. However it made it useless as a missile weapon since the shaft would tend to tumble if thrown as opposed to a javelin that, weighted towards its front, tends to maintain a much straighter alignment when thrown.

The new design of the spear gave it greater reach in melee combat than the multi-purpose spear of the Archaic period, whose point of balance was either midway along the shaft or slightly towards the spearpoint. With this weapon, the hoplites at Marathon had a striking range well beyond the short 2-metre spears of the Persians that were weighted for throwing as well as being used in melee combat.

How the Spear was Wielded

There are four possible ways of holding a spear: low underarm, high underarm, low overarm and high overarm. All four holds appear in classical Greek art.

Diagram 54: Low underarm.

Diagram 55: High underarm.

Diagram 56: Low overarm.

Diagram 57: High overarm.

The low underarm hold appears in the artistic record but usually in the context of individual combats or the pursuit of a defeated enemy. In a phalanx, with shields overlapping, it would have been impossible to use a spear in this manner with any kind of flexibility, and it would have been equally impossible to raise a spear past the shields to any of the other holds.

The high underarm hold consists of holding the shaft along the forearm, thumb pointing forwards and fingers curled around the far side of the shaft with palm facing the body. This grip has several advantages. The arm does not quickly tire in this position, especially if the spear is rested on the hoplite's shield rim where it overlaps the shield of the neighbour to his right. The spear can be manipulated easily, especially for parrying thrusts of opponents' spears as it is braced against the forearm and capable of strong sideways and up-and-down movement, and the spear is at the right height for thrusts against an opponent's shield or face.

For the low overarm hold, the hand grips the shaft in the same manner as the high underarm hold, but in this case the arm and wrist rotate so as to keep the spear above the forearm. The spear does not touch the forearm. This is a somewhat awkward grip, its principal advantage being that it is the highest way of holding a spear with the same grip as is used for the underarm holds. It also does not expose the forearm as this can be kept below the top edge of the shield.

The high overarm hold uses a different grip. With the forearm raised vertically, the thumb points backwards whilst the palm faces the body and the fingers curl over the shaft in the direction of the body. This is the classic throwing hold used for javelins and is the hold used by the majority of Greek warriors depicted on vases and amphorae. A strike with a spear held this way can be done in two ways: the first is a conventional throwing action in which all the muscles employed for casting a javelin are used to drive the spear at an opponent. The second involves keeping the arm straight whilst using the shoulder muscles to bring the spear down in an 'ice pick' configuration.

The greatest advantage of the high overarm grip is that, of all the grips, with the classic throwing action it imparts the greatest momentum to the spear. Gabriel and Metz recorded velocities of 7.3 m/s for low underarm hold strikes and 16.8 m/s for high overarm hold strikes. Connolly *et al.* recorded 4.8 m/s for low underarm, 3.8 m/s for high underarm, and 6.7 m/s for high overarm holds.[5] Christopher Matthew recorded only 6.5 m/s for high overarm, compared to 8.1 m/s for low underarm, 8.3 m/s for high underarm, and 6.5 m/s for low overarm holds. But it is clear from his diagrams that his high overarm strikes used the 'ice pick' method, with the arm kept straight rather than moving flexibly whilst holding the spear a little above shoulder height as for a throwing action.

Despite the differing figures for the velocities, the overall trend shows that a spear cast overhead with a throwing motion will travel much faster than a spear thrust forwards with the other three holds, or thrust overhead with an ice pick movement. This means that a spear strike with the high overarm hold has the greatest chance of penetrating enemy armour. Furthermore, it is quite possible to extend the range of a spear used in this manner by loosening the grip on the shaft at the moment of release without actually letting go of the spear, and pulling the spear back from the sauroter (which acts as a natural stop to this sliding movement) if the strike is not successful. Naturally a spear that penetrates an opponent's shield and armour cannot be easily pulled back. This sliding technique has been successfully demonstrated by Thegn Thrand.[6]

The weakness of the high overarm grip is an inability to parry an opponent's spear thrust. Only the wrist can be used to swivel the spear in place, and it is not strong enough to impart powerful lateral movements to the spear shaft. A strike with the high overarm hold can itself be easily parried by an opponent using the high underarm grip as he will have no difficulty knocking the spear aside. Contrary to Matthew, the high overarm is not tiring on the arm muscles provided the spear is held at the level of the shoulder with the arm bent close to the chest, and then raised and drawn back for a strike.

Which hold was employed by hoplites? There are examples of all four holds in the artistic record, and whereas most of the weapons held with the high overarm grip on Greek vases and amphorae are clearly javelins, there remains a minority that are equally clearly spears with a centre of balance well back from the shaft's midpoint. It is probable that all four holds were used in battle. The low underarm hold in open combat or whilst pursuing routed troops, as it is the most practical hold whilst running. The high underarm when sparring defensively, and the high overarm when executing a strike aimed at penetrating an opponent's armour. It is quite easy to change between the high underarm and high overarm holds. The hoplite moves the spear up from the high underarm to the low overarm position. He then momentarily releases his grip on the shaft, rotates his hand 180 degrees so his palm faces his body, and resumes his grip on the shaft. It takes a split second to accomplish.

The Shield

The one big change to the shield was the material used for its construction. Leather was replaced with wood which was sometimes covered with a layer of bronze between 0.2 and 0.5mm thick. This round shield, called an *aspis*, consisted of a bowl with a depth of about 10cm and a diameter of 80cm to 120 cm, averaging at about 90cm. Around the bowl was a rim 4–5 cm wide. The wood was 5–6mm thick over much of the bowl, thickening to 8mm at the centre and 14mm at the edges. The rim was also thick and accounted for 20–40 per cent of the total mass of wood in the shield. The wood was sometimes made up of criss-crossing layers that negated its weakness against a strike by a spear blade that entered the wood parallel to its grain.

Inside the shield in the centre was a cuff generally made of wood or bronze, the *porpax*, into which the forearm was inserted. The weight of the shield hung from the forearm at a point near the elbow. A hand grip, the *antelabe* was fixed inside the bowl near the rim. Gripping the antelabe kept the forearm tightly in the porpax and prevented the shield from rotating around the arm.

The advantage of this double grip is that it required little muscular effort to keep the shield at the ready. The shield could also be rotated around the elbow and remain in the same position relative to the body. There were however several disadvantages. The shield could not be extended far from the body hence could not be used as an offensive weapon against an opponent. Although the lower edge of shield could be extended the shield itself could not be lowered to protect the legs – if the hoplite found it impractical to extend his shield he was obliged to bend down if he wished to use it to block strikes against his shins or feet. Finally, although the shield adequately covered the front of his body it did not offer equal protection against attacks angling in from either side since nearly half its surface area extended left of the hoplite's left elbow, leaving the hoplite more vulnerable to a strike from his right.

The domed shape of the shield, reinforced by the thick sides of the dome and the thick rim, gave one crucial advantage: it made a concerted push by a file possible, with the shield of one hoplite pressed into the back of the hoplite in front of him. The dome enabled a hoplite to breathe with his diaphragm despite the pressure, and the thick sides of the dome plus the reinforcing rim prevented the shield's bowl from collapsing. Paul Bardunias conducted tests during the Marathon Archeion Dromena re-enactment event of 2015. Up to 11 men pushed shield-to-back against a pressure scale fixed to a tree. Pressures of more than a quarter of a ton were recorded but the shields did not break and no-one was injured.[7]

The Sword

The principal weakness of the classical hoplite's spear was, paradoxically, its reach. Extending 5 – 6 feet or more in front of his hand, he could not use it against an opponent that came into close contact with him. It is for this reason that hoplites were armed with the *xiphos* – a stabbing sword – or the *kopis* (or *machaira*), a sword used principally as a cutting weapon. Spartans used the smaller *enchiridion*, a dagger-like weapon (though it also appears on Theban stelai from the early 4th century onwards and in Athenian art). These swords, ideally suited to fighting in a limited space, would have been devastating in the crush of close combat, with shield pressed against shield as the two hoplite phalanxes pushed against each other.

Body Armour

Helmet

Helmets came in a variety of styles. Corinthian helmets – the most popular kind – offered maximum protection to the head and neck, the offsetting disadvantage being a certain loss of peripheral and downward vision, and an inability to tell the direction sound was coming from (later

Corinthian helmets had ear holes to correct the latter defect). Other helmets were more open, offering less protection for the face and throat, and the simple and easily manufactured pilos offered no protection to the face and neck at all, its only advantages being its cheapness and protection from descending strikes.

Cuirass

The bell cuirass in Archaic Greece had been made of bronze, whilst its classical version, the linen corselet, was made of an ingenious combination of linen and leather that was lighter, cheaper to manufacture, and just as effective.

The original bronze cuirass had been elaborately moulded to imitate human musculature – and provide plenty of angled surfaces for spears to glance off. Many cuirasses bore leather or textile *pteryges*, arranged in overlapping double rows to protect the body below waist level.

By the fifth century BC, the bronze cuirass had been largely replaced by the linen corselet. It consisted of a tube of leather or textile that covered the torso from hips to pectoral muscles, and was fastened shut on the left side. Two shoulder guards, the *epomides*, were attached to the back of the tube and wrapped round each shoulder to the front where they were tied. Like for bronze cuirasses, *pteryges*, dangling leather strips, were hung to protect the lower torso and upper legs.

There are endless debates as to what the linen corselets were made of. Multiple layers of twinned linen offer adequate protection against arrow fire, and if reinforced by kaolin (the 'white clay' or *argilos* that Aelian describes as appropriate armour for light troops), are resistant against spear and sword thrusts, as has been proven for Kevlar armour. What is more interesting is that 8 layers of kaolin-treated linen, 4–5mm thick, offered as much protection as 3 layers of leather, 6mm thick.[8]

Linen corselets were often augmented with iron or bronze scales covering a greater or lesser area of the linen.

Greaves

Since the aspis offered no protection for the lower legs, clip-on greaves were worn to remedy this defect. Originally made of bronze and extending to below the knee, by the classical period they covered the leg from knee cap to ankle and were anatomically correct renditions of the knee and calf. At the end of the fifth century BC many hoplites exchanged greaves for high sandal boots, the invention of which was attributed to Iphicrates.

4. The Hoplite

The single most important fact about a Greek hoplite is that he was not a trained professional. With the exception of Sparta, no Greek city-state had a standing army though a few, like Thebes, kept small bodies of professional soldiers maintained at state expense. In time of war eligible citizens – i.e. citizens wealthy enough to supply their own arms and armour, which was actually a minority of the adult male population – were called up for a campaign season that began after the spring sowing and was concluded before the winter harvest.

Earlier hoplite clashes were border disputes between neighbouring *poleis*, usually over land that was often not optimal for agriculture but became valuable as the cities' populations expanded and the need for land grew. A single battle was usually enough to decide the issue, after which everyone could go home. These were not wars of conquest, just a means of settling ownership of marginal border land (any Greek city-state that tried to play the conquest game would rapidly find itself outmatched by a hostile alliance of neighbours determined to put the upstart in its place). Hence there was no need to keep an army in the field for years, even less on a permanent basis.

This meant that a hoplite who went into battle had very little training though he might have some combat experience from previous engagements. Since he was a man of substance, he could generally afford to be accompanied by a personal servant who carried his equipment and rendered general service. These servants also served as skirmishers (*psiloi*) on the battlefield, armed with javelins, or perhaps bows or slings, and little else. Hoplites and their retainers were neither paid, equipped nor supplied by the state until the mid-5th century, after which they received a very small stipend. It was the cheapest way for a Greek polis of modest means to field a well-equipped army that was reasonably sized, but it meant that the hoplite's drill routines were very elementary, usually limited to forming up in files of regular depth that assembled into a line and then advanced into battle.

As time wore on and the original limited border clashes gradually developed into full-scale wars between coalitions, this lack of battlefield manoeuvrability became an increasing problem, particularly in battles against highly-trained Spartans, and some Greek states created small, professional units, the *epilektoi*, to compensate for this defect. These were the Argive One Thousand, the Syracusan Six Hundred, the 300-man Sacred Band of Thebes, the Arcadian *Eparitoi*, and the Three Hundred and the Four Hundred at Elis. These men, paid, equipped and fed by their *poleis*, could train up to a level that matched Sparta's best troops. Epilektoi could either operate as independent units or stand in the front rank of citizen hoplites, acting as the best fighters of the army. Wealthier rulers hired mercenaries, though these likewise were usually small bodies of troops. But no Greek state was prepared to undertake the kind of drastic social reformation *a la* Sparta necessary to enable all of its wealthier male citizens to become professional soldiers. The average hoplite remained an amateur to the end.

5. The Structure of the Phalanx

By the time of Thermopylae, the individual combats between heroes of the Iliad were a thing of the past. The hoplite, in adopting a shield that he could not use offensively and a spear that he could not throw, had become a specialist whose mode of fighting was effective only as part of that formation unique to Greece that was the phalanx.

The phalanx was a battle line and battle lines tended to form naturally, settling into their linear configuration from a natural bottom-up self-organising process rather than being imposed by top-down regimentation. A man who fights does not want more than one enemy to deal with at a time otherwise he will be overmatched. To ensure that happens, he needs to put himself in a position where he can be attacked from only one direction by one opponent. The most natural way for a group of men to do that is to form a line, facing their opponents to their front whilst their rear is secure from attack.

Once a basic line is formed it takes a little additional hierarchical structuring to refine this line into a row of files: grouping the men into file units with one man as file leader, a second-in-command, and a number three. The file leader, the best fighter in the file, takes the front place. His second-in-command, also a redoubtable fighter, is right behind him to replace him should he fall in combat. The number three stands at the back of the file and ensures the file remains straight as well as preventing any man from playing the coward during battle.

Once the file is organised this way the rest is easy. The file leaders stand side-by-side to give each other mutual protection. They ensure the files are properly spaced from each other, not so near that their movement and fighting is restricted, but near enough to close any gaps between one file and the next that the enemy might exploit. To determine the correct distance the aspis was a practical yardstick. Shield rim touching shield rim gave each file about three feet of lateral space, the standard interval for infantry in combat formation. In fact three feet was a tad too wide for the hoplite style of combat as hoplites needed their shields to overlap in order to give maximum protection, so they compensated by closing their files up as they advanced towards the enemy. But shields still provided the easiest and most reliable method for lining up files during deployment in an evenly-spaced line.

Phalanx Depth

Phalanxes varied in depth from possibly 1 rank (in one extreme case) to 50 ranks deep in the case of the Theban column, but the most common depth was 8 ranks. Christopher Matthew gives the depths of phalanxes in all engagements recorded in the sources.[9] There is one mention of a depth of 1 rank, two mentions of 2 ranks, two mentions of 4 ranks, ten mentions of 8 ranks, two mentions of 9–10 ranks, one mention of 12 ranks (in fact 12 or less ranks), two mentions of 16 ranks, three mentions of the Theban column at 25–50 ranks, one mention of an Athenian line formed 50 ranks deep in a street, and three mentions of very deep formations in special circumstances.

A phalanx rarely if ever deployed less than 8 deep for a regular battle, the one notable exception being at Marathon, where the Athenians were obliged to thin out their centre in order to be able to pack more hoplites on the flanks and still match the width of the Persian deployment. This led to the centre of their line being ruptured by the Persians.[10]

It has been proposed that hoplites regularly deployed two ranks deep for battle, as described by Xenophon in his *Cyropaedia*: a fictional account of the Persian King Cyrus but which gives insights into Greek and Persian military systems in Xenophon's time. In one passage Cyrus orders his generals to deploy his army, anachronistically Greek in character, in lines shallower than those of the much larger army of Croesus who had drawn up his troops 30 ranks deep with the Egyptian contingent deployed 100 deep:

> 'So instruct your taxiarchs and locharchs to form a line with each separate lochon [in this passage a lochon is roughly equivalent to a Spartan enomotia] two deep'. Now each lochos contained twenty-four men.
>
> 'And do you think, Cyrus', said one of the generals, 'that drawn up with lines so shallow we shall be a match for so deep a phalanx?'
>
> 'When phalanxes are too deep to reach the enemy with weapons', answered Cyrus, 'how do you think they can either hurt their enemy or help their friends?' – *Cyropaedia*: 6.3.21–23.

'Two deep' however is a mistranslation of the Greek: εἰς δύο – *eis duo* 'in two', which means, not two ranks, but two **files**. Xenophon uses the same term when describing the Spartan deployment at Leuctra:

> Coming now to the infantry, it was said that the Lacedaemonians led each enomotia three files abreast [εἰς τρεῖς – *eis treis* 'in three'], and that this resulted in the phalanx being not more than twelve men deep. – *Hellenica*: 6.4.12.

Thus, Cyrus' infantry were to be deployed in two files per lochon which, at 24 men per lochon (Xenophon supplies the number to allow the reader to make the calculation), created a line 12 ranks deep – a standard depth for a phalanx but much shallower than the infantry lines of the Fertile Crescent.

A phalanx rarely exceeded 16 deep. Besides the Theban column – a special formation which will be examined later – very deep formations were adopted only in narrow places, such as a pass,[11] the confines of a port,[12] or as a sally from a besieged city's gate.[13]

Phalanx Subdivisions

The phalanx was not a single homogeneous unit but, like any army, was subdivided into smaller units which were themselves subdivided, and so on. The only Greek state for which we have any detailed information on this structuring is Sparta. Thucydides describes the strength and composition of the Spartan army at the first Battle of Mantinea (418 BC):

> There were seven lochoi in the field without counting the Sciritae, who numbered six hundred men: in each lochos there were four pentekostyes [*pentekostues*], and in the pentekosty four enomotias [*enomotiai*]. The first rank of the enomotia was composed of four soldiers: as to the depth, although they had not been all drawn up alike, but as each lochagos chose, they were generally ranged eight deep; the first rank along the whole line, exclusive of the Sciritae, consisted of four hundred and forty-eight men. – *History of the Peloponnesian War*: 5.68.

Each subdivision is one quarter the size of the unit it is part of. At Mantinea an *enomotia* has four files of eight men, 32 men in all. A *pentekosty* has 128 men, a *lochos* 512 men, and the entire Spartan component of seven *lochoi* totalled 3,584 men, which at eight ranks per file comes out at 448 files.

An enomotia seems to have been flexible in size, as Xenophon describes enomotias at Leuctra in 371 BC as being arranged 'three files abreast, and that this resulted in the phalanx being not more than twelve men deep'. – *Hellenica*: 6.4.12. Three files times twelve men per file = 36 men, however the 'not more than' implies that each enomotia was actually less than 36 men, some files having eleven men or even fewer.

Shortly after Mantinea the Spartan army underwent a refinement to its organisation. A new level of command was inserted between the pentekosty and the enomotia and had a strength of two enomotias. This new unit retained the name of the pentekosty, whilst the old pentekosty was renamed the lochos and the former lochos was now called a mora. In this new arrangement there were two enomotias in a pentekosty, two pentekostyes in a lochos, and four lochoi in a mora.

A mora was commanded by a *polemarchos*,[14] a lochos by a *lochagos*, a pentekosty by a *pentekoster* and an enomotia by an *enomotarchos*.

> The men so equipped were divided into six morai of cavalry and infantry. The officers of each citizen regiment comprise one polemarchon, four lochagous, eight pentekosters and sixteen enomotarchous. These regiments at the word of command form enomotias sometimes [here a word is missing], sometimes three, and sometimes six abreast. – Xenophon, *Constitution of the Lacedaemonians*: 11.

It is worth noting that Thucydides, in the same passage where he describes the old Spartan structure, gives the ranks of command for the reformed Spartan army:

> For whilst the king has the army in the field, all things are commanded by him; and he signifies what is to be done to the polemarchois, they to the lochagois, these to the pentecontersin, and these again to the enomotarchois, who lastly make it known, every one to his own enomotia. – *History of the Peloponnesian War*: 5.66.

However in this passage he is speaking of the Spartan army *in general*, in which an efficient command structure carries out the orders of the Spartan king. This structure does not necessarily apply in every detail to the army that fought at Mantinea.

Given that an enomotia has 32 men (at a standard muster), it could be deployed at 10–11 deep at three men abreast and about 5–6 deep at six men abreast, which means that the missing word in the passage from the *Constitution of the Lacedaemonians* is either a 'four', a 'one' or a 'two'. The entire unit could deploy either into a single file 32 deep, making it comparable to the deep formations used by the Thebans and others, or it could deploy into two files each 16 deep, the maximum standard depth for a phalanx. There is no record however of the Spartan army ever using either of these deployments.

If deployed in 4 files a 32-man enomotia would be 8 ranks deep – the most common depth – which makes '4' the most likely choice for the missing number, and which also corresponds to the Spartan deployment at Mantinea and elsewhere. '4' would be mentioned first as it is the most frequent arrangement of the enomotia, followed by '3' and finally by '6' – a shallow formation only occasionally used (Diodorus Siculus also describes one instance of the Spartan phalanx deploying 4 deep before the walls of Athens, which means the enomotias formed up 8 files wide, but this was done to envelop the city and not as a true battle formation).

Why the new subdivision between the 32-man enomotia and the old 128-man pentekosty? Since Greek phalanxes, Spartan included, habitually formed up 8 ranks deep, the new 64-man pentekosty would form a perfect square, measuring 8 files by 8 ranks. This makes it the ideal size and shape to wheel on the battlefield. A phalanx never wheeled as a single unit, but did so by subunits whose shape had to be square to enable following subunits to line up on the wheeled subunit and wheel in turn, as described by Asklepiodotus, who names the syntagma, a unit measuring 16 files by 16 ranks, as the wheeling formation in a pike phalanx (See Chapter 1: 3. *Heavy Infantry – Manoeuvres*). The ability to wheel a line in this manner on the battlefield was a crucial factor in deciding the outcome of hoplite battles, as will be seen later. The mention by Xenophon of the Spartan general summoning his polemarchs and pentekosters to a war council[15], omitting the lochargous and the enomotarchs, makes sense if the new pentekosty was now the manoeuvring unit on the battlefield.

With 36 men the arrangement of the enomotia is neater: 12 men deep at 3 files abreast, 6 men deep at 6 abreast, and 9 men deep at 4 abreast. Two enomotias of this size grouped into a pentekosty of 72 men could deploy 8 files wide and 9 ranks deep, near enough to a square as no matter and perfectly serviceable for wheeling as described above.

It has been pointed out[16] that if a mora numbering about 512 men or possibly a little more at a full muster of Spartan citizens who were part of the professional army, the entire Spartan army of 6 morai would number no more than about 3,500 men. This is small compared to the armies raised by other Greek states and Lazenby (who argues for a larger Spartan regular army) proposes that many Spartans who were citizens but not fully-qualified to serve as professional soldiers in the regular army could in fact form part of the Spartan military establishment though not on a full-time basis, either as part of the regular morai or in separate units. This would enable Sparta to increase the size of its army well above the normal muster when the need arose. It would also suggest that Sparta, not an especially wealthy state, could not afford to maintain a permanent professional army at state expense that was equal in size to the temporary citizen levies raised free-of-charge by the other Greek poleis.

However it is simpler and better fits with the sources to accept that for most of its battles the regular Spartan army did not make use of the non-professional Spartan citizens and never numbered more than about 3,500 men, the balance being supplied by Sparta's allies who outnumbered the Spartan contingent:

> Moreover, the allies of the Lacedaemonians were offended at Agesilaus, because, as they said, it was not upon any public ground of complaint, but by reason of some passionate resentment of his own, that he sought to destroy the Thebans. Accordingly, they said they had no wish to be dragged hither and thither to destruction every year, **they themselves so many, and the Lacedaemonians, with whom they followed, so few.** – Plutarch, *Life of Agesilaus*: 20.

Agesilaus reigned from 398–360 BC. During that period the armies fielded by Sparta of which we have numbers and that were composed of its own troops and those of its Peloponnesian allies incorporated around 10,000–15,000 hoplites: 13,500 at Nemea and 10,000–11,000 at Leuctra. Diodorus describes a Spartan army of 18,000 infantry[17] that invaded Boeotia under Agesilaus, however the Greek word for 'infantry' used here is στρατιώτας *stratiotas* – a general term referring to any kind of foot soldier, not just hoplites. Agesilaus had many light troops – psiloi – in his army, as Diodorus describes him using them to assault the Athenians:

As for Agesilaus, he led out his army in battle array against the Boeotians, and, when he had drawn near, in the first place launched his light-armed troops [*psiloi*] against his opponents, thus testing their disposition to fight him. – *Library*: 15.32.4.

The hoplite component would clearly have been considerably less than 18,000 men.

Hence a composite Spartan army would have incorporated between about ¼ and ⅓ actual Spartan hoplites, which fits well with the passage from Plutarch. Besides allies, Sparta sometimes also used perioiki – dwellers in Spartan territory that were not full citizens – as additional troops.[18] In an emergency the unfree non-citizens – helots – would also be called up.[19]

The Spartan contingent at Nemea totalled 6,000 men of which about 2,500 were Spartan troops and the balance were 'Lakedaimonians', a term that is not synonymous with 'Spartans'. All Spartans were Lakedaimonians but not all Lakedaimonians were Spartans. Whether they correspond to perioiki or helots or both is debated.

We know less about how the other Greek poleis organised their phalanxes. Only one subdivision of the phalanx is mentioned in the sources: a unit about 1,000 hoplites strong. Aristotle describes Athens as having 10 taxiarchs who each commanded a *taxis*. The largest army fielded by Athens numbered 9,000 hoplites[20] led by 10 generals (*strategoi*), which suggests that an Athenian taxis was in the region of 900 men, possibly 1,000 by the time of Aristotle as the Athenian population would have increased in numbers. Boeotia appointed eleven boeotarchs, each in command of a *meros* of 1,000 hoplites and 100 cavalry.[21] One can assume that other Greek city states organised their armies on similar lines. The absence of any mention of smaller subunits suggests that the larger units were adequate for what was expected of them: to march in column to the battlefield, form up in a line, and then advance upon the enemy. Since the citizen hoplites were not professionally trained there was no need for subunits that could execute more complex manoeuvres during a battle.

Besides these citizen hoplite formations there were also the professional military units maintained at state expense by several of the larger poleis. Composed of full-time soldiers, these units were able to train up to a level that matched the Spartan elite.

6. Deploying the Phalanx for Battle

According to Xenophon, the Spartan army marched in column with one enomotia following another.[22] How was each enomotia configured? For Connolly and Sekunda, it marched in a one-man-wide line 36 men deep, with three files each with 12 men following each other. When deploying for battle the frontmost file of the leading enomotia stopped. The second file behind it marched to the left alongside it. The third file marched to the left of the second file until parallel with it. The next enomotia deployed to the left of the first enomotia, file by file, and so on until the entire army was deployed in a battle line 12 ranks deep.

There are three problems with this theory. The first is that the marching column would be very long, probably about 6km in length or more (at 4–5 feet per rank in loose marching order) not including Spartan allies, making it difficult to deploy quickly in line should an enemy suddenly appear which, according to Xenophon, happened frequently enough for the Spartans to require a drill tailored for the event. Secondly, there is no proof that enomotias ever formed up one file wide. Xenophon describes them forming units 3 and 6 files wide, with a third missing width that is probably 4 files wide. Thirdly, there is no recorded instance of a Spartan army actually deploying 12 ranks deep.

Armies in Antiquity had no problem marching off-road across the countryside, hence their columns could easily be wider than the width of the tracks available to them. The ideal width for a column would be narrow enough to negotiate around difficult terrain but wide enough to keep the length of the army short and able to deploy quickly into a battle line. Given that a phalanx usually deployed 8 ranks deep, it makes sense to suppose that an enomotia in column was 4 files wide, each file having 8 men. When deploying for battle, one enomotia could march up alongside the enomotia in front and immediately be at the correct depth. The length of a full-strength Spartan army (minus allies) marching 4 files wide would be around 1½ km – short enough to react quickly to a sudden threat as the men at the back of the line could reach the front in about 15 minutes or less.

Enomotias could deploy into line in this fashion facing ahead, right or left. To deploy facing right, the lead enomotia would wheel right. The following enomotia would wheel right and move up alongside its right. The next enomotia would follow suite, and so on. The same process was followed when deploying to face the left.

Diagram 58: The Enomotias marching in open order.

Diagram 59: The Enemotias halt and close up to intermediate order.

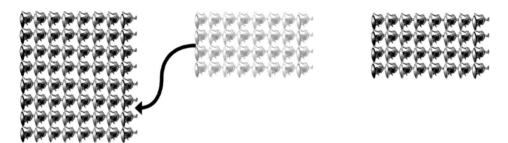

Diagram 60: The second Enomotia moves up alongside the first.

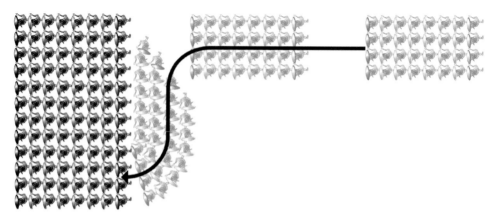

Diagram 61: The third Enomotia moves up alongside the second,
and the process continues for the remaining enomotias.

Given that enomotias also deployed 3 and 6 files wide, this would enable phalanxes to be formed that were about 10–11 ranks deep (as was the case at the Battle of Leuctra) or about 5 ranks deep, though there is no record of the last deployment ever being used.

When deploying, did hoplites overlap their shields? Christopher Matthew gives examples of hoplites deploying in close order – which for him means files 45cm wide though in reality they could not be narrower than about 60cm.[23] However none of the instances he cites (except perhaps one) refer to a regular deployment of a hoplite phalanx on the battlefield. The fact that despite several mentions of hoplites bunching up, presumably with overlapping shields, there is no mention of them doing so before the onset of a battle, makes it reasonable to conclude that hoplites generally formed up in intermediate order, i.e. with shield rims touching and each file about 3 feet wide.

Thucydides confirms an initial intermediate deployment when he states that a phalanx would move to the right as it advanced as each hoplite sought the protection of his neighbour's shield:

> All armies are alike in this: on going into action they get forced out rather on their right wing, and one and the other overlap with this their adversary's left; because fear makes each man do his best to shelter his unarmed side with the shield of the man next him on the right, thinking that the closer the shields are locked together the better will he be protected. – *History of the Peloponnesian War*: 5.71.

This rightwards drift was more a contraction of the line than a movement as the files compacted together to the right to enable the shields to overlap and give each hoplite the protection on his right side he needed (the officer on the rightmost file would move as he saw fit, having no reason to edge towards the right as there was no shield there to shelter behind – and certainly his subordinate file leader on his left would not try to jostle him rightwards).

How was this overlapping of shields done? There were three possible ways:

a) a shield overlapped the shield to its left and was overlapped by the shield to its right (see Diagram 62);

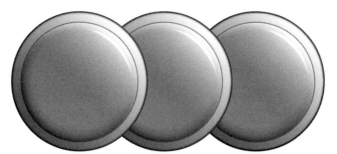

Diagram 62: Shields overlapping to the left.

b) a shield overlapped the shield to its right and was overlapped by the shield to its left (see Diagram 63);

Diagram 63: Shields overlapping to the right.

c) every other shield was in front of its two neighbours, such that, say, all odd-numbered shields overlapped both their neighbours and all even-numbered shields were overlapped by their neighbours (see Diagram 64).

Diagram 64: Mixed overlap.

Of the three options, a) is the most effective. Bardunias[24] states that b) has the disadvantage of the shield to the right getting between hoplite's chest and his shield-arm, compromising the ability of his shield's bowl-shape to allow his diaphragm to breath during othismos (see below). Furthermore, any pressure on the left half of his shield tends to rotate it as it is not braced against anything. Matthew points out that given the shape of the shield, the rightmost hoplite would be slightly in front of the hoplite to his left, who in turn would be slightly ahead of the hoplite to his left, and so on, creating an oblique line with the right projecting ahead of the left. This is not a problem since the opposing hoplite line would also be oblique, its right projecting ahead of its left, and hence both lines would meet more or less simultaneously along their lengths (see Diagram 65).

Diagram 65: Oblique hoplite lines meet.

Alternatively, hoplites could simply tilt their overlapped shields, with the left side slightly ahead, and maintain a straight line (see Diagram 66).

Diagram 66: Tilted overlaps.

With option a) the shield to the right overlaps the hoplite's shield, leaving him free to breathe during othismos. Furthermore, the right side of his shield overlaps the shield of his neighbour on the left who gives it firm support against pressure. He himself supports the shield of the neighbour on his right. This mutual support of shields against pressure creates a rigid shieldwall that cannot cave in to pressure at any point. Option a) also helps the second hoplite in a file to take up the post of the frontmost hoplite who has fallen in combat. To do so he must turn his shield so the left side faces forward and then advance and insert the left side of his shield in front of his neighbour's shield on the left. Since the left side projects well past his forearm, he remains well protected on the left whilst not exposing himself on the right.

Option c) is better than option b) but not as good as option a), as some hoplites will find their breathing obstructed by the shields of the neighbours to their right, whilst others will find their shields easily rotated during othismos. But the main disadvantage of this arrangement is the near-impossibility of the hoplite standing behind a hoplite whose shield is in front of those of his neighbours to replace him should he fall in combat. The second hoplite would need to angle his shield forwards in order to fit it through the narrow gap between the neighbouring shields, which would expose him to an enemy strike. If he simply takes his place with his shield behind those of his neighbours the shieldwall risks eventually becoming ruptured (see Diagram 67).

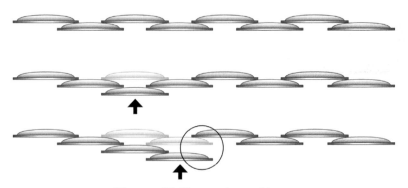

Diagram 67: Non-overlap problems.

To what extent did shields overlap, or in other words, how close together were the files? Christopher Matthew puts the width of each file at 45cm, basing his figure on the close order interval of 1 cubit (1½ feet) given by the Hellenistic manuals. This interval however clearly applies to the pike phalanx, the phalangites of which had smaller shields. It is not actually possible to wield a 3 foot wide shield in an overlapping shield wall with each hoplite having only a foot and a half of lateral space, since the distance from the elbow in the porpax to the edge of the shield is greater than half the width of the shield, meaning one cannot get half of one's shield width behind that of a neighbouring hoplite, and trying to put one's shield in front would result in his shield edge striking against one's forearm. According to Bardunias the minimum file width that is practical for hoplite combat is about 60cm, with up to a third of a shield overlapping that of its neighbour.

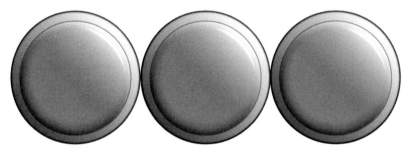

Diagram 68: Shields with files 90cm wide.

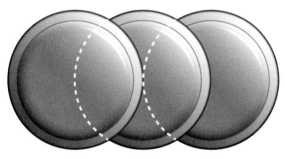

Diagram 69: Shields with files 45cm wide.

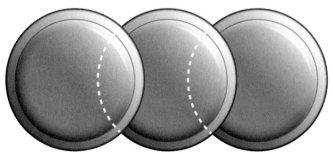

Diagram 70: Shields with files 60cm wide.

Order of Deployment

In a phalanx, the right front corner of an enomotia, a pentekosty, a lochos and a mora (or taxis) was where the commanding officer was positioned. An officer of a unit would move to the file on his left to make way for a superior officer, as shown in Diagram 71:

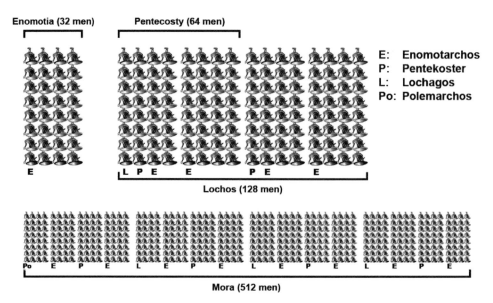

Diagram 71: The placing of officers.

This predilection for the right also applied to the units themselves, with the elite formations generally taking up position on the right flank of a line. There were good reasons for placing officers and the best units on the right which will be examined below.

7. The Phalanx in Combat

A battle between two phalanxes typically went through six stages: preliminary skirmishing; the advance; the charge; fighting with spears; othismos and, lastly, the rout.

The Preliminary skirmishing

The two opposing lines generally formed up several hundred yards apart, waiting sometimes for several hours whilst opposing skirmisher infantry or cavalry engaged in the space between them.

Hoplite battles had originally consisted of the hoplites themselves throwing javelins at their opponents before closing to hand-to-hand fighting with spears. Once the hoplite's weaponry became adapted exclusively to melee combat, light troops were used to cast javelins, arrows and sling-bullets at the enemy line to disorder it before their own heavy infantry closed for melee. The inevitable result was that the light troops, originally meant to harass the hoplites, became a screen against each other, deploying in front of the infantry to absorb the missiles of their opponents. Tribal warfare in New Guinea, recorded on camera in 1962,[25] shows that there are surprisingly few casualties from this kind of combat, which can go on for hours without any appreciable result.

The initial skirmish combat hence became a way of enabling both sides to deploy and reshuffle their units without fear of a sudden attack, and to try and ascertain the intentions of their opponent. If skirmisher foot were involved these preliminaries were usually concluded without incident but in the case of cavalry if one troop of horse was defeated by the other that could have adverse effects on the phalanx of the losers, as when the Spartan cavalry at Leuctra were driven back against the Spartan phalanx and disrupted it, though this did not have a decisive effect on the outcome of the battle.

The Advance

A phalanx formed up for battle was an impressive sight, and hoplites did everything they could during their advance to turn the awe of their opponents into terror.

The first part of the advance was primarily concerned with keeping order, not an easy thing to do with a line of men that could be more than a kilometre long advancing over ground that was usually overgrown with tall grass interspersed with shrubs, bushes, rocks and the odd tree. Hoplites didn't fight on football fields. Several methods were used to ensure the phalanx remained orderly. Before moving, the commander, posted on the right wing, would shout a watchword that was repeated down the line by his officers. When it reached the end of the line it would be shouted back until it reached the commander, telling him that every unit was in place and ready to advance. Trumpets (the *salpinx*) would be used to order the entire line to begin advancing simultaneously.

Most hoplites were not trained to march in step, except Spartans who advanced in cadence to the sound of flutes. Other hoplites would sing a battle hymn, the paean, to raise their morale and possibly also aid in keeping their marching rhythm, if not immaculately synchronised like the Spartans, then at least fairly regular.

The phalanx would advance remaining intact, until within a certain distance of the enemy,[26] at which point the hoplites would lower their spears to a fighting position, either underarm or overarm as described above. If the hoplite initially held his spear vertically at his side in a grip with his thumb pointing downwards he could raise it immediately to the high overarm position. If he held his spear with his thumb pointing upwards he would lift and then level his spear into the high underarm position. It would depend on the preference of the individual hoplite.

Now disposed for battle, the phalanx would continue its final advance into contact. At this time – or more likely before – the hoplite files will have begun moving together, shields overlapping to create a sturdy and protective shieldwall:

> In the conflict they extend their right wing so as it comes in upon the flank of the left wing of the enemy: and this happens for that every one, through fear, seeks all he can to cover his unarmed side with the shield of him that stands next to him on his right hand, conceiving that to be so locked together is their best defence. The beginning hereof is in the leader of the first file on the right hand, who ever striving to shift his unarmed side from the enemy, the rest upon like fear follow after. – Thucydides, *History of the Peloponnesian War*: 5.71.

This shrinkage of the line would have been impressive. If the phalanx initially deployed with files 3 feet wide, by the time it neared the enemy each file would have contracted to between two and two and a half feet in width, corresponding to the overlap of the shields. Thus a line a kilometre wide consisting of approximately 1,000 files and containing about 8,000 hoplites would shrink to a width of between 830 and 670 yards, leaving about 170 to 330 files on the right flank facing fresh air. The general and his elite troops on the right flank would be 300 yards from the enemy.

This is too much: up to a third of the phalanx, including its best troops, would be unengaged and out of the battle. This leads to the natural conclusion that the commander on the right, who determined the direction the phalanx moved, would have angled his advance towards the **left**, ensuring that the greater part of the phalanx engaged the enemy line frontally but leaving a certain portion on the right free to overlap the enemy's left flank. The commander, lacking any protection by heavy infantry on his vulnerable shieldless side (as Thucydides mentions), would naturally not want the enemy line to overlap his right flank, and so would ensure that he was the one who did the overlapping. His opposite number in the enemy line would do likewise. But it is a reasonable assumption that each hoplite commander would want the overlap to be as little as possible in order to ensure that he was not completely out of the fight. Even with this leftward advance of the commander, the overall progress of the contracting phalanx would have seemed to be towards the right (see Diagram 72).

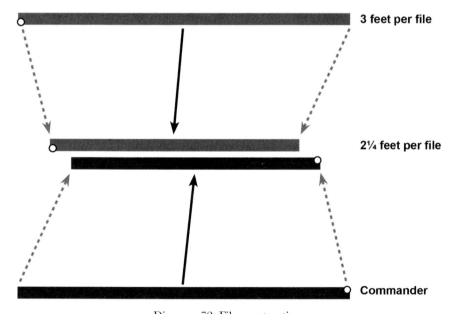

Diagram 72: Files contracting.

Spartan commanders took advantage of this rightwards contraction of the hoplite line to advance more to the right, allowing more of their army to overlap the enemy. According to Xenophon a Spartan commander would position himself between 'two morai and two polemarchs'.[27] Thus if the Spartan phalanx was deployed a standard 8 ranks deep the general would be 64 files from the right flank of the line, which meant that if he personally advanced towards the leftmost file of the enemy, he would have a completely unengaged mora on his right – eight pentekosty units free to advance past the rear of the engaged enemy phalanx, wheel to the left and then move, one behind the other until they were behind the enemy line. They could then wheel left into line again and charge the enemy rear. This ability to wheel around the enemy's flank was a Spartan tactic that decided many of their battles. Less-trained amateur hoplites could not perform it, limiting their own overlapping files to a right-turn in place, followed by an attack on the left edge of the enemy's line.[28]

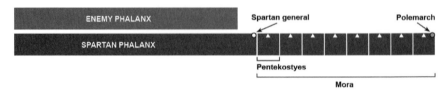

Diagram 73: The Spartan line contacts the enemy.
A Mora remains unengaged to the right of the Spartan general.

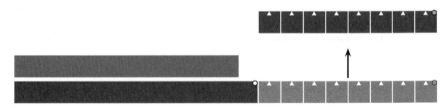

Diagram 74: The Mora advances past the enemy phalanx.

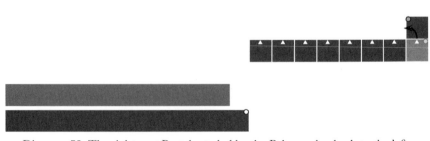

Diagram 75: The rightmost Pentekosty led by the Polemarch wheels to the left.

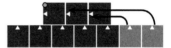

Diagram 76: As the rightmost Pentekosty advances toward the left, the other Pentekostyes wheel and follow it.

Diagram 77: The leading Pentekosty reaches the end of the enemy line, wheels left and advances enough to clear the way for the following Pentekostyes.

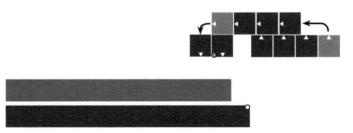

Diagram 78: The second Pentekosty stops when it reaches the far edge of the leading Pentekosty, wheels left and advances alongside the leading Pentekosty. Meanwhile the following Pentekostyes continue to wheel left and advance.

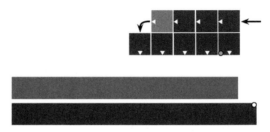

Diagram 79: The remaining Pentekostyes advance and wheel left to reform the line facing the enemy rear.

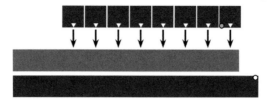

Diagram 79b: The Mora, now in a line again, charges the enemy.

The Charge

Once near the enemy and in battle posture, shields overlapping in front and spears at the ready, the phalanx would cover the last stretch of ground to engage the opposing line. At this point most phalanxes shouted their war cry and closed at a run. The hoplites did this to raise their aggression to fever pitch and quell all feelings of fear and trepidation.[29] It also served to intimidate their opposition. As Ancient warfare was to a large extent an affair of morale, much depended on the individual fighting man's perception of the determination and combat readiness of the enemy. The charge would to a certain extent disorder the phalanx, and some contingents could pull ahead of others.[30]

The run need not have been a sprint. Herodotus affirms that the Athenians charged the Persians at Marathon when the two armies were 'no less than 8 stadia (1440m) apart'.[31] For Matthew this is a literary embellishment, but one need not discount Herodotus if one assumes that the Athenians, carrying their shields at their sides and their spears underarm, advanced on the Persians at a trot calculated to confuse the timing of their volley, in the same way Alexander charged the Persian foot at Issus to get past their arrow fire.[32]

A jogger moves at about 10km/h. Presuming the Athenians moved at this speed, they would cover the distance between themselves and the Persians in less than nine minutes. The Persians 'saw them running to attack and prepared to receive them, thinking the Athenians absolutely crazy, since they saw how few of them there were and that they ran up so fast without either cavalry or archers'. [33] The mention of archers preceding an infantry engagement implies that a preliminary missile exchange was a standard component of Persian battles, and the absence of any mention of Persian archers shooting at the Athenians suggests that the Persians did not have the time to form up properly and loose their arrows in a co-ordinated volley before the Athenians fell upon them.

There was one Greek army that did not close with their opponents at the run or trot: the Spartans. Invariably, the Spartan phalanx advanced at a measured pace, the hoplites keeping time to marching songs accompanied by flutes.

> And when at last they were drawn up in battle array and the enemy was at hand, the king sacrificed the customary she-goat, commanded all the warriors to set garlands upon their heads, and ordered the pipers to pipe the strains of the hymn to Castor; then he himself led off in a marching paean, and it was a sight equally grand and terrifying when they marched in step with the rhythm of the flute, without any gap in their line of battle, and with no confusion in their souls, but calmly and cheerfully moving with the strains of their hymn into the deadly fight. – Plutarch, *Lycurgus*: 22.

This steady advance by the Spartans in silence and perfect array, signalling a cool and confident professionalism, was sometimes enough by itself to cause the enemy to flee.[34]

A battle line composed of Spartan morai and non-Spartan allies invariably split before reaching the enemy, the allies contacting their opponents before the Spartans did. This however had little effect on the subsequent battle since there is no record of appreciable gaps appearing between the Spartan and non-Spartan components of the phalanx once all its elements had reached the enemy.

Once the two opposing phalanxes contacted each other they did not usually charge home like mediaeval knights. As Bardunias points out, infantry charging into infantry did not confer the impetus that was better gained by stopping, reforming the phalanx with ranks compressed shield against back, and then shoving against its opponents with a concerted push.[35] If a running man collides with another running man he will accomplish nothing other than come to a very abrupt halt. Charging at infantry with horses is a very different matter as a horse weighs between a quarter and half a ton, and galloping at about 40km/h has tremendous inertia, quite capable of knocking down several men in succession. The hoplite charge however was all about psychologically intimidating one's enemy, and once the two lines were within spear sparring distance they halted and the real fighting began.

The Sparring of Spears

A hoplite's spear projected for about ⅔ to ¾ of its length ahead of the hoplite himself. The two phalanxes then would have been about six feet apart. Homer describes the front ranks as so closely compressed that 'buckler [was] pressed on buckler, helm on helm, and man on man; and the horse-hair crests on the bright helmet-ridges touched each other, as the men moved their heads, in such close array stood they one by another, and spears in stout hands overlapped each other, as they were brandished'. This refers to a spear combat between two proto-phalanxes of his time, but the mechanics of hoplite spear fighting had not changed in classical Greece, and the close order between the frontmost ranks – to maximise the reach of the second and even third rank spears – would have been the same.

Sophocles describes this initial contest as a 'spear storm', however care must be taken over the term. There were few casualties during the initial stages of a battle, typically 5 per cent for each side, which included not only the initial spear contest but also the ensuing *othismos*. That translates to about 40 per cent of the front rank only of a standard phalanx 8 ranks deep. Movie productions of hoplite battles usually depict a free-for-all: hoplites killing and being killed with wild abandon in the few minutes assigned to the scene. But the reality was very different. Reenactors, like actors, tend to go at each other hammer and tongs, however in a situation where the spearpoints are not blunted and your opponent fully intends to kill you, everything changes. Breaking ranks to lunge at your opponent is tantamount to suicide as you expose the vulnerable parts of your body to a potentially fatal counterblow.

Keeping their shieldwall intact, hoplites would have fenced cautiously, jabbing at their opponents without exposing themselves, and waiting for the right moment to strike with lightning speed before whipping back to the defensive posture again. The 'right moment to strike' would have been when the hoplite perceived a momentary lapse in his opponents' ability to parry his strike and strike back, a lapse possibly caused by their having to deal with his comrades behind or on either side of him. In any case, his strike would have been one of tremendous force as he attempted to penetrate his enemy's armour and ram his spear into the head or chest. Possibly switching from his high underarm to high overarm grip in the blink of an eye, the hoplite would have cast his spear at his opponent with a powerful throwing motion that engaged all the muscles of the arm and shoulder, trying to hit his opponent's shield or helmet at the correct angle so the spearpoint would not glance off but penetrate through the metal and wood. If the spearpoint was not firmly wedged in his opponent's armour the hoplite would whip the spear back, changing his grip to high underarm in an instant and bringing his spear down to the level of his shield, ready to knock aside any counterthrusts by his enemies' spears.

Another kind of strike – best done in this case with a high underarm grip – would have involved trying to slip the spear through the chinks in his enemy's armour: hitting the exposed spear-wielding arm, the legs, the face and the neck. But these could all be parried or blocked by the spear or shield. However the one thing the hoplite could not do was give ground to avoid a strike. His shield was part of an interlocking shieldwall, difficult to disengage from, and he had the hoplite of the second rank right behind him, literally breathing down his neck, whose shield was likewise part of an overlapping shieldwall. The front rank hoplite's shield or armour would have to stop a spear strike; if they could not he was done for.

A successful strike could kill the opponent or at least incapacitate him. A failed strike very often broke the striker's spear shaft.[36] A broken spear put its wielder at an immediate disadvantage: besides lacking its spearpoint, his spear no longer had the reach of his opponent's spear. If he wanted to continue fighting he would have to close in. As more spears were broken the need to close became more imperative and a tipping point was eventually reached when the hoplites came together for the second phase of the battle: the push of shield against shield, or *othismos*.

There is no mention in the sources of hoplites in the rear ranks passing their spears to those fighting in the front. Besides being his personal property, a spear was the hoplite's principal weapon, necessary even in victory when pursuing the fleeing enemy besides being his only effective means of warding off any enemy cavalry in the vicinity. The only recorded example of a weapon being passed on in this manner is during the Battle of the Granicus, in which Alexander, leading his lance-armed cavalry in a charge across the river at the Persian elite cavalry and their commanders, broke his lance and was given another by one of his Companions. But this is probably an exceptional event as the Companion cavalry were committed to keeping their commander alive and aiding him in any way they could. There is no evidence that supporting ranks of infantry felt any similar obligation to give their weapons to their front rankers.

The Shove of Shields

A confrontation between two phalanxes could end during the initial charge, as one line fled in terror from the other. It could also end with the spear contest as one side, feeling itself outmatched by the combat skills or determination of the other, decided on the better part of valour and likewise fled. But most hoplite battles moved on to the third stage when hoplites, their spears broken or simply feeling they were not getting the better of the spear fencing match, moved in past the reach of their enemy's spears and rammed shield against shield for the shoving match that was *othismos*.

Othismos as a viable tactic

Of those who have written books on othismos, Paul Bardunias is unique in that he recreated a simulation of the process, using hoplite reenactors during the 2015 Archaeon Dromena in Marathon, Greece.[37] A pressure sensor was fixed to a tree. A reenactor then pressed his shield against the sensor and the pressure he exerted was recorded. After about 20 seconds a second reenactor leaned against the first reenactor, shield pressing on his back. 20 seconds later a third reenactor pressed against the first, and so on, until 10 hoplites were shoving against each other. The process was repeated three times.

The reenactors discovered that if braced by two adjacent files the central file was able to exert much more pressure. During this process the hoplites' bodies faced forwards, the top rim of their shields pressed against the front of their shoulder and upper chest and the bottom rim against their thighs. They were able to breathe thanks to the space within the cavity of their shields, and although the shields creaked they did not break. The file braced by two adjacent files reached a pressure of 368kg, even though it was only six men deep.

What is of interest is that as each man added his weight to the file, the pressure exerted against the sensor went up, but by less each time. By the time the eighth man added his weight, the pressure increased by less than 10kg per man.

Eight of the reenactors also tried freestyle pushing, each man pressing his shield with his left shoulder inside the bowl of the shield against the man in front whilst his body was angled at about 45 degrees. This worked less well, the pressure increasing after the fourth man only because the bodies of the men in the front were turned to face forwards by the pressure behind them.

A phalanx with files packed close together and composed of fit hoplites for whom pushing determined victory could have exerted pressures reaching half a ton. This mattered. The phalanx was designed to prevent one thing happening – recoil. Recoil was the precursor of rout, as a buckling line signalled to its men that it could not withstand the enemy and they were doomed if they did not run. Individual hoplites, their shields locked together and with fellow hoplites right behind them also with shields locked, could not recoil to avoid their opponents'

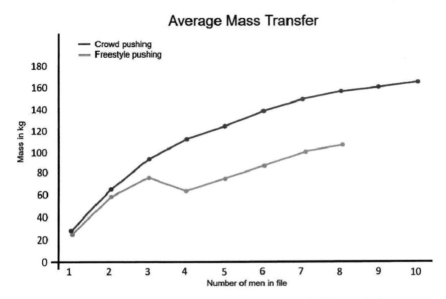

Diagram 80: Graph © Paul Bardunias. Reproduced with permission.

blows, but had to rely on their armour to protect them. A phalanx being pushed back gave the clearest signal that it was outmatched and could not do what, as a formation, it was supposed to do. The only option was to run, which is why whoever won the othismos contest won the battle. Othismos then was clearly a viable tactic.

One problem with this practical examination of othismos remains: Bardunias established that from the 8th man onwards, a hoplite file exerted very little additional pressure. Why then did the Theban columns use files of 25 or 50 hoplites to push against their opponents, and successfully as well?

There are two reasons for these great depths: first, that whereas adding more men to a file did very little in general to increase the pressure that file was able to exert, there would be moments when all the men of the file exerted pressure in unison, creating a brief peak in the pressure that forced an opposing file backwards. Secondly, the pressure exerted by hoplites was not continuous, but applied in bursts, with pauses to rest the muscles. In those pauses the opposing phalanx could press forwards and push its opponents back until those hoplites began pushing again, stopping their recoil and even resuming their advance. However, if the hoplites had a deep mass of additional hoplites behind them, they could not be pushed back, even when resting, whereas they could themselves push a shallower phalanx back. Bit by bit, a deeper phalanx could drive a shallower phalanx before it until the shallower phalanx finally broke.

What is also clear is that if a deep phalanx did not help in an othismos contest, then it served no purpose. The men in the rear ranks could not help the men in front, nor were they needed to replace them, nor did they do anything to boost the overall morale of the phalanx, which depended entirely on the men in front holding the line against the enemy. A deep phalanx meant a shorter line and a greater danger of being outflanked, and getting outflanked was one of the principal ways of losing a phalanx battle. If a deep phalanx did not give a clear advantage in hoplite combat – which means an advantage in othismos – it would have been nothing more than a huge liability.

The uses of the word othismos

Othismos is a noun with the meaning of 'a thrusting' or 'a pushing'. It is derived from the verb *otheo*: 'to push', 'to thrust', 'to force back', and with associated meanings of 'to banish', 'to push matters on,' 'to crowd,' 'to jostle,' and 'to throng'. Like the English 'thrust' or 'push' it can be used in a literal or metaphorical sense, and in which sense it is being used depends on the context.

To cut a long story short, othismos is used in a literal sense in the sources frequently enough for it to be clear that the phalanxes actually did press against each other, in two instances explicitly affirming that shields were actually being pushed against shields:

But the rest with violent combat and the **pushing of shields**.

τὸ δὲ ἄλλο καρτερᾷ μάχῃ καὶ **ὠθισμῷ ἀσπίδων** ξυνειστήκει – *to de allo kartera mache kai **othismo aspidon*** – Thucydides: 4:96 (Battle of Delium).

At this point one may unquestionably call Agesilaus courageous; at least he certainly did not choose the safest course. For while he might have let the men pass by who were trying to break through and then have followed them and overcome those in the rear, he did not do this, but crashed against the Thebans front to front; and **setting shields against shields they shoved**, fought, killed, and were killed.

ἐξὸν γὰρ αὐτῷ παρέντι τοὺς διαπίπτοντας ἀκολουθοῦντι χειροῦσθαι τοὺς ὄπισθεν, οὐκ ἐποίησε τοῦτο, ἀλλ᾽ ἀντιμέτωπος συνέρραξε τοῖς Θηβαίοις: καὶ **συμβαλόντες τὰς ἀσπίδας ἐωθοῦντο**, ἐμάχοντο. ἀπέκτεινον, ἀπέθνῃσκον. – *exon gar auto parenti tous diapiptontas aklouthounti cheirousthai tous opisthen, ouk epoiese touto all' antimetopos sunerraxe tois Thebaiois: kai **sumbalontes tas aspidas eothounto**, emachonto.* – Xenophon, *Hellenica*: 4.3.19 (Battle of Coronea).

There are plenty of cases of phalanxes closing with their opponents and fighting shield to shield without that implying they used othismos, as is clear from Homer and later writers who cite examples of archaic hoplites using shields that could never have stood up to the pressure of an othismos push. These passages however don't refute othismos; they just prove that it was easy to get past the spear guard of a phalanx. This was the principle weakness of any spear-armed formation: the spears alone could not stop the advance of a determined and well-protected foe, and once he got past the reach of the spears they became useless, obliging their bearers to resort to a secondary weapon. It was this weakness that would ultimately drive the spearman from the ancient battlefield.

There are other objections against othismos. Here is a selection of the more cogent ones:

1. *Carrying off wounded commanders during othismos:*

> Nevertheless, the fact that Cleombrotus and his men were at first victorious in the battle may be known from this clear indication: they would not have been able to take him up and carry him off still living, had not those who were fighting in front of him been holding the advantage at that time. – Xenophon, *Hellenica*: 6.4.13.

This is easily explained. The Spartans initially succeed in driving the deeper Thebans back. In doing so they pass over the prone body of Cleombrotus until the men of the rear rank are able to lift him up and carry him away.

2. *Commanders getting wounded by spears during othismos (when spears had become useless):*

> But they received him with a vigour that matched his own, and a battle ensued which was fierce at all points in the line, but fiercest where the king himself stood surrounded by his fifty volunteers, whose opportune and emulous valour seems to have saved his life. For they fought with the utmost fury and exposed their lives in his behalf, and though they were not able to keep him from being wounded, but many blows of spears and swords pierced his armour and reached his person, they did succeed in dragging him off alive, and standing in close array in front of him, they slew many foes, while many of their own number fell. – Plutarch, *Agesilaus*: 18.

Reading this passage in context, it is clear that it applies to the initial spear contest between the Spartans and the Thebans, with an allusion to othismos coming only after Agesilaus is removed from the battle: 'But since it proved too hard a task to break the Theban front, they were forced to do what at the outset they were loath to do. They opened their ranks and let the enemy pass through.'

3. *A commander gives orders during an othismos crush (when no orders would have been necessary or even possible):*

> In the battle at Leuctra, Epaminondas commanded the Thebans, and Cleombrotus commanded the Lacedaemonians. The battle remained finely balanced for a long time, until Epaminondas called on his troops to give him one step more, and he would ensure the victory. They did as he asked; and they gained the victory. The Spartan king Cleombrotus was killed in the fighting, and the Laconians left the enemy in possession of the battlefield. – Polyaenus, *Strategems*: 2.3.2.

This hints to the nature of othismos – that is it not constant but alternates between efforts of pushing and pauses to rest. It is quite possible that both sides could momentarily break off to rest after an extended bout of othismos, giving a general like Cleombrotus time to encourage his men.

4. *Weapons are seen in the hands of dead hoplites after battle, i.e. after othismos when weapons would not have been wielded:*

> Now that the fighting was at an end, a weird spectacle met the eye, as one surveyed the scene of the conflict – the earth stained with blood, friend and foe lying dead side by side, shields smashed to pieces, spears snapped in two, daggers bared of their sheaths, some on the ground, some embedded in the bodies, some yet gripped by the hand. – Xenophon, *Agesilaus*: 2.14.

A hoplite engaged in othismos still has his right arm free and has enough room to wield a sword or knife. What is of interest in this passage is that only daggers are still gripped by the hand, not spears. What is also of interest is the mention of shields 'smashed to pieces' διατεθρυμμένας – *diatethrymmenas*. An aspis was extremely strong. What in an infantry fight could break it to pieces? Certainly not victorious hoplites walking over it. The only force strong enough in those circumstances would be the pressure from othismos, which could overcome the strength of an imperfectly made shield and collapse it inwards, shattering it (and killing its bearer). Rather than refute othismos, this passage tends to confirm it.

The Rout

Very few soldiers are prepared to fight to the death when they know a battle is lost. This knowledge comes as a sense that their unit cannot hold against the enemy, it no longer protects them, and they are now vulnerable individuals. For hoplites in battle there were several indicators that the game was up: troops appearing on the flank and rear; the phalanx being pushed back; neighbouring sections of the line breaking and running. The job of the file closer or *ouragos* was to prevent file members from quitting the field, but if the members of the file decided together that it was time to leave there was nothing he could do to stop them pushing past him and bolting for safety. When the rout commenced, all that mattered was speed, and hoplites often discarded their shields and spears to lighten themselves and run faster. This could be their undoing as they were now helpless against pursuing troops like cavalry or skirmishers who could outstrip them. Hoplites who kept their arms were often more likely to escape alive as they were left alone for easier pickings.[38]

8. Conclusion: the Effectiveness of the Hoplite Phalanx

To measure the effectiveness of a battle formation it would be unfair to match it against opponents it never faced in battle. Hoplite vs. Hunnic horseman or hoplite vs. Indian elephant is a theoretical exercise the conclusions of which cannot be proved. Any good formation is not only inherently strong but is also at least to some degree flexible, able to adapt to different situations and enemies. Greek hoplites may have been nonplussed by their first encounter with elephants but, like the Romans, they may well have learned eventually how to deal with them. Ditto for Huns.

To evaluate the hoplite phalanx properly we need to measure its performance against its historical enemies as described in historical accounts. What were the hoplites' historical enemies? Broadly-speaking there were four: the tribal armies of the Balkans, the Persians, the Romans and the Carthaginians.

The Balkan tribes of Thrace, Paeonia and Illyria generally employed javelin-armed cavalry and lightly-equipped infantry. Whilst mobile in difficult terrain their armies were no match in pitched battles against the heavily armed and armoured hoplites.

The Achaemenid Persian Empire had a large cavalry component but lacked heavy infantry and its cavalry were not up to assaulting hoplites properly disposed to oppose it.[39] However if the Persian cavalry could catch a phalanx not properly disposed and surround it in the open they were able to destroy it, as they did during the Ionian revolt.[40] Persian infantry consisted of archers equipped with a short spear that was easily outreached by the Greek *doru*. They had no body armour and only the front rank had large pavises, designed for protection against arrow fire and of little use in melee with a phalanx that used othismos to knock them over. If the phalanx could ensure its flanks were safe it could beat any Persian troop-type.

There is one description of a Greek phalanx confronting Carthaginian heavy infantry. The Corinthian general Timoleon surprised a much larger Carthaginian army crossing the Crimissus river and defeated its elite heavy infantry, armed with bronze helmets and iron breastplates and carrying large aspis-like shields. The initial spear contest was undecided, but once Timoleon's hoplites had closed with the Carthaginian foot the latter were at a disadvantage, being weighed down with heavier equipment on a muddy riverbank in the middle of a thunderstorm.[41] How the Greeks would have coped with the Carthaginians in different circumstances is unclear as both were similarly equipped and fought in much the same way. But Carthage's inability to subjugate a significant part of the Greek diaspora may be in part due to a superior Greek military tradition.

There is no detailed record of a Roman army facing off against a Greek phalanx, however the Roman army initially fought in a phalanx formation that was similar to the Greek version and was equipped like them. After Tarquin the Proud was deposed as king of Rome, he returned in 509 BC with an army strengthened by his Etruscan allies to reclaim his throne. He was met by an army commanded by the Consuls Valerius and Brutus. After an initial cavalry clash the two infantry lines met:

> The battle raged with varying fortune, the two armies being fairly matched; the right wing of each was victorious, the left defeated. – Livy, *History*: 2.6.

This is a classic battle of phalanxes, in which the right wing of each line overlaps and defeats the enemy left. It was not long after this that the Romans reformed their tactical thinking, imitating their Latin neighbours to the south by making the sword the infantryman's principal weapon and equipping them all with long shields that did not overlap when in line, but permitted the soldier to fight with complete freedom of movement. The soldier's tendency to recoil before superior opponents was countered by organising the army into multiple lines, which permitted sections of the hard-pressed front line to retire through the line behind it, confronting the enemy with fresh troops.

This system gave the Roman infantryman a distinct advantage over the classical hoplite. The principal weakness of a spear phalanx was its inability to stop a well-armoured enemy from getting past its spear guard and into direct contact with the spearmen. The Roman soldier, protected by his large shield, could rush a phalanx line and engage hand-to-hand with the hoplites. Trained to use a sword, he was better skilled in a swordfight than his opponent, but more importantly he had *fighting mobility*: he could recoil momentarily from his enemy's blows whilst his enemy could not recoil from his. Chapter 1 showed just how important this mobility is in close-quarter combat. Once the Roman soldier had got in close and personal the hoplite stood little chance.

After a time this fighting technique spread across central and southern Italy as the spear gave way to the sword. The point would eventually be reached when Hannibal equipped his African spearmen with Roman arms and retrained them in the Roman way of fighting after the legions at the Trebia, despite being surrounded, were able to burst through the centre of his infantry line. The Greek hoplite or his imitators were no match for the Roman legionary.

The legions, however, found it a very different story when facing the hoplite phalanx's far deadlier successor.

Notes

1. J.M. Edmonds, *Elegy and Iambus*: Volume I.2.2.
2. *Iliad*: 2.540.
3. Matthew, *A Storm of Spears*: 3.
4. Matthew, *A Storm of Spears*: 1.
5. Bardunias, *Hoplites at War*: 1.
6. https://www.youtube.com/watch?v=U5E1vKsDUBo
7. Bardunias, *Hoplites at War*: 9.
8. Bardunias, *Hoplites at War*: 3.
9. Matthew, *A Storm of Spears*: 12.
10. The single line of Spartans at Dipaea, as mentioned by Pausanias, 8.8.4, describes a severely depleted Spartan army obliged to fight a numerically superior Arcadian coalition. Nonetheless the notion of a line one man deep defeating a regular enemy phalanx is distinctly odd.
11. Thucydides, *The Peloponnesian War*: 7.79.
12. Xenophon, *Hellenica*: 2.4.34.
13. Diodorus Siculus: 17.26.4.
14. First mentioned by Xenophon, *Hellenica*: 3.5.22, when the Spartan general Pausanias calls a conference of his polemarchs and pentekonteres (395 bc).
15. Xenophon, *Hellenica*: 3.5.22; 4.5.7.
16. J. F. Lazenby: *The Spartan Army*.
17. Diodorus Siculus, *Library*: 18.32.
18. Herodotus, *History of the Peloponnesian War*: 9.11.3.
19. Herodotus, *History of the Peloponnesian War*: 10.1.
20. Cornelius Nepos, *Lives of Eminent Commanders*: Miltiades.5; Pausanias: 10.20.2; Plutarch, *Moralia*: 305 B.
21. Matthew gives a list from the sources of all references to a close order or bunched formation during a battle. Only one, Timoleon bunching up his vanguard to charge Carthaginian infantry, can be considered as deploying in close order, i.e. with shields overlapping, before the start of a regular battle.
    Asklepiodotus 3.6 – This describes the close order of a pike phalanx

Herodotus 9.18 – The Phocian contingent, already deployed, draws together to stand against the Persian cavalry that surrounds it.

Thucydides 1.63 – Aristeus and his elite hoplites, have beaten their opposition but their Potidaean allies are defeated, and Aristeus decides to close up charge through the enemy to reach the safety of Potidae.

Thucydides 2.4 – The Thebans bunch up when attacked by surprise in the streets of Plataea.

Thucydides 5.10 – The Athenian right wing of army is already in line and bunches up when under attack.

Hellenica 4.3.18 – The Thebans at Coronea have already won on their part of the field. The Spartans have wheeled to face them. The Thebans gather in close order to smash through them – i.e. this is a bunching up on the move.

Plutarch Pelopidas 17 – The 300-strong Sacred Band bunch up to smash through the Spartan line – their advance is preceded by a cavalry charge.

Plutarch Pelopidas 23 – The Spartans extend their wing against the Thebans at Leuctra and cannot close up again to normal order before being charged by the Theban Sacred Band.

Hellenica 7.4.22 – The Arcadians besieging Cromnus form up to fight Spartans. συντεταγμένοι – means forming up for battle, not forming close order.

Xenophon Agesilaus 6.7 – Same as above. Agesilaus leads army on the march arrayed for battle, not in a loose column.

Diodorus 15.86.4 – At the Battle of Mantinea Epaminondas leads the elite group in close order *after* the start of the battle in order to push through the enemy.

Diodorus 16.3.2 – Philip invents the Macedonian phalanx with its close order.

Plutarch Timoleon, 27 – After deployment Timoleon bunches up his vanguard to charge Carthaginian infantry. This is probably one case of actually deploying in a closer order before the start of a regular battle.

Diodorus 17.26.4 – A dense phalanx charges out of city gates during a siege.

Plutarch Philopoemen 9 – This concerns the formation of a pike phalanx.

Plutarch Philopoemen 10 – The 'close array' here is of a pike phalanx.

22. Xenophon, *Constitution of the Lacedaimonians*: 11.8.
23. Bardunias, *Hoplites at War*: 3.8.
24. Bardunias, *Hoplites at War*: 3.8.
25. As shown in the 1963 documentary, *Dead Birds*.
26. Xenophon, *Hellenica*: 4.2. The Spartans habitually stopped a stadium (about 200m) from the enemy in order to sacrifice a goat to Artemis

Agrotera, goddess of the hunt, as a final morale-booster. They then advanced on the enemy in attack formation.

27. Xenophon, *Constitution of the Lacedaimonians*: 13.6.
28. Asklepiodotus 10.2: *Right- or left-facing, then, is the movement of the individual men, 'by spear' to the right, and 'by shield' – called in the cavalry 'by rein' – to the left; this takes place when the enemy falls upon the flanks and we wish either to counter-attack, or else to envelop his wing, i.e., overlap the wing of the enemy.*
29. Thucydides, *History of the Peloponnesian War*: 5.70.
30. Xenophon, *Anabasis*: 1.8.18.
31. Herodotus, *Histories*: 6.112.1.
32. Arrian, *Anabasis*: 2.10.
33. Herodotus, *Histories*: 6.112.2.
34. Xenophon, *Hellenica*: 4.3.17.
35. Bardunias, *Hoplites at War*: 9.
36. Xenophon, *Agesilaus*: 2.14 – broken spears were a common sight on the Greek battlefield.
37. Bardunias, *Hoplites at War*: 9. See also: https://www.youtube.com/watch?v=xxFLymbGT_Y
38. Plato, *Symposium*: 221a.
39. Herodotus, *Histories*: 9.18.
40. Herotodus, *Histories*: 5.102.
41. Plutarch, *Timoleon*: 28.

Chapter 3

The Macedonian Phalanx

1. The Battle of Sellasia, 222 BC

In 229 BC Sparta made a last effort to reassert its ancient dominance over the Peloponnesian peninsula. The Achaean League, an alliance of Peloponnesian states established in 280 BC to counter the power of Macedonia, had succeeded in its aim of breaking the Macedonian stranglehold over southern Greece, retaking Corinth and the key fortress of Acrocorinth from their Macedonian garrisons. The league reached its high watermark when Antigonus Gonatas of Macedonia made peace in 240 BC, ceding the territories he had lost.

But this was Greece, where success inevitably bred jealousy and the desire to put down those who had succeeded. The Aetolian League of central Greece along with Elis and Sparta were especially hostile, but it was Sparta who undertook to break the Achaean League once and for all.

The Spartan king, Cleomenes III, had spent the previous six years revitalising the decadent Spartan state, implementing an extensive land reform and creating thousands of new citizens. Military reforms went along with social reforms. In addition to the regular Spartan infantry he already disposed of that were 'less than 5,000 strong',[1] he raised an additional 4,000 foot 'whom he taught to use the two-handed pike, instead of the spear, and to hold their shields by an ochane, and not by a porpax as before'.[2] This was the first time Spartan infantry ceased fighting as hoplites and fought like Macedonian phalangites instead.

An able general, he utterly defeated the Achaean League in several battles and had driven it to agree to discuss terms with him when a sudden illness obliged him to return to Sparta. It was the turning point. Aratus, the League's premier politician and general, turned to his erstwhile enemy Macedonia, agreeing to surrender the Acrocorinth in return for military aid. Cleomenes meanwhile extended his control over the entire Peloponnese, capturing for a brief moment some of Sparta's former glory as victor of the Peloponnesian War.

The new Macedonian king, Antigonus III Doson, arrived with his army. Initially held up at the Corinthian isthmus by fortifications that sealed off the Peloponnese, he acquired Argos after its inhabitants rebelled against Cleomenes, obliging the Spartan king to abandon Corinth and fall back to Laconia. Cleomenes was able to win a few local successes against the Achaeans whilst the Macedonian army wintered in Macedonia, but he could do nothing to avert the inevitable battle between himself and Antigonus.

The battle took place in the summer of 222 BC at Sellasia, in one of the passes that led to Sparta. Antigonus came with an army of 15,600 Macedonian, mercenary and allied phalangites, 7,000 allied hoplites, 3,000 light troops, 1,000 Gauls, 1,000 Agrianes and 1,200 cavalry.

Against him Cleomenes was able to assemble an army of 20,000 infantry[3] and 650 cavalry, consisting of 6,000 phalangites (his original 4,000 plus an additional 2,000 helots 'trained in the Macedonian manner'[4]), about 6,000 Perioeci and allies the composition of which were probably hoplites, something in the region of 8,000 mercenary light troops, and 650 cavalry. Badly outnumbered in heavy infantry and cavalry, Cleomenes made the best possible use of terrain, dividing his infantry into two wings that deployed on two hills overlooking the pass, whilst his cavalry and about 3,000 mercenary light infantry sat on the low ground between them. His two infantry lines on the hills were each strengthened by field works: a palisade and a ditch.

Antigonus waited several days, using the time to probe unsuccessfully for weaknesses. Finally he attacked. Cleomenes' brother, Eucleidas, commanded the Perioeci and allies on the hill of Euas, whilst Cleomenes commanded the 6,000 phalangites and 5,000 mercenary light troops[5] on the hill of Olympus.

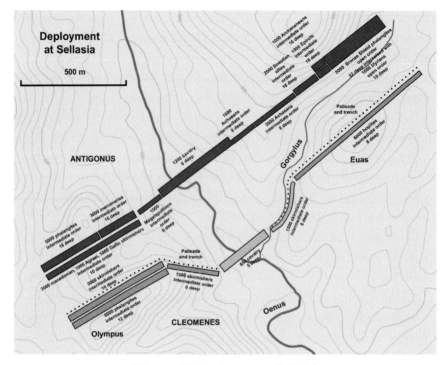

Diagram 81: Deployment at Sellasia[6]

Eucleidas most likely commanded hoplites since he did not use the terrain to offset the 'peculiar armament and battle array'[7] of the Macedonian phalangites (implying his own armament and array were different), but met them at the top of the hill, forfeiting the advantage of high ground.

> … by allowing the enemy to reach his position, unharmed and in unbroken order, he was placed at the disadvantage of having to give them battle on the very summit of the hill; and so, as soon as he was forced by the weight of their armament [*kathoplismou*] and their battle array [*suntaxeos*] to give any ground, it was immediately occupied by the Illyrians; while his own men were obliged to take lower ground, because they had no space for manoeuvring on the top. The result was not long in arriving: they suffered a repulse, which the difficult and precipitous nature of the ground over which they had to retire turned into a disastrous flight. – Polybios, *Histories*: 2.68.

Cleomenes, seeing the collapse of his brother's phalanx, abandoned his position behind his palisade wall and advanced down the hill to engage the Macedonian phalangites deployed against him. The battle on the slopes of Olympus, between phalangite and phalangite, was a much closer affair:

> But when Cleomenes saw that his brother's division was retreating, and that the cavalry in the low ground were on the point of doing the same, alarmed at the prospect of an attack at all points at once, he was compelled to demolish the palisade in his front, and to lead out his whole force in line by one side of his position. A recall was sounded on the bugle for the light-armed troops of both sides, who were on the ground between the two armies: and the phalanxes shouting their war cries and with sarissas lowered [note that **both** phalanxes used sarissas], charged each other. Then a fierce struggle arose: the Macedonians sometimes slowly giving ground and yielding to the superior courage of the soldiers of Sparta, and at another time the Lacedaemonians being forced to give way before the overpowering weight of the Macedonian phalanx. – Polybios, *Histories*: 2.69.

It looked like a draw, but Antigonus had a trick up his sleeve:

> Finally, the troops around Antigonus, packing their sarissas closely together and making use of the phalanx's unique close-order disposition, attacked the Lacedaimonians with force, driving them back from their field-defences. – *Ibid.*

Cleomenes was a novice in phalangite warfare and had deployed his phalanx in the standard Greek intermediate order of three feet per file (or perhaps a little less with shields overlapping). Confronted with a Macedonian close order arrangement of 1½ feet per file, his own files, outnumbered 2:1 (or 3:2 at best) by the Macedonians, could not withstand them. The battle was lost and with it Sparta's independence. Even before the battle was over however the rout of Eucleidas showed that the day of the Greek hoplite was done. But why had it fared so badly against the Macedonian phalangite?

2. Origins of the Macedonian Phalanx

The Pezhetairoi

According to Anaximenes of Lampsacus (380–320 BC) a certain king Alexander was the first to establish a full-time Macedonian soldiery:

> Anaximenes, in the first book of the Philippika, speaking about Alexander, states: Next, after he accustomed those of the highest honour to ride on horseback, he called them 'Companions' [*hetairoi*], and, after he had divided the majority of the infantry into companies [*lochoi*] and files [*dekads*] and other commands, he named them 'Infantry Companions' [*pezhetairoi*], so that each of the two classes, by participating in the royal companionship, might continue to be very loyal. – Harpocration, *Lexicon*: s.v. pezhetairoi.

Before this time Macedonia, like every other state in the area, had relied in time of war on a temporary levy of males of combat age who were rich enough to possess arms (as tombs of archaic Macedonians show). Alexander, following the example of Thebes, Arcadia, Elis and Sparta, created a professional core of troops paid by the state. This core of troops would have been small as Macedonia was no more capable than any other Greek polis of supporting a large standing army. During the campaign season the bulk of the Macedonian foot would continue to be supplied by the temporary levies. 'Majority of the infantry' in the quote refers to the organisation of the majority of the new **full-time** infantry created by Alexander. Theopompus makes clear that not all the Macedonian infantry, regular and levy, were *pezhetairoi*, but just a chosen few:

> Theopompus says that men, chosen as tallest and strongest, served as bodyguard to the king and were called foot companions [*pezhetairoi*] – Theopompus, FGrHist 115, F348.

Which Alexander was responsible for the creation of the pezhetairoi is a subject of endless dispute. Alexander III the Great is ruled out as the *pezhetairoi* were already in existence under his father Philip II.[8] Alexander II (370–368 BC) reigned for only two years, but that would be long enough to institute a military reform of this nature. Alexander I (498–454 BC) however seems the most likely candidate. The timing is right: he creates a force of hoplites just as hoplites demonstrate they are the supreme infantrymen of the Eastern Mediterranean. Furthermore, he had a successful military career. After the departure of Xerxes he expanded the Macedonian state by force of arms:

> But Alexander enlarged his dominions **not less by his own valour** than through the munificence of the Persians. – Justin, *Epitome of the Philippic History of Pompeius Trogus*: 7.4.

A final piece of proof is the way the new *pezhetairoi* were organised. They were divided into lochoi and each lochos into individual files of ten men (*dekads*). Ten was not a file depth commonly used by Greeks at that time, but it was used by Persians, and it makes sense that Alexander I, who acceded to his throne as a vassal of Persia, would have been influenced by their military system.

It has been argued[9] that Homer mentions Greek soldiers at Troy organised in tens and this might have been the source of the *dekad*:

> For should we be minded, both Achaeans and Trojans, to swear a solemn oath with sacrifice, and to number ourselves, and should the Trojans be gathered together, even all they that have dwellings in the city, and we Achaeans be marshalled by tens, and choose, each company of us, a man of the Trojans to pour our wine, then would many tens lack a cup-bearer; so far, I deem, do the sons of the Achaeans outnumber the Trojans that dwell in the city. – *Iliad*: 2. 124–9.

But it is highly unlikely that a Macedonian king would have used an unit of organisation employed centuries before his time and mentioned only in passing by Homer, rather than something more contemporary.

It has also been argued that Alexander I could not have created a professional Macedonian army as Macedonia was militarily weak after his reign.[10] Four examples of Macedonian weakness are cited:

1. *Macedonia submits to Persian overlordship during the Persian wars.*

Given the size of the Persian army the Macedonian kings, even with a force of professional troops at their disposal, would have had no chance alone against the Achaemenid Empire. Submission was their only recourse.

2. *The infantry of Perdiccas II (413–399 BC) cannot face the Thracian army in battle.*[11]

In 429 BC Sitalces, king of the Odrysian tribe in Thrace, led a Thracian coalition of 150,000 men into Macedonia. Perdiccas II did not dare face such a huge army in battle, but limited himself to hit-and-run tactics with his cavalry (abandoning even that after the cavalry were surrounded). This does not argue weakness in the Macedonian infantry as even the best infantry stands no chance if it is heavily outnumbered and surrounded – the fate of the Spartans at Thermopylae.

3. *Perdiccas II leads only 200 cavalry at the Battle of Potidaea.*[12]

Reading the context around Thucydides' account of Potidae makes clear that Perdiccas had no real interest in fighting for the Spartans against the Athenians but was hoping to use their differences to extend his own power in Chalcidice and along the Thracian coast. His contribution of 200 cavalry can hardly represent the entire army at his disposal and it did not take part in the battle. It looks more like a token force. It is noteworthy that a force of Macedonian horsemen also fought for the Athenians, suggesting that the Macedonian kingdom was less than united at that time.

4. *Demetrios of Phaleron claimed the Macedonian army of 400 BC was weak.*

> ... only these last fifty years immediately preceding our generation, you will be able to understand the cruelty of Fortune. For can you suppose, if some god had warned the Persians or their king, or the Macedonians or their king, that in fifty years the very name of the Persians, who once were masters of the world, would have been lost, and that the Macedonians, whose name was before scarcely known, would become masters of it all, that they would have believed it? – Polybios, *Histories*: 29.21.

To use this passage to argue a weak Macedonian army 50 years before the time of Demetrios (b. 350 BC) is a real stretch. What he said *a propos* Macedonia could have been said of any Greek *polis* in 400 BC, or of any state bordering the vast Achaemenid Empire for that matter (or of any state in the world at that time, bar China).

The strongest proof for a professional corps of Macedonia infantry from the time of Alexander I however comes from archaeology.

Pierre Juhel[13] notes a striking difference between the funerary contents of middle rank Macedonians from the archaic and classical period, with the dividing line around the year 500 bc. Before that date, all Macedonian men of some substance, i.e. not just rich aristocrats, were buried with their defensive and offensive armament: shields, spears, swords, helmets and cuirasses. Macedonians of the same middle social rank after this date were buried with hunting weapons but not with ordinary combat weaponry. The implication is that archaic Macedonian soldiers owned their own weapons whilst classical Macedonians used state equipment (also evidenced by the appearance of kings' names on Macedonian shields, e.g. 'Of King Demetrios'). State equipment means a professional soldiery, paid and equipped by the Macedonian king, and the year 500 points to Alexander I as the one who instituted it.

How were the 'infantry companions' or *pezhetairoi* armed? Following the dazzling success of the Greek phalanx at Marathon, Thermopylae and Plataea, it is almost certain they were equipped and trained as hoplites.

This impression is strengthened by the character of the Macedonian infantry at the Battle of Lyncestis (423 BC). At the outset of the Peloponnesian War, the Spartan

Diagram 82: Late 5th century funeral stele from Pella, showing a Macedonian hoplite with a pilos helmet. Archaeological Museum, Istanbul.

general Brasidas marched to Chalcidice to support local insurrections against Athens who controlled the area as part of its naval empire. The Macedonian king, Perdiccas II, formed an alliance with Sparta in his strategy to expand his own influence along the north Aegean coastline. In return for his assistance against Sparta, Brasidas was inveigled into supporting Perdiccas against Arrhibaeus, client king of Lyncestis on the western Macedonian border who had recently revolted against his Macedonian overlord.

> In the meantime Brasidas and Perdiccas, with joined forces, marched into Lyncus against Arrhibaeus the second time. He [Perdiccas] led with him the power of the Macedonians and the Greek hoplites who dwelt among them. He [Brasidas], besides the Peloponnesians that were left him, led with him the Chalcideans, Acanthians, and the rest, according to the forces they could severally make. The whole number of the Greek hoplites were about three thousand. The horsemen, both Macedonians and Chalcideans, somewhat less than a thousand; but the other throng of irregular barbarians was great.
>
> Being entered the territory of Arrhibaeus, and finding the Lyncesteans encamped in the field, they also sat down opposite to their camp. And the foot of each side being lodged upon a hill, and a plain lying between them both, the horsemen ran down into the same, and a skirmish followed, first between the horse only of them both. But afterwards, the infantry of the Lyncesteans coming down to aid their horse from the hill, and offering battle first, Brasidas and Perdiccas drew down their army likewise, and charging, put the Lyncesteans to flight; many of which being slain, the rest retired to the hill-top and lay still. – Thucydides, *History of the Peloponnesian War*: 4.124.

Perdiccas has 'Greek hoplites' that fight alongside the hoplites of Brasidas and successfully rout the infantry of Arrhibaeus (whom Thucydides is careful to point out are not 'hoplites' but 'infantry' – *pezous*). Brasidas had originally arrived with 500 Peloponnesian hoplites and 300 Chalcidean peltasts.[14] With these he has troops from the 'Acanthians and the rest, according to the forces they could severally make'. How many hoplites did he have in total?

If Perdiccas' Greek hoplites were professional troops maintained at state expense, then it makes sense to look at the sizes of the paid professional units of other Greek states to form an approximate idea of how large the Macedonian contingent was. Greek *poleis* maintained full-time troops that numbered between 300 and 1,000 men.[15] Putting the Macedonians at the upper limit of 1000, that would have left Brasides with about 2,000 hoplites in total. After the battle the Macedonians and barbarians fled, leaving Brasides to face the enemy alone. He was able to form a square with his hoplites large enough to protect his light troops in the middle and make his escape. 2,000 hoplites formed up 8 deep would have created a square measuring about 60 x 60 yards, and leaving a free area in the middle measuring roughly 45 x 45 yards, adequate to accommodate 300 peltasts in a loose formation. So 1,000 Macedonian hoplites at the most looks about right.

Besides the hoplites and levies of Perdiccas, there is a large mass of 'barbarians' – non-Macedonian tribal allies. It is clear that these 'barbarians' were not Macedonians as the two are described as distinct from each other after the battle:

> The next night, the Macedonians and multitude of barbarians (as it is usual with great armies to be terrified upon causes unknown) being suddenly frightened, and supposing them to be many more in number than they were, and even now upon them, betook themselves to present flight and went home. – *Ibid*: 4.125.

Were the Greek hoplites of Perdiccas mercenaries, at least in part? Demosthenes mentions Philip II as having mercenaries (*xenoi*) side by side with *pezhetairoi*:

> Hence it is not difficult to see how the majority of the Macedonians regard Philip. As for his mercenaries [*xenoi*] and footguards [*pezhetaroi*], they have indeed the name of admirable soldiers, well grounded in the science of war; but one who has lived on the spot, a man incapable of falsehood, has informed me that they are no better than other soldiers. – Demosthenes, *Olynthiac*: 2.17.

Hence it is reasonable to assume that Perdiccas, who died just 54 years before Philip's accession, had a similar mix of hired and home-grown personal troops. In this light Thucydides conflates the two, describing a force that fights in the Greek manner and lives in Macedonia but is distinct from ordinary Macedonians since it is supported by the Macedonian king.

The introduction of the Pike and Pelta

When did the *pezhetairoi* abandon hoplite for phalangite gear? The answer – if one accepts the testimony of Diodorus Siculus – is clear:

> Yet even so, with such fears and dangers threatening them, Philip was not panic-stricken by the magnitude of the expected perils, but, bringing together the Macedonians in a series of assemblies and exhorting them with eloquent speeches to be men, he built up their morale, and, having improved the organization of his forces and equipped the men suitably with weapons of war, he held constant manoeuvres of the men under arms and competitive drills. Indeed he devised the compact order and the equipment [*kataskeuen*] of the phalanx, imitating the close order fighting with overlapping shields of the warriors at Troy, and was the first to organize the Macedonian phalanx. – *Library*: 16.3.

Diagram 83: Reconstruction of a Macedonian *pezhetairos*.

This passage is important for several reasons. Firstly, it shows that Philip II did not create Macedonia's professional soldiery but trained it in a new way of fighting (seasonal levies would not have had the time for 'constant manoeuvres' and 'competitive drills' and there is no mention of any change from a seasonal to a full-time soldiery). Secondly, he introduced the weaponry of the pike phalanx, and lastly he invented the close order formation that gained the phalanx victory at Sellasia.

Philip may have invented the close order, but it is unlikely he invented the phalanx pike, or sarissa, *ex nihilo*. Iphicrates, an Athenian military commander, is sometimes credited with being its originator. Very long spears however were nothing new in warfare, having been used before Philip and Iphicrates' time by the Egyptians,[16] the Chalybians in northern Anatolia[17] and the Thracians (probably by cavalry),[18] but Iphicrates was the first to introduce them in Greece in the year 373 BC (after returning from Egypt where he would have seen the Egyptian spears).

Two sources describe Iphicrates' military reforms, Cornelius Nepos and Diodorus.

For example, he changed the arms of the infantry. While before he became commander they used very large shields [*maximus clipeis*], short spears [*brevibus hastis*] and little swords [*minutis gladius*], he on the contrary exchanged aspis for the pelta [*peltam pro parma fecit*], for which reason the infantry have since been called peltasts, in order that the soldiers might move and charge more easily when less burdened. He doubled the length of the spear and increased that of the swords; he changed the character of their armour, giving them linen in place of bronze or chain armour. In that way he made the soldiers more active; for while he diminished the weight of their armour, he contrived to protect their bodies equally well without overloading them – Nepos, *Iphicrates*: 1.3–4.

Hence we are told, after he had acquired his long experience of military operations in the Persian War, he devised many improvements in the tools of war, devoting himself especially to the matter of arms. For instance, the Greeks were using aspis shields which were large [*megalais aspisi*] and consequently difficult to handle; these he discarded and made light shields [*peltas*] of the same size, thus successfully achieving both objects, to furnish the body with adequate cover and to enable the user of the pelta, on account of its lightness, to be completely free in his movements. After a trial of the new shield its easy manipulation secured its adoption, and the infantry who had formerly been called hoplites [*hoplitai*] because of their heavy shield [*aspidon*], then had their name changed to peltasts [*peltastai*] from the pelta they carried. As regards spear [*doratos*] and sword [*xiphous*], he made changes in the contrary direction: namely, he increased the length of the spears by half, and made the swords almost twice as long. The actual use of these arms confirmed the initial test and from the success of the experiment won great fame for the inventive genius of the general. He made soldiers' boots that were easy to untie and light and they continue to this day to be called 'Iphicratids' after him. – Diodorus: 15.44.1–4.

Notice that Nepos refers to the Greeks using 'short spears'. Given that the typical *doru* could hardly be considered short, it is possible that Nepos had a shorter spear in mind which he doubled to give the length of an Iphicratean spear, whereas Diodorus, who speaks of the doru being increased by one half, was thinking of a more standard length hoplite spear. In this view both authors come out at approximately the same length for Iphicrates' spear. Hoplite spear lengths varied between 230cm and 280cm with an average length of 255cm or 8½ feet. A spear half as long again would be a little under 13 feet. 12 feet is about the maximum length a spear can be wielded single-handed, which suggests that the Iphicratean spear was intended to be as long as possible whilst being held with one hand.

Besides lengthening the spear, Iphicrates adopted a lighter shield, the *pelta*. Aristotle describes it:

Aristotle in his 'Thessalian Constitution' says: 'The *pelte* is a shield [*aspis*] that has no rim nor is it covered with bronze and it is not cut round from oxhide but of goatskin or the like. – scholia on Euripides' *Rhesus*: fr. 498.

He also replaced metal greaves with lighter boots that protected the lower legs. What is emphasised by both sources is that the new peltast (actually a reformed hoplite) was meant to have combat **mobility**. This is highly unusual as mobility was the last thing necessary for hoplite combat. The light round shield, lengthened sword, lighter boots and

– possibly, following Nepos – lighter body armour suggest that the Iphicratean peltast was meant to fight in a very different manner – more like a legionary than a hoplite, able to strike at opponents with his longer sword without having to come into shield-to-shield contact, and give ground as necessary. He could outreach a classic hoplite's spear with his own, and when the hoplite closed for othismos, he did not need to press forward in othismos himself but could give way whilst outfighting his opponent since he was lighter and more agile, had combat mobility and possessed a longer weapon.

Philip knew Iphicrates. The Athenian was a family friend, having been adopted by Philip's father Amyntas (king of Macedonia 393–370 BC). He was also a close friend of Philip's brother Alexander II who reigned 370–368 BC. In 368 BC Alexander was assassinated by Ptolemy. Philip's other brother, Perdiccas, was the legitimate heir but he was too young to rule. A rival claimant to the throne, Pausanias, was driven from Macedonia by Iphicrates, which allowed Perdiccas to keep the crown until he was old enough to rule effectively (assassinating the regent Ptolemy in order to do so). Perdiccas was killed in battle by the Illyrians in 359 BC. His son, Amyntas, inherited the throne but was too young to rule. Perdiccas' last surviving brother, Philip, became regent before deposing Amyntas and declaring himself king in the same year.[19] Iphicrates died in 353 BC, when Philip was 29 years old and had been king for six years.

It is often assumed that Philip did not invent the Macedonian pike but merely adopted the Iphicratian reforms.[20] Philip would have been well aware of Iphicrates' innovations but he did not just copy him. In the long spear he saw a possibility that Iphicrates had missed, a formation that was eminently **not** mobile but didn't need to be since it could drive any enemy from the battlefield by sheer mass of spearpoints.

Philip reworked the pelta, making it smaller, stronger and ensuring it was concave – othismos would remain a feature of his new formation. He also reworked the spear, increasing its length by half as much again, from about 12 feet or more to between 16 and 19 feet, and turning it into a pike that its user had to wield with two hands. This was possible since the smaller shield allowed the left hand to project beyond the shield rim and grip the pikeshaft.

But the shield's advantages didn't stop there. A smaller shield meant the soldiers could form their files up closer together, virtually shoulder to shoulder, whilst their shields could still overlap to form a new, condensed version of the hoplite shieldwall. Three pikemen would now face two hoplites.

Furthermore, with such long shafts, up to five ranks could project their pikes past the front rank. This, along with the more compact files, made it very difficult for hoplites to get past the spearpoint-tipped forest of pikes and engage in othismos. And even if hoplites did succeed in driving past the pikes to shield-to-shield contact, or just pushing against the pikes themselves, there were still three pikemen to every two hoplites. The othismos contest was lost in advance. The hoplite simply had no answer to the phalangite.

3. The Phalangite's Panoply

The Sarissa

The sarissa consisted of three components: the pike head, the shaft, and the butt or sauroter.

The pike head, or spearpoint, was small, according to the Roman poet Grattius:

> What if I allow myself to speak of the immense contoi of the Macedonians? How long are the shafts and how mean the teeth they spike them with! – *Cynegeticon*: 117–118.

This is the unique reference in the primary sources to the size of the pike head. There are unfortunately no clearly identifiable pikeheads in the archaeological record to serve as confirmation.[21] In 1970 what was assumed to be a large leaf-shaped spearhead was discovered in the Vergina cemetery in Macedonia, along with a large sauroter and a smaller spearhead and metal tube. The large 'spearhead' was 51cm long and weighed 1,235g. The sauroter was 44.5cm long and weighed 1,070g. What is immediately obvious is that the spearhead weighs more than the sauroter and a weapon made of the two would have its centre of balance forward of its midpoint. A large pikehead like this not only contradicts Grattius but also defeats the purpose of a sarissa: a weapon with its centre of balance near the rear end, enabling it to be wielded with ease and outrange any other melee weapon. Matthew is probably correct in identifying the large spearhead as the butt of a cavalry lance, since it resembles the spear-like lance butt visible in the Alexander Mosaic discovered at Pompey.

The smaller spearhead closely resembles a javelin head discovered in another tomb nearby, leading to the probable conclusion that the smaller spearhead in fact belonged to a javelin. Hence the finds in the Vergina tomb are incomplete, grave robbers taking away the pike head and cavalry spearpoint as something useful. One is hence left with the quote from Grattius. For practical purposes, it is probably reasonable to assume that the pikehead was similar to the doru's spearhead since, as will be seen below, there is no need to suppose a significantly larger or smaller implement for the sarissa to function as described by the sources. The doru spearhead would be 27.9cm long and weigh 153g.

The metal tube was 17cm long. A replica of it weighs 200g. It may have served as a connector between two halves of a sarissa shaft, which would have been joined together when the pike was used in regular phalanx combat. Dividing a sarissa shaft in two served several purposes. It made the sarissa easier to carry when the army was on the march, especially when passing through heavily forested terrain. It also allowed the phalangite to use the top half of the shaft as a short spear. Arrian hints at the possible use of a sarissa in this manner when describing Alexander's killing of Cleitus:

> … for according to some he leaped up and snatched a spear from one of his bodyguards; according to others, a sarissa from one of his ordinary guards, with which he struck Cleitus and killed him. – *Anabasis*: 4.8.

A sarissa is too long to serve as a bodyguard's indoor weapon, but the top half of a sarissa – which can conveniently be called a spear – is ideal for the purpose.

A sarissa in two halves could also be used as a javelin if need be since the top half with a pikehead and connecting tube would have a centre of balance around the midpoint, making it serviceable as a missile weapon. Finally, it would be easier on the march to find suitable wood long enough for the a replacement shaft if that shaft were in two parts.

All this is speculative, as besides the Vergina tube (whose purpose is not known for certain) there is no literary or archaeological evidence for a sarissa in two halves joined by a connecting tube, and the spears in the Alexander mosaic, comparable to sarissas in length, do not show any such tube.

There is no reference in the primary sources either of sarissas having sauroters but it is inconceivable they did not. The sarissa was a development of the hoplite doru which did have a sauroter (there are plenty of archaeological examples) and which served as a counterweight besides being a convenient way of sticking the spear in the ground whilst on campaign. The sarissa, like the doru, needed to have its centre of gravity well towards the back end so it could be wielded comfortably whilst maximising its reach. Without a sauroter that would have been impossible. It is also difficult to conceive the sauroter in the Vergina cemetery being used for anything other than a sarissa as it is considerably heavier than the typical *doru* sauroter.

According to Statius[22] the sarissa shaft was generally made of ash, as this tree supplies hard straight wood without weaknesses and is not too heavy. Dogwood may also have been used as Arrian mentions it being used for Macedonian cavalry lances.[23] On campaign an army would use whatever wood was available to make replacement shafts.

How long was a sarissa? There is no extant example of a sarissa shaft in the archaeological record so we are dependent on the written record. There are several references to sarissa lengths:

... their spear, moreover, is not shorter than ten cubits, so that the part which projects in front of the rank is to be no less than eight cubits – in no case, however, is it longer than twelve cubits, so as to project ten cubits. – Asklepiodotus, *Tactics*: 5.1.

The spear should not be shorter than 8 cubits and the longest pike should not exceed a length that allows a man to wield it effectively. – Aelian, *Tactics*: 12.

Both Asklepiodotus and Aelian call the sarissa a 'spear' in these passages but are clearly referring to a pike. Aelian's shortest length for a sarissa does not match Asklepiodotus', however Aelian, writing at the end of the 1st century AD – 200 years after the phalanx had fallen out of use – clearly drew on Asklepiodotus (1st century BC) and other authors who were familiar with it. It is possible that Aelian included the long spear of Iphicrates, about 8 cubits or 12–13 feet in length, with the Macedonian pike when giving his range of lengths. In any case Aelian is not careful in reconciling his sources, giving different lengths two chapters later (and calling the pikes 'sarissas'):

> The length of the sarissas, when the phalanx was first created, was 16 cubits but is, in fact, now 14 cubits. – *Tactics*: 14.

This range of 14 to 16 cubits corresponds to Polybios (c.200 – c.118 BC):

> … the length of the sarissae is sixteen cubits according to the original design, which has been reduced in practice to fourteen. – *Histories*: 18.29.

Theophrastos, writing at the time of the death of Alexander, gives 12 cubits as the longest length of a sarissa:

> The height of the 'male' tree [of the Cornelian Cherry] is at most twelve cubits, the length of the longest sarissa, the stem up to the point where it divides not being very tall. – *Causes of Plants*: 3.12.

Polyaenus, describing Cleonymus's (end 4th century – beginning 3rd century BC) siege of Edessa in Macedonia, gives 16 cubits:

> At the siege of Edessa a breach was made in the walls, the phalangites, whose sarissas were sixteen cubits long, sallied out against the assailants. – *Stratagems*: 2.29.

The sources then give two sets of lengths: a) 10–12 cubits, and b) 16 cubits later reduced to 14 cubits. Matthew resolves the apparent contradiction.[24] Asklepiodotus and after him Arrian described the sarissa as it was originally conceived under Philip and Alexander. This is the 10–12 cubit weapon. Theophrastes, writing in 322 BC, gives this length. Polyaenus gives a length of 16 cubits for Macedonian sarissas around the year 300 BC. This is the 'original design' of Polybios, which had been reduced to 14 cubits by the battle of Pydna (168 BC). This 16 to 14 cubit reduction is echoed by Aelian. The sarissa started out as a shorter weapon but quickly increased to 16 cubits as rival Successor pike phalanxes tried to gain an advantage in reach against each other, eventually settling back to 14 cubits as the longest realistically manageable length.

There is some dispute on the length of a cubit. To cut a long story short (Matthew does a thorough job of analysing cubit lengths), 48cm is the distance that best satisfies the ancient use of the measurement by later classical Athens and subsequently by Macedonia and Alexander's empire. To give two examples: Diodorus describes the height of Porus as 4 cubits and one palm[25] (a palm is one sixth of a cubit), which at 48cm per cubit comes out at 2 metres, though Arrian rather unrealistically calls him 'a magnificent example of a man, over 5 cubits high', a literary exaggeration. – *Anabasis*: 5.19.1. Alexander's land surveyors, or *bematists*, recorded the distance between Alexandria Arieon (modern day Herat) and Prophthasia (modern day Juwain) as 1,600 stades. A stade equals 600 Greek feet. A Greek foot equals ⅔ of a cubit. So using a 48cm cubit the distances comes out at 307.2 km. The actual distance is 304 km.[26]

Taking a cubit as 48cm, the earlier sarissa was up to 576cm or a little over 19 feet long. The later version reached a length of 768cm or 25½ feet before scaling back to a little under 22½ feet.

Where is the point of balance of a sarissa? To calculate it, one needs to take into account the mass of the sauroter, spearhead, shaft and connecting tube. In Diagram 84, the shaft sections have been foreshortened for clarity. The sauroter, connecting tube and spearhead are to scale.

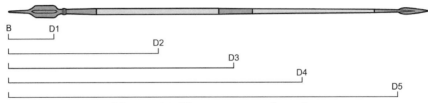

Diagram 84: The components of a sarissa.

To calculate the weight of the shafts for a sarissa that incorporates the Vergina sauroter, connecting tube and a typical hoplite spearhead, it can be assumed that the lower half of the shaft has a diameter at one end matching that of the sauroter (34mm) and at the other end matching the diameter of the wider end of the connecting tube (32mm). The upper half of the shaft will have a diameter matching the narrower end of the connecting tube (28mm) and the diameter of the spearhead's tube (19mm). The lower half of the shaft can be considered a regular tube for practical purposes whilst the upper half of the shaft has a significant taper.

European Ash has a dry weight of $0.68g/cm^3$.[27] The lower shaft tube has a length of 251.8cm and weighs 1.64kg. One can assume its centre of balance is halfway up the tube (125.9 cm). The upper shaft tube can be assumed to have the same length as the lower tube. It weighs 0.77kg.[28] Its centre of balance is 92cm from its wider end.[29]

With this data it is possible to calculate the point of balance of the entire sarissa:

Point of Balance = (M1 x D1) + (M2 x D2) + (M3 x D3) + (M4 x D4) + (M5 x D5) / (M1 + M2 + M3 + M4 + M5)

B = the end of the sauroter

M1 = mass of sauroter

M2 = mass of lower half of shaft

M3 = mass of connecting tube

M4 = mass of upper half of shaft

M5 = mass of pike head

D1 = distance from end of sauroter to point of balance of sauroter

D2 = distance from end of sauroter to point of balance of lower half of shaft

D3 = distance from end of sauroter to point of balance of connecting tube

D4 = distance from end of sauroter to point of balance of upper half of shaft

D5 = distance from end of sauroter to point of balance of pike head

The final answer is 195.46cm from the end of the sauroter. This approximates to 4 cubits (192cm). It is an important measurement as will be seen below.

The entire sarissa (if the shaft is made of ash) weighs 3.833kg, not an especially heavy weapon, and lighter than most estimates.

The Shield

Several types of shield were used by phalangites. The tacticians describe one which in their estimation is best suited for a pike phalanx, the Macedonian shield:

> ... the best shield for use in the phalanx is the Macedonian: of bronze, 8 palms in diameter, and not too concave. – Asklepiodotus, *Tactics*: 5.1.

> ... the Macedonian shield, made of bronze, is best. It must not be too concave and should be 8 palms in diameter. – Aelian, *Tactics*: 12.

A palm is 7.7cm which makes the shield 61.6 cm wide. This width is confirmed by a complete limestone mould used to create the metal face of a phalangite shield in the Ptolemaic army, and dated around 300 BC.[30] The mould is 69–70cm in diameter, but the metal disc created from it would need to be large enough to fold around the edges of the wood shield it was attached to, which would leave a diameter of about 65cm, corresponding to the measurements of the manuals. The fragments of a shield facing found at Dodona and dated from the 3rd century BC has been estimated to have a diameter of 66cm, but this is approximate as 80 per cent of the metal facing is missing and the surviving fragment is very buckled.

Besides the Macedonian shield there were larger kinds that were fairly common. Life-size reliefs from the shield monument at Veria have diameters between 73 and 76cm.[31] This corresponds to the remains of shields found at Vegora,[32] Pandamis and Staro Bonče.[33]

This larger shield came in at least two types. The first was 'not too concave.' The shields at Veria were 8–10cm deep, the monument dating around the beginning of the 3rd century BC. These shields are accompanied with reliefs of hoplite shields, themselves between 10.5 and 13mm deep (see Diagram 85).

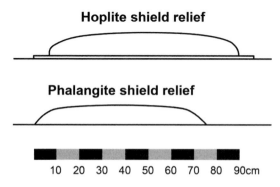

Diagram 85: The Hoplite and the Phalangite shields.

The second type that first appears on coins of Philip II is bowl-like in shape and much more concave: a profile image of this shield on a tetradrachm of Seleucus I (about 303–300 BC) indicates it was about 25cm deep presuming it is about 76 cm in diameter (see Diagram 86).

All types of phalangite shield had a strap, the *telamon*, which was slung over the shoulder and bore the weight of the shield. One can see it in a Macedonian tetradrachma from about 336–328 BC (see Diagram 87).

Besides the telamon, the shield had an *ochane*. What exactly an *ochane* is is disputed. For Richard Taylor[34] it is identical to an *ochanon*, which is the same word just with a different gender. An ochanon resembles a porpax and functions much like it.[35]

Ochanon is sometimes used to denote the porpax and antelabe:

For the Greeks are fond of heavy, full armour: they have a double helmet, a breastplate covered with scales, a concave bronze shield

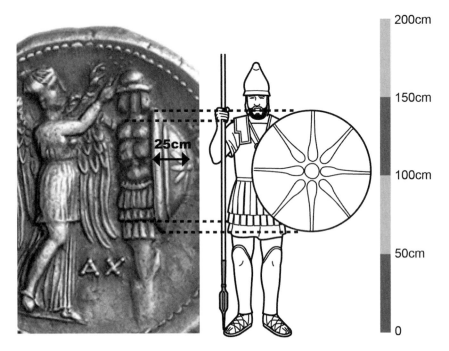

Diagram 86: The Tetradrachm shield.

Diagram 87: The Telamon dangles below the shield.

held by two handles [*ochanois duo*] (of which the one surrounding the forearm avails for othismos, while the other is grasped by the end of the hand), two greaves, a hand-held javelin, and a spear for hand-to-hand combat. – Julius Africanus, *Kestoi*: 7.1.10.

An ochane is not the same thing as a shield-strap or telamon, slung over the shoulders to bear the weight of the shield:

> They invented three things in which they were followed by the Greeks: it was the Carians who originated wearing crests on their helmets and devices on their shields, and who first made grips [*ochana*] for their shields; until then all who used shields carried them without these grips [*ochanon*], and guided them with leather belts [*telamosi*] which they slung round the neck and over the left shoulder. – Herodotus, *The Histories*: 1.171.4.

The main difference between an ochane/ochanon and a porpax is that the latter obliged the left hand to grip the antelabe in order to keep the left forearm firmly wedged in the porpax and prevent the shield from rotating, whilst the former allowed the left hand to remain free to grasp the sarissa. The phalangite shield's ochanon is probably best understood as a rather narrow, flexible leather strap in which the arm fitted loosely.

The Sword

The sword of the phalangite, like that of the hoplite, came in two kinds: a twin-edged, leaf-shaped version (commonly called a *xiphos* though this was also a generic term for a sword) 45–60cm long, and a heavier, single-edged version (called a *makhaira* though, again the term was also a generic name for a sword) 35–70cm long, with one example 77cm long. The smaller version was a thrusting weapon whilst the larger version was ideally suited for hacking. Since Iphicrates doubled the size of the hoplite's sword as part of his reforms, it is probable that hoplites in general used shorter versions of these two swords, between 35 and 45cm long, lengthened by Iphicrates to a weapon around 80cm long – any longer would have rendered it impractical.

It is difficult to determine how long the swords were that were used by phalangites, but it is reasonable to assume they were quite short, since there is little room for longer weapons in the packed confines of a phalanx. It is possible that the longer versions of these swords were used by cavalry.

The probability that phalangites used short swords is reinforced by the fact that they were sometimes equipped with daggers instead:

> … and now that the Macedonians engaged man to man or in small detachments, they could only hack with their small daggers [μικροῖς ἐγχειριδίοις] against the firm and long shields of the Romans – Plutarch, *Aemilius Paulus*: 20.5.

Armour

Helmet

According to Sextus Julius Africanus (*Kestoi*: 1.1.45–50) Alexander the Great issued pilos helmets to his infantry, seemingly towards the end of his reign. From this time onwards pilos helmets appear on one side of Macedonian coins with the Macedonian shield (or the larger shield used by phalangites) on the other. These helmets gradually replaced the Phrygian helmet[36] which itself was sometimes masked, covering the lower half of the face with metal moulded into the pattern of a moustache and beard.

Phalangite pilos helmets sometimes had crests, frequently depicted in coinage, that emerged from a small rectangular crest box fixed to the top of the helmet. There are also examples of small tubes fixed on other points on the helmet that held feathers. There is however no evidence of helmets with large crest supports as appear on hoplite helmets, running from forehead to neck, or transverse across the helm from ear to ear. This is important as will be seen later.

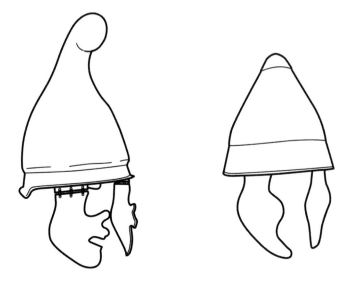

Diagram 88: Left: Phrygian helmet; right: Pilos helmet.

Body Armour

It is possible that Philip's phalangites did not originally wear any body armour. Polyaenus' list of their panoply excludes it:

> Philip accustomed the Macedonians to constant exercise, before they went to war: so that he would frequently make them march three hundred stades, carrying with them their helmets, shields, greaves, and spears; and, besides those arms, their provisions likewise, and utensils for common use. – *Stratagems*: Philip, 10.

After Philip however linen armour became the standard body armour for Hellenistic phalanxes, as shown in wall paintings and coins. Metal cuirasses however continued to be worn at least by some men of rank, as shown on the Stele of Nikolaos.[37]

Greaves

Polyaenus notes that Philip II's infantry were equipped with greaves as seen in the above quote. Greaves are depicted in the Tomb of Lyson and Kallikles, on the Ephesus relief, and the figure on the stele of Zoilos.[38] Many paintings and reliefs however depict phalangites without greaves, wearing the Iphicratean high boots instead that offered some protection to the lower legs. It is possible that only the front rank, made up of officers, wore greaves since only they needed them.

4. The Phalangite

The phalangite was a full-time professional soldier, necessarily so since the pike phalanx, by its structure and function, was a good deal more complex than a hoplite phalanx. Phalangites were obliged to be precise in the wielding of their pikes, positioning them correctly in relation to the other pikes so as to form a hedge of spearpoints in which the pikes worked together and did not foul each other. Furthermore using a pike whilst bearing a shield was a tricky business since the pikeman was obliged at times to keep the shield at his side and at times to bring it in front of him – all whilst holding the pike with both his hands. Unlike the hoplite spear, there was little that was natural or intuitive about wielding a sarissa. It required constant training.

This obliged Philip to create and pay for a standing army that was capable of matching the seasonal levies of other Greek and Balkan states. Not even the Spartans had managed this, relying on their allies and their perioiki or helots if necessary to bolster the numbers of their small professional army. The effort nearly bankrupted Macedonia. Three years after acceding to the throne in 359 BC Philip took possession of the gold mines near Krinides. He expanded their production to a revenue of over 1,000 talents,[39] yet despite this income he had trouble paying his troops[40] and after his death, according to his son Alexander, the treasury held only 60 talents, with a debt of 500 talents.[41] And this after a string of successful wars and conquests that had brought large parts of Thrace and Illyria and all of Thessalia under Macedonian control. Philip was not profligate, being a hard, practical man bent on conquest,[42] but the upkeep of an army composed entirely of full-time troops was almost more than he could manage. When Alexander began his Persian campaign he had 70 talents and owed 200. He had supplies for only 30 days.[43] He would be freed of the burden of supporting a large professional army only after conquering the vast resources of the Persian Empire.

5. The Structure of the Pike Phalanx

The Phalanx File

The pike phalanx formed up much like the hoplite phalanx, in a line composed of files of equal depth with a file leader or *lochagos* according to Asklepiodotus and a filer closer or *ouragos* at the back.

For the tacticians files varied in depth: 8, 10, 12 or 16 men. All three tacticians emphasise the usefulness of the 16-man option, where the file can double to 32 men in depth or halve to 8 men.[44] This doubling or halving refers to the three file spacings: open order with each file occupying a width of 4 cubits or 192cm, intermediate order at a width of 2 cubits or 96cm, and closer order at one cubit or 48cm (see Chapter 1). For the rest of their discussions on phalanx depths and organisation the tacticians use the 16-man file, which suggests it was the standard depth.

Polybios, in an attempt to refute the account of the battle of Issus by Callisthenes (Alexander's official chronicler who was present at the battle), actually confirms the three spacings:

> He [Callisthenes] goes on to say 'that Alexander heard of the entrance of Darius into Cilicia when he was a hundred stades away from him, having already marched through the pass: that he therefore retraced his steps through the pass, his phalanx in the van, his cavalry next, and his baggage on the rear. But that as soon as he had debouched upon the open country, he gave general orders to form up into a phalanx, at first thirty-two deep; then sixteen; and lastly, when they were nearing the enemy, eight deep'.
> – *Histories*: 12.19.

Polybios assumes that the spacing of the 16-deep formation is six feet per file, and then demonstrates that such a formation would be too wide for the available space at Issus between the mountains and the sea. Polybios gives that space as 14 stades wide (1 stade = about 600 feet or 180m). Assuming an infantry line of 32,000 men, he calculates its width when 16-deep as 20 stades – too wide for the available space.

Oddly enough though, he misses the obvious. Callisthenes is clearly describing the phalanx as forming up in open, then intermediate, and finally close order. As will be demonstrated below, Alexander had about 16,000 pikemen composed of 12,000 phalangites and 4,000 hypaspists, the remainder of his infantry being hoplites and light troops. Since only pikemen formed up in three different file intervals, it is reasonable to assume that Callisthenes was talking about these 16,000 heavy foot. Initially deploying from column into an open order line 32 deep[41] (ideal for covering large distances) at 4 cubits or 192cm per file, they would have been about 960 metres wide, or about 5,33 stades. As they advanced they doubled files to 16 deep and two cubits (96cm) wide whilst maintaining the same frontage. Once near the enemy they doubled again to 8 deep and one cubit (48cm) wide, still keeping the same frontage. This deployment left plenty of space on either side for the cavalry and light troops, with the hoplites following behind.

A 16-man file was broken down into 8-man half-files which themselves were broken down into 4-man quarter-files.[45] The quarter-file does not seem to have been used much, if at all, on the battlefield, though it may have been used when the phalanx marched in column, advancing by rank so that the files were transformed into 4-man ranks. The half-file would be used when the phalanx doubled from intermediate to close order, the rear half of a file moving up alongside the front half of the file.[46]

The existence of the 16-man file with two 8-man half-files is confirmed by Arrian:

> ... he [Alexander] enlisted them [the Persians] into the Macedonian ranks, with a Macedonian *dekadarchos* leading each *dekad* and, following him, a Macedonian *dimoirites* and a *dekastateros* [ten-stater man] – so named after his pay – which was less than that of the *dimoirites*, but greater than that of the soldiers with no supplement. Added to this were twelve Persians and, last in the *dekad*, a Macedonian who was also a *dekastateros*; so within the *dekad* there were four Macedonians, three of whom were on increased pay, the commander of the *dekad*, and twelve Persians. – *Anabasis*: 7.23.3–4.

Breaking this down, a Macedonian file in intermediate order has 16 men: one file leader (the *dekadarchos* – 'leader of ten', the term most likely inherited from the old Macedonian hoplite structure), followed (in order of importance) by the next senior officer, the *dimoirites*; after that two *dekastateros* officers of which one is at the back of the file. For the tacticians a *dimoirites* is a half-file leader, which makes the two *dekastateros* officers file closers, the eighth and sixteenth man in the file. The *dimoirites* stood at the head of the rear half file, i.e. ninth place in the entire file. This enables the 16-man file in intermediate order to double to two 8-men half-files in close order, with each half-file's leader in front and file-closer at the rear.

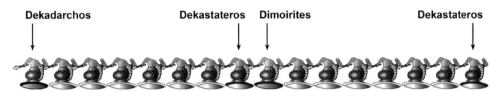

Dekadarchos   Dekastateros   Dimoirites   Dekastateros

Diagram 89: The Macedonian file.

Phalanx Subdivisions

The manuals[47] give a detailed breakdown of the organisation of the phalanx into units and subunits. Starting with the individual file, each subunit was made up of two of the subunits below it:

Name	Commanding Officer	Files	Number of Men
lochos, dekad, enomotia	lochagos, hegemon	1	16
dilochia	dilochites	2	32
tetrarchia	tetrarch, exarchos	4	64
taxis	taxiarch, hekatonarch	8	128
syntagma, xenagia	syntagmatarch, xenagos	16	256
pentacosiarchia	pentacosiarch	32	512
chiliarchia	chiliarch	64	1,024
merarchia, telos	merarch, teleiarch	128	2,048
phalangarchia, strategia	phalangarch, strategos	256	4,096
diphalangarchia, keras, meros	kerarch	512	8,192
tetraphalangarchia	general of the army	1,024	16,384

Officers from the file leader to the kerarch took their place in the front rank, which meant that the entire front line of a phalanx was composed entirely of officers. An officer also occupied the position of the officer of one of the two subunits he commanded. So a dilochites took the place of one of the lochagoi, the tetrarch took the place of one of the dilochites, and so on.

The position of officers and their units was arranged according to a merit system.[48] This was done in groups of four to ensure a balance of merit and hence command ability throughout the phalanx. Diagram 90 shows how it was achieved.

Starting with the largest 4-unit group of the phalanx – the four phalangarchias – each phalangarch is graded best, second-best, third-best and fourth-best, or 1st, 2nd, 3rd, 4th, and are arranged as shown in Diagram 90, Row A.

This arrangement ensures that the vulnerable flanks of a phalanx are headed by the best officers (1st and 2nd) who are the most capable of dealing with any problems and who inspire the most confidence in the men near them. The less-effective officers are in the middle, but so arranged that the combined merit of the left half of the phalanx (2 + 3) matches the combined merit of the right half (1 + 4).

The combined merit of the two merarchs on the left wing matches that of the right, but the best merarchs command the teloi of the two outermost phalangarchias. If these two advance ahead of the rest of the line and expose their flanks they will have the best commanders of the phalanx to deal with any threats. Notice that all phalangarchias have their highest-ranking commanders at each end of the unit where they can best manage any trouble should one phalangarchia advance ahead of the others. Notice also that of two adjacent phalangarchias, one is the mirror image of the other, in that the positions of the officers in one are reversed in the other.

A similar setup is used for the phalangarchia itself, divided into four chiliarchies (Diagram 90, Row B). In this case however the place of precedence at the extreme right is occupied by the most senior officer of the unit, the phalangarch. The second place at the extreme left is taken by the next most senior officer, the merarch, who commands a telos (later called a merarchia). The remaining two places at the centre are occupied by chiliarchs.

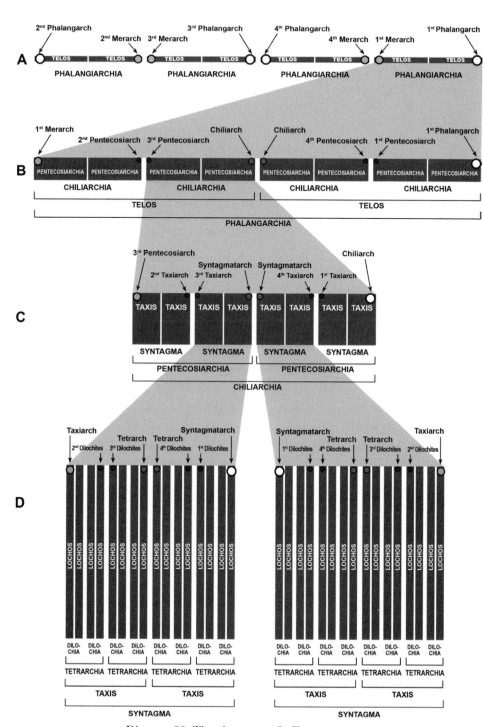

Diagram 90: The placement of officers.

Each chiliarchia is similarly subdivided into four syntagma (Diagram 90, Row C) in which the officers are distributed in the same way, and each syntagma in turn subdivides into four tetrarchies which in turn subdivide into four files (Diagram 90, Row D).

This arrangement of officers applies to all the levels of subunits in the phalanx. The guiding principle is that officers are distributed evenly by merit, and that every subunit has the most senior and hence most meritorious officers at each corner, ensuring that the vulnerable flanks of that subunit are well commanded should the unit be separated from the rest of the phalanx.

6. The Structure of the Macedonian Phalanx of Alexander

Alexander's phalanx is the one historical phalanx for which we have some detailed information on its organisation. Does his phalanx correspond to the structure described by the tacticians?

There are four battles for which we are given subunits of the phalanx and the officers who commanded them: Granicus, Issus, Gaugamela and Hydaspes. Starting with these subunits, is it possible to determine what they are and if they correspond to any unit type described by the manuals? It is commonly assumed that they numbered about 1,500 men, with the elite infantry unit, the hypaspists, numbering 3,000 men.[49] This is based on two factors:

a) Diodorus Siculus' breakdown of Alexander's army that crossed the Hellespont into Asia minor:

> There were found to be, of infantry, twelve thousand Macedonians, seven thousand allies, and five thousand mercenaries, all of whom were under the command of Parmenion. Odrysians, Triballians, and Illyrians accompanied him to the number of seven thousand; and of archers and the socalled Agrianians one thousand, making up a total of thirty-two thousand foot soldiers. – *Library*: 17.17.

The 12,000 Macedonians are generally accepted as being phalangites.

b) The number of heavy units this army deploys at the Battle of Granicus a few weeks later, as described by Arrian:

Close to these were posted the hypaspists of the Companions under the command of Nicanor, son of Parmenio. Next to these the phalanx of Perdiccas, son of Orontes, then that of Coenus, son of Polemocrates; then that of Craterus, son of Alexander, and that of Amyntas, son of Andromenes; finally, the men commanded by Philip, son of Amyntas. – Anabasis: 1.14

Phalanx is used here by Arrian to describe a heavy infantry unit of indeterminate size. Altogether there are six commanders, hence six units. But in describing the cavalry deployment on the left flank Arrian goes on to say:

Close to these [the right wing cavalry] were the infantry, the phalanxes of Craterus, Meleager, and Philip, reaching as far as the centre of the entire line.

Craterus and Philip are already mentioned in the initial description of the infantry deployment, leading to the conclusion they are in fact the same individuals whose names have been duplicated. That leaves Meleager. Hence, according to the common interpretation, there are a total of 7 commanders, 6 commanding the regular pike infantry and one commanding the hypaspists. Since the hypaspists are assumed to number 3,000 men, the remaining units must number 1,500 men to reach a total of 12,000 infantry. These units however do not correspond to any classification in the manuals.

How many hypaspists were there?

Near the end of Alexander's reign the hypaspists numbered 4,000 men. The Argyraspides, or Silver Shields, the new name for the hypaspists (i.e. agema and other hypaspists combined) after the death of Alexander, numbered 3,000 men, as described by Diodorus:

After them he drew up the Macedonian Silver Shields, more than three thousand in number, undefeated troops, the fame of whose exploits caused much fear among the enemy – *Library*: 19.28.

This however proves that the original hypaspists were in fact 4,000 strong. After returning to Babylon from India Alexander send home 10,000 Macedonians, replacing them with Persians:

He selected the oldest of his soldiers who were Macedonians and released them from service; there were ten thousand of these. – *Library*: 17.109.

1,000 of those replacements were assigned to the hypaspists:

> In the archonship of Anticles at Athens, the Romans installed as consuls Lucius Cornelius and Quintus Popillius. In this year Alexander secured replacements from the Persians equal to the number of these soldiers whom he had released, and assigned a thousand of them to the hypaspists stationed at the court. – *Library*: 17.110.

After Alexander's death all Persians were removed from Macedonian units by the Successor generals, who continued to make use of non-Macedonians but always in separate units. The remaining hypaspists, now renamed Argyraspides and minus their Persian reinforcement, numbered 3,000 of their original 4,000 men.

Were the hypaspists always 4,000 strong? This is more difficult to establish. The assumption that the hypaspists numbered 3,000 men comes from five sources (including the number of Argyraspides mentioned above). On the face of it they seem conclusive, and historians generally accept them as such. It is possible however, on closer examination, to view them from a different perspective.

The fight against the Aspasians

During his campaign against the Aspasians not far from India, Alexander led a select force which he divided into three divisions under the command of Leonnatus, Ptolemy and himself:

> Over one part he placed Leonnatus, the confidential body-guard, joining the brigades of Attalus and Balacrus with his own; the second division he put under the lead of Ptolemy, son of Lagus, including the third part of the royal hypaspists, the brigades of Philip and Philotas, two *chiliarchia* of the archers, the Agrianians, and half of the cavalry. The third division he himself led towards the place where most of the barbarians were visible. – *Anabasis*: 4.24.

'Third part' suggests that the hypaspists contained three subunits. If one assumes these subunits are chiliarchies each with 1,000 men (see below) then the hypaspists number 3,000 men in total.

However the Greek for 'third part' is τὸ τρίτον μέρος, which can mean one-third in quantity – 'a third' – but can also mean the third of three parts which may or may not be equal to each other. If one assumes that the hypaspists were split three ways, Leonnatus retaining the one part he already commands, Ptolemy receiving another part, and Alexander keeping the final part, then it is possible they may have been composed of four or more subunits divided into three unequal groups. This passage is not conclusive either way.

The Siege of Sangala

Whilst besieging the Indian city of Sangala, Alexander created a separate force for Ptolemy:

> He accordingly stationed Ptolemy, son of Lagus, there giving him three chiliarchia of the hypaspists, all the Agrianians, and one line of archers, pointing out to him the place where he especially conjectured the barbarians would try to force their way. – *Anabasis*: 5.23.

Chiliarchia is a specific term, referring to a unit of 1,000 men. So the hypaspists, composed of 3 *chiliarchia*, numbers 3,000 men.

This passage however, is a strong argument **against** the hypaspists numbering 3,000 men. Ptolemy receives 'three chiliarchia' of the hypaspists and 'all' (ξύμπαντας – all together) the Agrianians. The implication is clear that Ptolemy does not receive all the hypaspists but only three subunits of them, whereas in contrast he does get the entire body of Agrianians.

Nearchus and Antiochus

Whilst passing through the territory of the Assacenians Alexander sends a reconnaissance force to sound out the countryside and get news of the local war elephants:

On the following day he sent out Nearchus and Antiochus, the chiliarchs of the hypaspists, giving the former the command of the Agrianians and the light-armed troops and the latter the command of his *chiliarchia* and two others besides – *Anabasis*: 4.30.

The nature of the two additional chiliarchia is not given, implying they are the same as the chiliarchia of Antiochus, but it is not clear that these three chiliarchia comprise the total force of the hypaspists. The passage can be interpreted as meaning three chiliarchia or more than three chiliarchia.

The Deployment at the Hydaspes

At the Battle of the Hydaspes, Alexander led the hypaspists across the river and then arranged them for battle:

When he had also crossed this piece of water, he selected the choice guard of cavalry, and the best men from the other cavalry regiments, and brought them up from column into line on the right wing. In front of all the cavalry he posted the horse-archers, and placed next to the cavalry in front of the other infantry the royal hypaspists under the command of Seleucus. Near these he placed the royal *agema*, and next to these the other hypaspists, as each happened at the time to have the right of precedence. – *Anabasis*: 5.13.

Three named units, each presumably a chiliarchia, hence 3,000 men in total. The translation of this passage however misses some vital nuances. Here is the relevant section in Greek, phrase by phrase:

τῶν δὲ πεζῶν – of the infantry
πρώτους – in front of/before **or** first in rank/dignity
μὲν τοὺς ὑπασπιστὰς τοὺς βασιλικούς – the royal hypaspists
ὧν ἡγεῖτο Σέλευκος – under the command of Seleucus
ἐπέταξε τῇ ἵππῳ. – he placed behind **or** next to the cavalry.
ἐπὶ δὲ τούτοις – Behind/after these ('These' could conceivably refer to the cavalry. 'Cavalry' in Greek is literally 'horse' – τῇ ἵππῳ – a collective feminine noun in the singular, i.e. it signifies a plural entity. 'These' – τούτοις – refers to either a masculine or neuter

plural noun. Relative pronouns do not necessarily agree with their antecedents though they usually do.[50] As τούτοις does not agree in number with ἵππῳ it would not agree in gender with it either.)

τὸ ἄγημα τὸ βασιλικόν – the royal *agema*.

ἐχομένους δὲ τούτων – Keeping close to these (the same rule applies here as for the agema behind the cavalry: τὸ ἄγημα is a singular noun whilst τούτων is in the genitive plural)

τοὺς ἄλλους ὑπασπιστάς – the other hypaspists

ὡς ἑκάστοις – as to each

αἱ ἡγεμονίαι – the seniority

ἐν τῷ τότε ξυνέβαινον – in that time corresponded.

There are then two ways of translating this passage into English. The first way has the royal agema after the royal hypaspists – ἐπὶ δὲ τούτοις referring to τοὺς ὑπασπιστὰς τοὺς βασιλικούς. The other hypaspists keep close to the agema or, since τούτων is also in the plural, the agema and the royal hypaspists together. This is the common interpretation.

Another way of interpreting the text is to have the royal agema after the cavalry, and the other hypaspists near the agema. Which gives:

> Of the infantry, the royal hypaspists under the command of Seleucus were placed first behind the cavalry: that is, the royal agema and, keeping close to them, the other hypaspists, following the seniority that corresponded to each of them at that time. [i.e. the same seniority evident at Gaugamela and Issus where the agema deploys before the 'rest of the hypaspists'.[51]]

There are hence **two** entities: the agema and the 'other hypaspists' who together are subunits of the royal hypaspists under the command of Seleucus. This interpretation solves the problem of why Seleucus is named commander of the royal hypaspists whilst the agema and the other hypaspists have no named commanders. Furthermore, to see the royal hypaspists as a distinct unit from the regular hypaspists – distinct enough to be a unit of greater prestige than the agema whilst the other hypaspists are of lesser importance – is strange. 'Hypaspists' and 'royal hypaspists' are interchangeable terms in Arrian. At the siege of Thebes, Perdiccas imprudently leads his unit in a precipitate attack against the

Theban stockade, followed by Amyntas. Alexander sends troops in support but holds back his elite infantry:

> He gave instructions to the archers and Agrianians to rush within the stockade, but he still retained the agema and hypaspists outside. – *Anabasis*: 1.8.3.

The attack fails and the Macedonians fall back to Alexander:

> Eurybotas the Cretan, the captain of the archers, fell with about seventy of his men; but the rest fled to the Macedonian agema and the royal hypaspists. – *Ibid.*

The hypaspists and royal hypaspists are evidently identical here.

'Royal hypaspists', like 'hypaspists', are also interchangeable as a generic term for all subunits of Alexander's elite infantry. The royal hypaspists that are split into three parts during the Aspasian campaign are called hypaspists earlier:

> Alexander now took command of the hypaspists, the archers, the Agrianians, the brigade of Coenus and Attalus, the royal body-guard of cavalry, about four regiments of the other Companion cavalry, and half of the horse-archers, and advanced towards the river Euaspla – *Anabasis*: 4.24.

Whenever the agema is mentioned however, it is always as a distinct subunit: at Thebes, Issus, Gaugamela and the Hydaspes. It is identical to the 'foot-companions' that take part in the battle preceding Alexander's siege of Sangala:

> Upon the right wing he posted the guard of cavalry and the cavalry regiment of Cleitus; next to these the hypaspists, and then the Agrianians. Towards the left he had stationed Perdiccas with his own regiment of cavalry, and the *taxeis* of foot-companions [*pezhetairoi*]. – *Anabasis*: 5.22.

The infantry force deployed in line across the Hydaspes numbered 'not much under 6,000 men'.[52] This force, according to Arrian, included the javelinmen and Agrianians, flank guards for the heavy infantry that were to advance 'at a slow pace and in regular order'.[53] It did not include the archers that moved off to accompany the cavalry[54] (see Diagram 91, Part A). Shortly before reaching the Hydaspes Alexander had 2,000 archers[55] and 1,000 Agrianians.[56] How many javelinmen were there? For Duncan Head[57] the javelinmen are identical with the Agrianians, a copyist's error putting an 'and' between them and the Agrianians. But that leaves a problem of numbers. If the royal hypaspists/agema/other hypaspists numbered 3,000 men as is commonly assumed, then with 1,000 Agrianians they would number only 4,000. Include a separate force of javelinmen about the same size as the Agrianians (which makes sense if they guard one flank of the heavy infantry whilst the Agrianians guard the other flank) and they number 5,000 men. The problem is solved if one assumes the heavy foot number 4,000 men, which then gives a total force of 6,000 men as stated by Arrian. Even if one presumes there were three subunits they could still total 4,000 men, with the royal hypaspists numbering 1,000, the agema 2,000, and the rest of the hypaspists 1,000 (see Diagram 91, Part B).

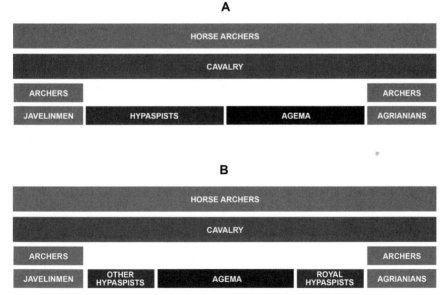

Diagram 91: The options for the deployment of the hypaspists and agema at the Hydaspes.

Somewhere behind this force were the two taxis of Cleitus and Coenus that were not mentioned by name in the deployment and hence not included in the tally.

The size of the phalanx subunits

Presuming there were only two subunits of the hypaspists, were they as large as the other units of the phalanx? After defeating Darius at Gaugamela Alexander marched on Babylon, which surrendered to him. He then celebrated his triumph by holding games and creating a new level of command, the *chiliarchia*, composed of 1,000 men and to be commanded by chiliarchs:

> He appointed judges and offered to those who wished to enter a contest in military valour prizes of a new kind; those who should have been judged the bravest were each to command a troop of 1,000 men – they called them *chiliarchae* – this being the first time that the forces were divided into that number; for previously there had been *lochoi* consisting of 500 men, and the prizes of command had not gone to bravery. – Quintus Curtius Rufus, *History of Alexander*: 5.2.

Notice the existence of the *lochoi*, 500-man units corresponding to the *pentechosiarchia* of the manuals.

There were eight winners in total. The new *chiliarchia* was created by dividing the next unit in size above it, the 2,000-man *telos*, into two *chiliarchia*, but each *telos* did not receive two chiliarchs as one of the new *chiliarchia* would continue to be under the direct command of the *telos'* commander, the *merarch*. This implies that Alexander's infantry had eight 2,000-man *teloi* each with its own commander.

There is evidence that the telos existed at least as early as 335 BC. In order to disengage from an attempt to besiege Pelium, Alexander deployed his army 'in such a way that the depth of the phalanx was 120 men'.[58] This was done on the spur of the moment, obliging Alexander to use an already-existing formation. A telos, deployed 16 deep, has 128 files. Turning it into a column by wheeling its syntagmas 90 degrees, or by simply having the men turn in place, converts its ranks into files, giving it depth of 128 ranks – close to Arrian's rounded off '120 men'.

A study of the Macedonian deployment at Gaugamela suggests that there were indeed eight teloi:

> Of the phalanx of Macedonian infantry, nearest to the cavalry had been posted first the agema of the hypaspists, and then the rest of the hypaspists under the command of Nicanor, son of Parmenio. Next to these was the brigade of Coenus, son of Polemocrates; after these that of Perdiceas, son of Orontes, then that of Meleager, son of Neoptolemus, then that of Polysperchon, son of Simmias, and last that of Amyntas, son of Andromenes, under the command of Simmias, because Amyntas had been despatched to Macedonia to levy an army. The brigade of Craterus, son of Alexander, held the left end of the Macedonian phalanx, and this general commanded the left wing of the infantry. – Arrian, *Anabasis*: 3.11.

The eight telos-sized units are the agema, the 'rest of the hypaspists' under Nicanor, and the six regular pike units under Coenus, Perdiccas, Meleager, Polysperchon, Amyntas, and Craterus. If the agema was equal in size to the other units then who was its commander? This could have been Craterus but more probably was Alexander himself. The Persians sent their scythe-bearing chariots against the place where Alexander is stationed, i.e. with the Companion cavalry near the right wing of the infantry:

> Meantime the foreigners launched their scythe-bearing chariots against Alexander himself, for the purpose of throwing his phalanx into confusion – *Anabasis*: 3.13.

'Phalanx' here means a unit of heavy infantry, not the entire pike phalanx. Arrian uses this term to describe the units deployed at the Granicus. Alexander would have assumed direct command of the agema since it formed a composite unit with his Companion cavalry, with which he launched his decisive attack against the Persian line once the Persian left had separated from the centre:

> Alexander wheeled round towards the gap, and forming a wedge as it were of the Companion cavalry and of the part of the phalanx which was posted here, he led them with a quick charge and loud battle-cry straight towards Darius himself. – *Anabasis*: 3.14.

Diagram 92: The deployment at Gaugamela.

One can see virtually the same deployment at Issus:

> First, upon the right wing near the mountain he placed the
> agema and the hypaspists under the command of Nicanor, son of
> Parmenio; next to these the taxis of Coenus, and close to them that
> of Perdiccas. These troops were posted as far as the middle of the
> heavy-armed infantry to one beginning from the right. On the left
> wing first stood the taxis of Amyntas, then that of Ptolemy, and
> close to this that of Meleager. The infantry on the left had been
> placed under the command of Craterus; but Parmenio held the
> chief direction of the whole left wing. – *Anabasis*: 2.8.

Diagram 93: The deployment at Issus.

'Taxis' is a generic term for a unit. Alexander again takes charge of
the agema (note that Nicanor commands only the hypaspists) and leads
it with his Companions in the decisive attack against the Persian line.
In the accounts of Diodorus and Arrian the right flank infantry and
cavalry act in concert:

> He set the cavalry along the front of the whole army, and ordered
> the infantry phalanx to remain in reserve behind it. He himself
> advanced at the head of the right wing to the encounter, having
> with him the best of the mounted troops. – Diodorus Siculus,
> *Library*: 17.33.

At first he still led them on in close array with measured step, although he had the forces of Darius already in full view, lest by a more hasty march any part of the phalanx should fluctuate from the line and get separated from the rest. But when they came within range of darts, Alexander himself and those around him being posted on the right wing, advanced first into the river with a run. – *Anabasis*: 2.10.

For the Macedonian phalanx had been broken and disjoined towards the right wing; because Alexander had charged into the river with eagerness, and engaging in a hand-to-hand conflict was already driving back the Persians posted there – *Ibid*.

At the Granicus, however, the arrangement was somewhat different. To return to Arrian's account reproduced earlier:

Close to these were posted the hypaspists of the Companions under the command of Nicanor, son of Parmenio. Next to these the phalanx of Perdiccas, son of Orontes, then that of Coenus, son of Polemocrates; then that of Craterus, son of Alexander, and that of Amyntas, son of Andromenes; finally, the men commanded by Philip, son of Amyntas. – *Anabasis*: 1.14.

Close to these [the right wing cavalry] were the infantry, the phalanxes of Craterus, Meleager, and Philip, reaching as far as the centre of the entire line. – *Ibid*.

This seems to imply that there were nine units, or if one accepts that Philip and Craterus' names were duplicated, seven units. Arrian however affirms that three of the seven units took up half the line. Why these duplications, and how to reconcile three units out of seven making up half the heavy infantry?

The first thing to note is the absence of the agema (which is mentioned by name in all the other major battles of Alexander). Arrian specifies that the hypaspists here were those of the Companions, hearkening back to their origin as shieldbearing infantry, possibly *hamappoi*, for the Macedonian elite cavalry, whereas the agema, also called the *pezhetairoi*, were originally the professional infantry unit created by Alexander I.

Diodorus affirms that Alexander left half his infantry – 12,000 foot – and nearly half his cavalry – 1,500 horse – in Europe under the command of Antipater.[59] This near-even split of the Macedonian army could well have been mirrored in Alexander leaving one of his two elite infantry units in Macedonia to help Antipater quell any trouble there.

The second thing to note is that the Macedonian infantry advanced to the Granicus in a double line:

> Meantime Alexander was advancing to the river Granicus, with his army arranged for battle, having drawn up his hoplites in a double phalanx, leading the cavalry on the wings, and having ordered that the baggage should follow in the rear. – *Anabasis*: 1.13.

'Hoplites' as used here is a generic term for heavy infantry and would include the Macedonian pikemen. 'Double phalanx' translates διπλῆν μὲν τὴν φάλαγγα which means a phalanx in two lines, as the primary meaning of διπλῆν – *diplen* – is 'twofold', as in cloth folded to make two layers. Doubling his phalanx into two shorter lines would ensure his army, advancing in battle array, could traverse the ground more easily without becoming disrupted. It would also ensure that the phalanx could defend itself if attacked in the rear by cavalry. Alexander would use the same arrangement later at Issus and Gaugamela.

Diodorus mentions that Alexander had 5,000 mercenary infantry along with his 12,000 Macedonian foot and 7,000 allies.[60] The mercenaries, like the Macedonians and unlike the allies, were professional troops, well-trained in maintaining formation whilst on the move. With this in mind, it is possible to create a plausible deployment that takes everything into account.

Alexander deploys his Macedonians and mercenaries into a double line. He has 12,000 Macedonians and only 5,000 mercenaries, so he orders the three teloi of Craterus, Meleager and Philip to form two lines, of which the rear line is a combination of Macedonians and mercenaries. The mercenaries themselves, occupying the width of three teloi, have an average depth of about 13 ranks (or a standard 12 ranks if they number 4,600 men). Philip, Amyntas and Craterus continue to command the front halves of their teloi whilst *ad hoc* commanders, of which Meleager is one, take charge of the rear halves (see Diagram 94).

Philip	Amyntas	Craterus	Coenus	Perdiccas	Nicanor
PHAL.	PHAL.	PHAL.	PHALANGITES	PHALANGITES	HYPASPISTS

| PHAL. | PHAL. | PHAL. | | MERCENARIES | |

Meleager

Diagram 94: The march to the Granicus.

As the army nears the Granicus Alexander orders the Macedonians to deploy in a single line. According to the manuals, only syntagmas, measuring 16 files x 16 ranks, can execute wheels.[61] In Diagram 94 each syntagma is marked with the first letter of the telos' commander (Meleager's half-telos is marked with an M). The syntagma of the rear line all wheel left and form a column.

Philip	Amyntas	Craterus	Coenus	Perdiccas	Nicanor
PHAL.	PHAL.	PHAL.	PHALANGITES	PHALANGITES	HYPASPISTS

P P P P M M M M C C C | MERCENARIES |

Meleager

Diagram 95: The first stage of the deployment.

The leading syntagma immediately wheels to the right and moves up alongside the leftmost syntagma of the front line (see Diagram 96).

Philip	Amyntas	Craterus	Coenus	Perdiccas	Nicanor
PHAL.	PHAL.	PHAL.	PHALANGITES	PHALANGITES	HYPASPISTS

P P P M M M M C C C | | MERCENARIES |

Meleager

Diagram 96: The second stage of the deployment.

The next syntagma behind it advances until its front edge is parallel with the side edge of the foremost syntagma, and wheels right.

Philip	Amyntas	Craterus	Coenus	Perdiccas	Nicanor
P PHAL.	PHAL.	PHAL.	PHALANGITES	PHALANGITES	HYPASPISTS

P P P M M M M C C C ← | MERCENARIES |

Meleager

Diagram 97: The third stage of the deployment.

The process is repeated for the following syntagmas.

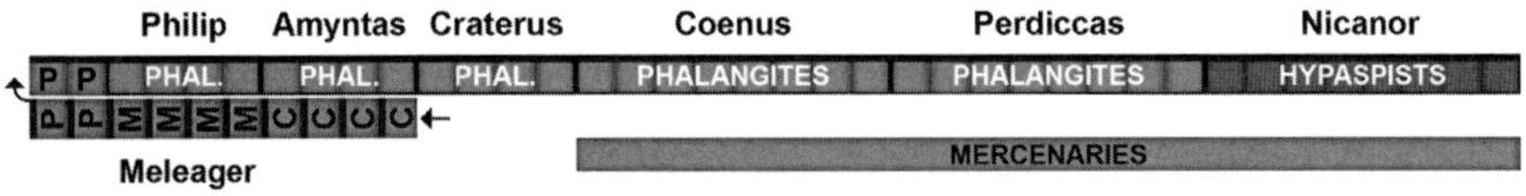

Diagram 98: Extending the line.

Finally the last syntagma wheels right and moves up to form a single line of phalangites.

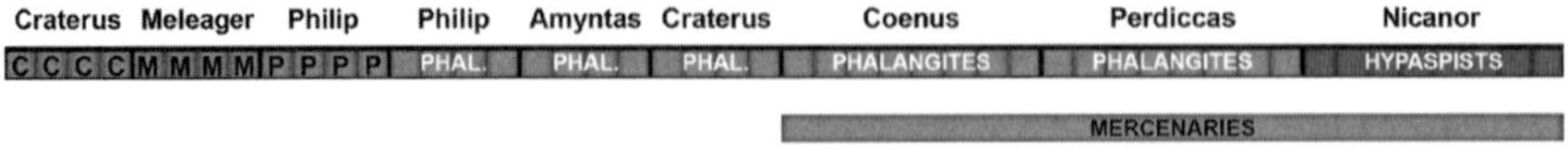

Diagram 99: The line is extended.

During this manoeuvre no syntagma ever exposes its vulnerable flank to the enemy. Syntagmas also never have to guess how far they must move before wheeling, but use each other as a reference point. The manoeuvre is simple, precise and safe.

Philip now resumes command of his entire telos. Meleager continues to command his half telos. Who commands the half-telos of Craterus? It is the unit at the edge of the line so, according to the manuals, it requires a senior officer. This may quite possibly have been Parmenion, who was given command of the left wing but did not take charge of any of the cavalry units there as Arrian names all their commanders.[62] For any Macedonian commander to be without a unit of his own would be unheard of. Parmenion would not be mentioned as commander since, unlike Meleager, he was not an integral part of the unit he commanded, but took charge of it in a temporary capacity.

This arrangement clarifies the passage from Arrian. The duplicated names correspond to the split teloi, and the three teloi of Philip, Amyntas and Craterus considered as complete units reach the middle of the line. Finally the six teloi, each numbering 2,000 men, come to a total of 12,000 Macedonians as given by Diodorus.

If Alexander had eight teloi, i.e. 16,000 pikemen, at Issus and Gaugamela, where did the reinforcements come from between the

Granicus and Issus? After taking Halicarnassus, Alexander marched through Phrygia and reached Gordium, where he cut the famous knot. There he received 3,000 Macedonian infantry along with some cavalry, under the command of Ptolemy, and another unspecified force under Parmenion.[63] Parmenion was Alexander's second-in-command which suggests he was bringing quality troops, possibly the agema from Europe which Alexander would soon use at Issus.[64] The 3,000 reinforcements were offset by 1,500 troops left at Celaenae as a garrison.[65] Presuming that 1,000 of these were Macedonians and the remainder allies, that leaves 2,000 Macedonian infantry – a complete telos – along with the 2,000-man agema. Alexander now had his full complement of 16,000 pike infantry.

Thus far there is evidence that shows the existence of units that in size if not always in name correspond to the *pentecosiarchia*, *chiliarchia* and *telos* of the manuals. Is there evidence for any other subdivisions in Alexander's army?

The Diphalangarchia

The diphalangarchia, or half-phalanx unit of 8,192 men, is visible in Alexander's army in his assignment of commanders for the left half of the phalanx, with himself by implication taking command of the right half. The left half commander at the Granicus was probably Parmenion (Craterus being in the wrong place) whilst at Issus and Gaugamela Arrian is explicit that it was Craterus. At the Hydaspes there is no mention of a left half infantry commander, probably due to the phalanx being divided into several separate units.

The Phalangarchia

At the Hydaspes Alexander split his army into three parts. One part under the command of Craterus, which included the two teloi of Alcetas, and Polysperchon remained at the camp.[66] The second part, incorporating the hypaspists and agema along with the two regular pike teloi of Cleitus and Coenus, accompanied Alexander. The third part, which included the remaining two pike teloi, positioned itself near the river between Alexander and Craterus.[67]

After defeating Porus' son, Alexander advanced towards Porus himself and then paused to draw up his infantry into an orderly phalanx, besides which this gave them the chance to catch their breath. The pike teloi of the detachment originally between Alexander and the camp most likely joined him at this point. Finally he departed with the cavalry, ordering the infantry to stay where they were:

> Seleucus, Antigenes, and Tauron were ordered to lead the phalanx of infantry, but not to engage in the action until they observed the enemy's cavalry and phalanx of infantry thrown into disorder by the cavalry under his own command. – *Anabasis*: 5.16.

Notice that there were three infantry commanders: Seleucus who led the hypaspists and agema, and Antigenes and Tauron who had four teloi between them.

This all suggests that by the time of the Hydaspes a new subunit was in play, the 4,000-man *phalangarchia*, made up of two teloi, whose origins may be seen in Alexander's earlier expeditionary operations that involved detachments composed of cavalry and the hypaspist and agema units.

The Syntagma

The manuals, when describing the 256-man syntagma, mention that it had five supernumeraries: a herald (στρατοκῆρυξ – *stratokeryx*), a standard-bearer (σημειφόρος – *semeiphoros*), a trumpeter (σαλπιγκτής – *salpinktes*), a rear commander (οὐραγός – *ouragos*), and an aide-de-camp (ὑπηρέτης – *hyperetes*).[68]

Asklepiodotus adds that the herald, standard-bearer and trumpeter were necessary to ensure the men understood orders during the noise and dust of the battlefield:

> The first was to pass on the command by a spoken order, the second by a signal, in case the order could not be heard because of the uproar, the third by the bugle, whenever the signal could not be seen for the dust. – *Tactics*: 2.9.

This underlined the *syntagma*'s role as the unit of manoeuvre on the battlefield. Of these supernumeraries the herald, standard-bearer and trumpeter would have stood in the first rank in order to receive orders from the commanding officer and be visible to the men. Does one see any evidence of this in Alexander's phalanx?

Quintus Curtius Rufus describes the eagerness of Alexander's infantry at the Battle of Issus:

> Proceeding in the front with the standards, Alexander with his hand repeatedly made signs to his men to restrain their impatient steps, lest, at the critical moment of coming up with the enemy, their accelerated respiration, interrupted and exhausted, should disable them from making a vigorous charge. – *History*: 3.10.3.

The standards fit in well with the standard-bearers of the *syntagma*.

There is evidence for the existence of the smaller units of the *dilochia*, *tetrarchia* and *taxis*, but at this point it can be affirmed with reasonable certitude that the infantry phalanx of Alexander, at least by the end of his reign, was indeed the phalanx of the manuals as Aelian claimed.

7. Deploying the Phalanx for Battle

When marching in column, if near enemy, the phalanx always advanced by rank, i.e. with the front at 90 degrees to its direction of march. That meant that file leaders were on one side of the column and file closers on the other. This enabled the column to respond with speed against a surprise attack by an enemy, countermarching if necessary to face an attack against the side with the file closers.[69] Deployment facing any direction could be done quickly, the leading syntagma wheeling so its front edge now faced the enemy and then advancing until the entire column was on the new alignment. The column would then stop and the individual men turn in place to form a line with the front edge nearest the enemy force.

The most detailed description we have of a pike phalanx in column deploying into line for battle is at Issus. Alexander had advanced as far as Myriandrus when he heard that the Persian army had advanced into his rear. He immediately retraced his steps, marching his infantry in column through the narrow pass north of Myriandus and then deploying them in line as the land widened beyond.

... as long as the space was narrow everywhere, he led his army in column, but when the mountains parted so as to leave a plain between them, he kept on opening out the column into the phalanx, marching one line of heavy armed infantry after another up into line towards the mountain on the right and towards the sea on the left. – Arrian, *Anabasis*: 2.8.

Curtius Rufus mentions that the column consisted of *ordines* of 32 men 'as the narrowness of the place did not permit the army to extend any wider' – *History*: 3.9. *Ordines* in a military sense means a line of men, either ranks or files. Here by implication it means ranks, i.e. that the column was 32 men wide.

Polybios, in a passage quoted earlier, repeats Callisthenes' description of the infantry narrowing its depth as it neared the enemy:

But that as soon as he had debouched upon the open country, he gave general orders to form up into a phalanx, at first thirty-two deep; then sixteen; and lastly, when they were nearing the enemy, eight deep. – *Histories*: 12.19.

Using the *syntagma* as the phalanx's unit of manoeuvre, it is possible to create a plausible picture of how Alexander formed up his column and how it deployed into line.

The phalanx is formed into a double column, or *diphalangia*, as described by the manuals. There are four kinds of diphalangia: the first have their fronts facing outwards, the second have them facing inwards, the third have all fronts facing to the right, and the fourth all fronts facing to the left.[70]

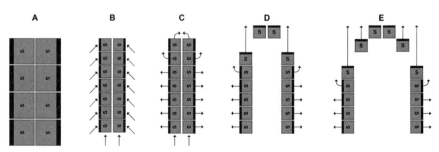

Diagram 100: The deployment of the diphalangia from column into line.

In this case the first kind of diphalangia seems the most appropriate as it best protects the phalanx from cavalry attacks on both sides and enables a quick deployment into line simultaneously to the right and left as described by Arrian. In Diagram 100, the diphalangia, two syntagmas wide, marches in open order, with each rank and file occupying about two yards. This is the 32-man wide column described by Curtius (A). Once through the pass the syntagmas contract to intermediate order and move up to close the gaps between them (B). The leading syntagmas wheel by their rear corners to face forwards whilst remaining side by side. The two syntagmas behind them wheel by their front corners to the right and left. The remaining syntagmas advance outwards, left and right (C). The second pair of syntagmas advance to line with the leading syntagmas. Meanwhile the third pair of syntagmas wheel right and left whilst the syntagmas behind them advance (D). The third pair of syntagmas move up alongside the leading syntagmas, the syntagmas behind them wheel, the remaining syntagmas advance, and the process continues until all the syntagmas are in line (E).

This method of deploying has several advantages: first, the officers keep their positions in their teloi throughout, preserving the structure of the units; secondly, no syntagma exposes its vulnerable flanks for any length of time; thirdly the deployment is quick, with all syntagmas moving simultaneously, and fourthly, the process is precise, with no need to estimate movement distances as each syntagma simply uses another as a reference point.

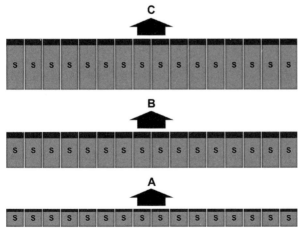

Diagram 101: The change in formation as the Phalanx advances to battle.

As shown in Diagram 101, the syntagmas, now in line (A), double their ranks from 16 to 32 men (B), creating open order files with 2 yards per file. As they advance they open the gaps between the ranks C) to enable easy marching over the remaining distance to the Persian army. This is the initial 32-deep line described by Callisthenes.

As the phalanx approaches the Persian army the syntagmas close up their ranks and advance their rear files forward alongside their front files, creating intermediate-order files with 16 ranks. Once near the Persians the syntagmas advance the rear half-files or *dimoirites* alongside the front half-files, creating close-order files with 8 ranks. This corresponds to the rest of Callisthenes' description.

Before deploying into line the column would have advanced in this order, with Alexander at the end near the accompanying cavalry:

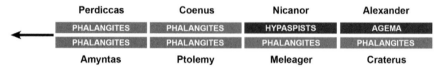

Perdiccas	Coenus	Nicanor	Alexander
PHALANGITES	PHALANGITES	HYPASPISTS	AGEMA
PHALANGITES	PHALANGITES	PHALANGITES	PHALANGITES
Amyntas	Ptolemy	Meleager	Craterus

Diagram 102: The order of march.

8. The Phalanx in Battle Formation

The Mobility of the Phalanx

It is commonly believed that the pike phalanx required level ground free of obstacles to function effectively and that on anything other than flat, smooth terrain its delicate formation would break down, exposing it to more flexible opponents. This notion comes from Polybios, echoed by Livy and Plutarch:

> Again, no one denies that for its employment it is indispensable to have a country flat, bare, and without such impediments as ditches, cavities, depressions, steep banks, or beds of rivers: for all such obstacles are sufficient to hinder and dislocate this particular formation. – Polybios, *Histories*: 18:31.

> [Philip V] had posted his men on ground of such a nature, that the phalanx (which even a small inequality of surface renders useless) could not advance on it. – Livy, *History of Rome*: 44.37.11.

The place [Pydna] afforded a plain for his [Perseus'] phalanx, which required firm standing and smooth ground – Plutarch, *Aemilius Paulus*: 16.5.

But Polybios' own descriptions of several battles involving the pike phalanx do not bear out his affirmation of the phalanx's extreme sensitivity to terrain. At Chaeronea Philip withdrew his phalanx to high ground from where he was able to defeat the Athenians:

> Engaging the Athenians at Chaeroneia, Philippus made a sham retreat: and Stratocles, the Athenian general, ordered his men to push forwards, crying out, 'We will pursue them to the heart of Macedonia'. Philippus observed, 'The Athenians know not how to conquer': and ordered his phalanx to keep close and firm, and to retreat slowly, covering themselves with their shields from the attacks of the enemy. As soon as he had by the manoeuvre drawn them from their advantageous ground, and gained an eminence, he halted; and encouraging his troops to a vigorous assault, he attacked the Athenians and won a brilliant victory. – Polyaenus, *Stratagems*: 4.2.2.

Philip was stationed with his phalanx on the right flank. The Athenians were on the slope of a spur whilst the Macedonian phalanx initially deployed on the slope of an adjacent spur. The average angle of the slopes was between 13 and 16 degrees (see Diagram 103).

Diagram 103: Philip's manoeuvre at Chaeroneia.

At Sellasia the Spartan phalangites and hoplites fought on hills behind trenches and palisades:

> Cleomenes strengthened both these hills by lines of fortification, consisting of trench and palisade. – Polybios, *Histories*: 2.65.

Eucleidas remained in his defensive position but nonetheless was overrun by the Macedonian phalanx even though he was behind a trench and palisade:

> As though victory were assured, he kept his original position on the summit of the hill, with the view of catching the enemy at as great an elevation as possible, that their flight might be all the longer over steep and precipitous ground. The result, as might have been anticipated, was exactly the reverse. For he left himself no place of retreat, and by allowing the enemy to reach his position, unharmed and in unbroken order, he was placed at the disadvantage of having to give them battle on the very summit of the hill; and so, as soon as he was forced by the weight of their heavy armour and their close order to give any ground, it was immediately occupied by the Illyrians – *Ibid*: 2.68.

The Euas slope has an average inclination of 15 degrees (see Diagram 104):

Diagram 104: Eucleidas' deployment at Sellasia.

Cynoscephalae would probably be considered the last place for a pike phalanx to fight a battle. The slopes are angled at an average of 22–26 degrees and yet the right wing of the phalanx was able to drive the Romans down them (see Diagram 105).

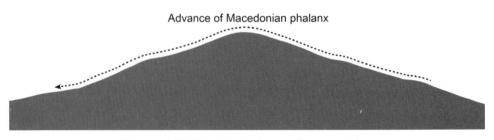

Diagram 105: The pike phalanx at Cynoscephalae.

These are the sharp tops of hills lying close alongside one another
– Plutarch, *Life of Flamininus*: 1.8.

For these hills, which are called Cynoscephalae, are rough, precipitous, and of considerable height – Polybios: 18.22.

The left wing of the phalanx however found its part of the hill too difficult to properly deploy in, and in any case was attacked by the Roman right wing before it had time to shake out the semblance of a line.[71]

At the Granicus the banks of the river were steep, nonetheless the phalanx was able to cross the river in battle formation and drive back the Persians on the far bank:

But most of the Macedonian officers were afraid of the depth of the river, and of the roughness and unevenness of the farther banks, up which they would have to climb while fighting. – Plutarch, *Alexander*: 16.1.

While Alexander's cavalry were making such a dangerous and furious fight, the Macedonian phalanx crossed the river and the infantry forces on both sides engaged. The enemy, however, did not resist vigorously, nor for a long time, but fled in a rout, all except the Greek mercenaries. – Plutarch, *Alexander*: 16.6.

Exactly the same thing happened at Issus, though in some places the river proved too much for the phalanx, with some parts advancing and others stalling before the excessively steep banks:

For Darius was no longer leading the foreigners against him, as he had arranged them at first, but he remained in his position, upon the bank of the river, which was in many parts steep and precipitous; and in certain places, where it seemed more easy to ascend, he extended a stockade along it. – Arrian, *Anabasis*: 2.10.

For the Macedonian phalanx had been broken and disjoined towards the right wing; because Alexander had charged into the river with eagerness, and engaging in a hand-to-hand conflict was already driving back the Persians posted there; but the Macedonians in the centre did not execute their task with equal speed; and finding many parts of the bank steep and precipitous, they were unable to preserve the front of the phalanx in the same line. – *ibid*.

In conclusion then, rough and sloping ground did not stop the phalanx either advancing or fighting unless it was too steep for the men to clamber up or too broken to form a continuous line.

The Problem of the Close Order

Askepiodotus and Aelian affirm the phalanx deployed in three orders: open, with each file occupying a width of 4 cubits or 192cm; intermediate at 2 cubits or 96cm; and close at one cubit or 48cm.[72] For Asklepiodotus the intermediate and close orders were used in combat: the intermediate order for advancing on the enemy and the close order when attacked by enemy.[73] Phalangite shields were between 64cm and 76cm wide.

In intermediate order there was plenty of space between shields for the pikemen to wield their sarissas as they saw fit (see Diagram 106):

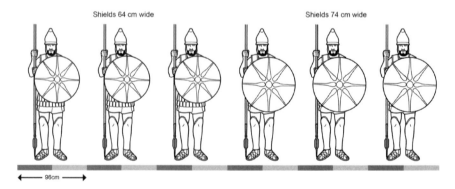

Diagram 106: Pikemen in intermediate order.

In close order however it was a different story. Shields of adjacent files would overlap as shown in Diagram 107.

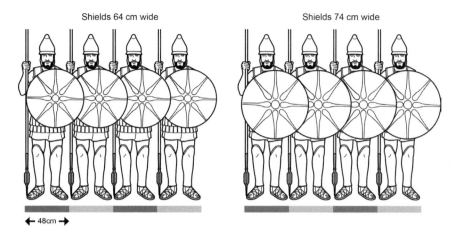

Diagram 107: Pikemen in close order.

There are several instances of the close order being used not just defensively but to advance in attack. At Sellasia, the Macedonian right flank, after unsuccessfully engaging the Spartan phalangites of Cleomenes in intermediate order, formed close order and advanced to drive the Spartans back.[74] Callisthenes' account of Alexander's infantry deploying 32, then 16 and finally 8 deep at Issus suggests a compacting of files from open to intermediate to close order that then assaulted the Greek mercenary hoplites and Persian infantry. Polybios states that when facing Roman legions two phalangites habitually faced one legionary, adding that the phalangites were in close order whilst the legionaries formed up with each file occupying a width of three feet (see Chapter 1), and at Cynoscephalae and Pydna the Macedonian phalanx advanced against the Roman legions, driving them back.

How did the phalangites wield their sarissas? It is almost universally assumed that phalangites held them underarm, with the shafts projecting past the lower right edge of the shields. This is the posture of the two standing phalangites to the left in the Pergamon plaque (Diagram 108, A).

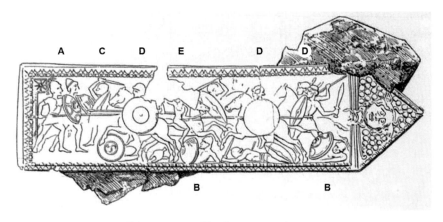

Diagram 108: The Pergamon plaque.

There are however several problems with using the Pergamon plaque as a reliable source for the pike phalanx. The scene probably indicates the charge by Eumenes' cavalry against the Seleucid left at Magnesia, which sent the auxiliary infantry next to the phalanx fleeing into it for protection, disrupting it.[75] Thus we see a phalanx in disorder, several phalangites already down (Diagram 108, B), legionaries past its sarissa-guard (Diagram 108, C) whilst it is being charged in the flank by Eumenes' cavalry (Diagram 108, D). The phalangites' low grip on their sarissas could be interpreted simply as an attempt to adopt as stable a posture as possible against the charge of the cavalry. The scene is a wild free-for-all, and one cannot use it as an indicator of how the phalanx looked when properly structured. Furthermore, the mixing together of troops types that were in fact widely separated on the battlefield – the Gallic cavalryman in the centre (Diagram 108, E) and the legionaries mixed with the Attalid cavalry – is an indication that the sculptor was not trying to be historically accurate but was creating a dramatic scene.

Assuming that the phalangites did indeed present their sarissas with a low underarm grip as shown in the plaque poses a problem for the second and subsequent ranks. The gap between 64cm wide shields of phalangites in closer order with the phalangites in battle posture is about 60cm above the ground, whilst that for 74cm wide shields is about 50cm high. In both cases the gap is about 15cm wide. Through this gap 5–6 ranks of phalangites must project their sarissas and keep their points from sticking in the ground when going up a riverbank or the slope of a hill. Any advance up a slope steeper than 9 degrees or so becomes impossible. If the phalanx traverses a dip or encounters any obstacle two feet or more in height it will stop dead in its tracks (see Diagram 109).

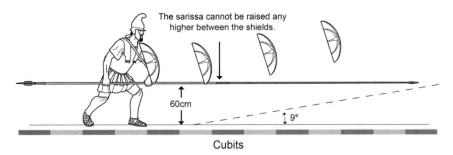

The sarissa cannot be raised any higher between the shields.

60cm

9°

Cubits

Diagram 109: The pike used underarm.

Several solutions have been offered. Connolly[76] proposes that the phalangite projected his left arm well forwards, which keeps the shield largely to the side of his body and opens a space between shields through which the sarissas can pass. But this would expose a large part of the phalangite's body to enemy weapons, and it contradicts all three tacticians who describe a literal touching or overlapping of shields.[77] It also contradicts the clear sense of overlapping or at least touching shields at the battle of Pydna as described by Plutarch:

> And when he saw that the rest of the Macedonian troops also were drawing their shields from their shoulders round in front of them, and with long spears levelled were withstanding his thureophoroi troops, and saw too the strength of their shields-together [συνασπισμός – *synaspismos*] and the fierceness of their onset, amazement and fear took possession of him. – *Aemilius Paulus*: 19.1.

Matthew proposes that the pike phalanx never fought in close order, and that the descriptions of the close order arrangement in the manuals actually refer to the hoplite phalanx.[78] This however contradicts the clear affirmations of the manuals, who describe the close order phalanx of one cubit per file as belonging to the pike phalanx.

Smith appears to have the right answer.[79] He proposes that the phalangites presented their pikes overarm, with the pikeshafts of the ranks further back passing between the heads and over the shields of the men in front. Matthew dismisses this as unworkable since the pikes would have been too heavy to carry overarm for any length of time. But presenting pikes overarm was done for centuries by another pike formation: the Mediaeval and Renaissance pike phalanx.

The trick of presenting a 4kg pike overarm whilst carrying the shield is to ensure both arms are supported. Renaissance pikemen achieved this by using pikes that were not counterweighted at the butt end, bearing the weight of the pike with the left arm held close to the chest whilst the right arm rested on the end of the pike, using its mass as a counterweight. The left arm carried the weight of the pike and right arm on its own bone structure, with little or no muscle strain (see Diagram 110).

Diagram 110: The Renaissance pike used overarm.

This could also be achieved with a shield, by suspending the shield from a strap around the shoulder whilst the left elbow rested on the shield's porpax (see Diagram 111):

Diagram 111: Renaissance pike used overarm with shield.

Could something similar be achieved with the sarissa and phalangite shield, bearing in mind the sarissa, unlike the Renaissance pike, is counterweighted? As an experiment I created a replica shield, 64cm wide, concave, with a telamon and ochanon improvised from some plastic cord and a piece of old leather belt (see Diagram 111b).

Diagram 111b: Reconstructed shield with *telamon* and *ochanon*.

After some trial and error I managed to attach the telamon to the shield in such a fashion that I was able to support my left arm with the elbow resting in the ochanon whilst the telamon bore the weight of the arm and shield. Using a pole-vaulter's grip the left hand was able to hold the sarissa (a trimmed tree branch) at the upper right edge of the shield whilst my right hand held the sarissa about two feet further back with my right arm bent close to my chest. In this position there was no muscle strain at all – I could have held the pose indefinitely.

A family friend, Kyle, kindly offered to pose with the shield and improvised sarissa. In Diagram 111c he is demonstrating the overarm grip. His right hand should have been using the pole-vaulter's hold, but I was too preoccupied trying to get the smartphone camera to work to notice and it isn't a perfect world.

Diagram 111c: Sarissa and shield using the overarm grip.

The shield leans somewhat forwards with the lower edge resting against the waist, but it is possible to extend the shield forwards and even raise it by using the left arm. Braced by the arm and the telamon, the shield is very rigid.

Using the same configuration of ochanon and telamon, Kyle had no trouble wielding the shield whilst holding the sarissa in an underarm grip, as shown in Diagram 111d. This time the top edge of the shield rests against the shoulder whilst the bottom edge extended outwards. One could extend it further by stretching out the left arm but one cannot raise the shield above the shoulder. Like for the high hold, the shield is very rigid. The shield sits lower than for the high hold and the projecting bottom edge gives good protection for the midriff.

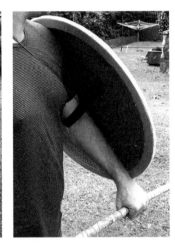

Diagram 111d: Sarissa and shield using the underarm grip.

Using these two holds, one can construct a model of the phalanx that not only allows the formation to present pikes in close order, but also permits the phalanx to traverse terrain that is not an obstacle if the individual pikemen are able to clamber over it. Each pikeman occupies a depth of 2 cubits and holds the pike with his left hand gripping the pikeshaft at its centre of balance, 4 cubits or about 6 feet from the tip of the sauroter. The entire weight of the pike, along with the shield, is borne by the telamon. The right arm does not actually support the pike or lean its weight on it but merely directs it and can be used to thrust it forward in a strike, similar to a hoplite striking with a dory. The front-rank pikeman holds the pike in an underarm grip as his shield can then better protect his waist and with this grip he can withstand a cavalry charge, kneeling down and ramming the sauroter in the ground behind him if necessary (see Diagram 112).

Cubits

Diagram 112: The phalanx using mixed grip.

Notice that all the pikemen can incline their pikes upwards when encountering a slope or other raised obstacle. All pikemen can use their pikes to strike at opponents, the second and subsequent ranks using the more effective overarm grip to deliver stronger pike-thrusts. The pikemen can also move their pikes laterally to a much greater extent than in an underarm grip, since there is about a foot of space between the pikemen's heads, enabling the pikes to be swivelled to the right or left to cover all the area in front of the phalanx.

My experiments with the homemade shield produced one other interesting result. Closing up a phalanx from intermediate to close order was achieved by the rear half-files marching up between the front half-files. This however would be impossible if the pikemen held their shields in front of them as there is less than a foot of space between the shields of each file in intermediate order, too narrow for the rear half-files to pass to the front. Plutarch hints at the solution to this problem:

As the attack began, Aemilius came up and found that the Macedonian battalions had already planted the tips of their long spears in the shields of the Romans, who were thus prevented from reaching them with their swords. And when he saw that the rest of the Macedonian troops also were drawing their shields from their shoulders round in front of them, and others on a prearranged signal sloping their sarissas to oppose the theureophoroi, and saw too the strength of their interlocked shields and the fierceness of their onset, amazement and fear took possession of him, and he felt that he had never seen a sight more fearful. – *Aemilius Paulus*: 19.1.

Notice the Macedonian troops who have their shields on their shoulders. With experimentation, I found that this was possible by pushing the ochanon up to around the upper arm. If I raised my left elbow so as to retain my left hand's grip on the sarissa, the shield then naturally swung to the side of my body alongside my shoulder. Kyle demonstrates this pose in Diagram 112b.

Diagram 112b: The shield carried at the shoulder.

The right arm supports the weight of the sarissa and the left arm, which does not require any effort to keep its position. More importantly though, the shield, snug against the left shoulder, enables one to pass through a gap not much wider than the shoulders. Phalangites, carrying their shields in this manner whilst in intermediate formation, would have no trouble doubling to close formation as the rear half-files would now have enough space between the front half-files to move up.

With my own experimenting I found it an easy process to bring the shield round to the front. First, I loosened my grip on the sarissa, letting its butt-end drop to the ground. Keeping a grip on the shaft with my left hand, I lowered my left elbow whilst using my freed right hand to pull the shield around to the front, such that the ochanon was now around my elbow. A few moments of adjustment and I had the stable overarm grip as described earlier. With a little practice I was able to keep the sarissa from moving much during this process.

Going back to Plutarch one can now form a coherent picture of what happened. The phalanx advanced in intermediate order whilst the front-rank pikemen kept their shields before them, presenting their pikes possibly in an underarm grip. The other ranks held their sarissas vertical or inclined forwards at an angle, shields at their shoulders. At around the time the front rankers jammed their sarissas into the Roman shields, the rear half-files marched up alongside the front half-files, then grounded their sarissas and brought their shields round to the front, creating the overlapping shieldwall that so impressed Aemilius Paulus. They then lowered their sarissas and the newly-arrived front rankers with possibly one or more ranks behind them struck at the Romans, adding to the force of the front-rank sarissas already implanted in the Roman shields.

All of this experimentation does not of course constitute conclusive proof, but it does demonstrate that a close order phalanx with overlapping shields was quite feasible and perfectly capable of advancing up steep riverbanks or over difficult terrain. There is no need to either disregard or explain away the sources.

9. The Push of Pikes

Once in battle order, shields to the front and sarissas lowered, how did the phalanx actually attack the enemy? The sources are abundantly clear: it engaged immediately in an othismos contest in which pressure was applied with sarissas rather than by shield pressing against shield.

> Just as a sword presents the effect of its edge, increased by the stroke and the weight of the iron towards its back, so the rank of

file leaders may be considered the edge of the phalanx, receiving its power, impetus and momentum from **the mass of men that presses forward from the rear**. Similarly, attention must be paid to those in the second rank, for the **pikes of those within it are projected forward** together with those of the front rank and, being positioned immediately behind the latter, are of great use in emergencies – Aelian, *Tactics*: 13.

Compactly [literally 'in a circle'] they stand back successively so that each hoplite [phalangite in this context] in the front **is covered by six sarissas and presses on with six forces** whenever they bear down. Those standing in the sixth **row press on with the weight of their bodies**, if not with their sarissas, so that the phalanx's push against the foes does not become endurable and flight [becomes] difficult for the front row men. – Arrian, *Tactics*: 12.

And the Macedonians, men say, with this **line of spears** do not merely terrify the enemy by their appearance, but also embolden every file-leader, protected as he is by the strength of five; while the men in the line behind the fifth, though they cannot extend their spears beyond the front of the phalanx, nevertheless **bear forward with their bodies** at all events and deprive their comrades in the front ranks of any hope of flight. But some, who wish to bring **all the projecting spear-points** to the same distance in front of the line, increase the length of the spears of the rear ranks. – Asklepiodotus, *Tactics*: 5.

Of these sixteen ranks, all above the fifth are unable to **reach with their sarissas** far enough to take actual part in the fighting. They, therefore, do not lower them, but hold them with the points inclined upwards over the shoulders of the ranks in front of them, to shield the heads of the whole phalanx; for the sarissae are so closely serried, that they repel missiles which have carried over the front ranks and might fall upon the heads of those in the rear. These rear ranks, however, during an advance, **press forward those in front by the weight of their bodies; and thus make the**

charge very forcible, and at the same time render it impossible for the front ranks to face about. – Polybios, *Histories*: 18.30.

For Aelian, Arrian and Polybios, the pressure of the rear ranks does not just keep the front ranks from taking early military retirement (as Asklepiodotus affirms), but also supplies an active pressure that propels the phalanx forward. How is this pressure transmitted to the enemy? Plutarch mentions that 'the Macedonian battalions had already planted the tips of their long spears in the shields of the Romans, who were thus prevented from reaching them with their swords'. The implication is that the phalangites aimed their sarissas at the enemy shields rather than at their faces or legs, partly because the shield was a target they could not miss, and partly because their purpose was to drive the enemy formation back, rather than try to kill front-rank enemy troops (though killing enemies was certainly a bonus).

Polybios affirms that the sarissas of the five first ranks could reach the enemy whilst Arrian maintains that those of the first six ranks could do so. This variability probably depends on the length of the sarissas. Taking the 12.5 cubit-long sarissa used in the diagrams above, it is certainly possible for the first five ranks to jam their pikeheads into the enemy's front rank shields if all ranks first close up shield against back (necessary for the rear ranks to apply pressure to those in front) and the front rank phalangite holds his sarissa a little forward of its centre of balance. Of course this would work better if the sarissas of the ranks further back were longer than those of the front ranks, which would explain Asklepiodotus' mention of variable pike lengths that ensured all pikes reached the same point in front, as demonstrated in Diagram 113.

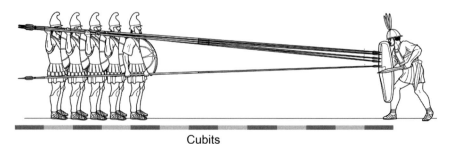

Cubits

Diagram 113: Reaching the enemy shield with five pikeheads.

To give more flexibility to the handling of the sarissas, half the phalangites would be able to wield their sarissas alongside their left shoulders, using their right arm to hold the shield, and half alongside their right shoulders with their left arm carrying the shield. This would mean 2–3 sarissas per side, few enough to avoid fouling each other, creating a battleline in which sarissas were no more than about 24cm apart – an impenetrable wall of spearpoints. This is offered as a possibility, not a certitude or even a probability, but it does correspond to the image evoked by Aelian: 'and each individual within the formation, surrounded [πεφραγμένου – with the sense of protected at all points: fenced in, walled around] by five or six pikes [wielded by the men of his file]…' – *Tactics*: 14. Diagram 114, showing just the first four ranks, illustrates this alternating method of presenting pikes.

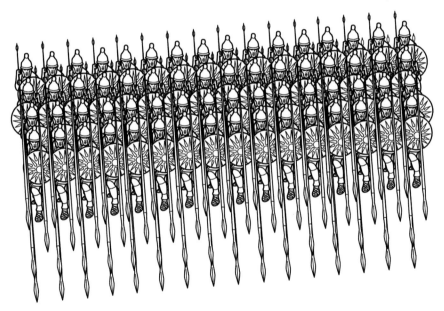

Diagram 114: Alternating pikes.

Experimenting with my homemade shield, I had no problem wielding it with either the right or left arm without changing the configuration of the telamon or ochanon. As a final point, phalangite helmets came in several forms as was seen earlier, but none that could hook on or obstruct a sarissa shaft.

What kind of force would be generated by this othismos of sarissas? Without testing it is impossible to know but it was enough in some cases to penetrate Roman shields and breastplates.[80] This however seems to have been the exception rather than the rule. Pike phalanxes generally drove shielded opponents back, as happened at Cynoscephalae, Pydna, Sellasia and elsewhere, rather than impaled them.[81]

The round concave shield of the phalangite enabled him – like the hoplite – to breathe during an othismos crush, with the top edge of the shield resting against his sternum whilst the bottom edge was pressed against his hip. Phalangite shields varied in size and bowl depth, but always remained within parameters suitable for othismos.

One objection to an othismos of sarissas is the comparison with hoplite othismos, where up to 400kg of pressure could be transmitted by the frontmost hoplite with file behind him pushing in concert (see Chapter 2). Besides being impossible for a phalangite to keep his grip on a sarissa shaft whilst 400kg propels him forwards, even if he did manage it the shaft would certainly snap under the strain.[82]

With othismos of sarissas however, all the force of the rear ranks is not transferred to the file leader. Part of the force of the phalangites pushing against the fifth man in the file is transmitted along his sarissa and the rest to the man in front him. The fourth man in the file transmits part of the force he receives to his sarissa and the rest to the man in front of him, and so on until the file leader receives the residue of the force, now only a fraction of its original strength. In addition, holding on to a sarissa shaft during this othismos would not unduly strain the arm muscles since the left arm is braced against the chest by the pressure of the sarissa being pushed against it, requiring only that the left hand keep its grip on the shaft.

How much force could a phalangite actually transmit along his sarissa? Polevaulters raise their own body weight – on average 79kg[83] – with ease and without their poles snapping. But is it likely these kind of pressures were generated? Two pike phalanxes would not want to engage in an all-out shoving match as that would mean death or serious injury for the file leaders of both formations. More likely an othismos contest between two pike phalanxes was a test of nerves: who would push a little harder and risk his shield and breastplate getting pierced, and who would get cold feet and back off?

Pike vs. pike combat was hence probably a question of morale, with more confident veteran units seeing greener troops off the field, as the Argyraspides did the inexperienced pikemen of Antigonus at Gabiene and Paraitakene. But against any other opponent the pike phalanx – provided it kept order and did not have exposed flanks – was invincible. It had no trouble beating hoplites at their own game. With smaller shields, phalangites could form close order files 48cm wide whilst hoplite files were about 60–70 cm wide. In a shoving contest that meant more phalangite than hoplite files, and the phalangites did not need to hold back as there was no danger of their own shields getting pierced by the hoplites' shorter spears. The hoplites' only chance was to take up a position on a slope (Chaeronea, Sellasia) or behind a steep riverbank (Issus) where the pike phalanx, struggling uphill, could not bring the full weight of its rear ranks to bear. But in that situation the hoplites could not win, only hold their ground and surrender the initiative to their opponents who were able to outflank them at leisure.

10. Conclusion: the Effectiveness of the Pike Phalanx

The effectiveness of the pike phalanx may be attested by the fact that of the infantry formations in Antiquity it was the only one that was successfully resurrected in a later age when, as it had done before, it dominated the battlefield for two centuries and more. In all the battles between the pike phalanx and the Roman legion – Heraclea, Asculum, Beneventum, Cynoscephalae, Magnesia and Pydna – the legion never beat the phalanx in a frontal fight provided the latter was on ground that permitted it to maintain its structure in an uninterrupted line. Difficult terrain was the legion's ace in the hole. An isolated maniple could respond to flank attacks by wheeling to face the threat or by the men simply turning in place; a syntagma with its sarissas lowered could do neither. Syntagmas could wheel on the battlefield to envelope an enemy line as the hypaspists enveloped the Greek mercenaries at Issus, but their phalangites had to raise their sarissas to a vertical position first, making them vulnerable against an attack.[84] And a phalangite without his sarissa was at a serious disadvantage against a legionary or any similarly equipped heavy infantry. His principal liability was his shield: slung around his neck by the telamon, he could not wield it freely in the way a legionary or hoplite could wield theirs. Its movement was limited and it could not be used offensively, e.g. for punching an enemy. And like his sword it was smaller than most enemy equivalents, offering less protection. Lastly, the phalangite may have had a sword but it was not his principal weapon, which meant he had far less training and experience with it than a legionary did: in a one-on-one duelling contest the phalangite stood little chance.

The phalanx suffered one other weakness: it was not really an offensive formation. Its overriding need to keep order meant it could not advance quickly, especially when in close formation, and with its sarissas lowered it could not wheel. When Philip II created the pike phalanx, he created lance-armed heavy cavalry to accompany it. The phalanx's job was to engage the enemy's heavy infantry, locking them into a fight they could not win. But it was the heavy cavalry that won the battles by punching a hole in a vulnerable point in the enemy line and attacking them from the rear. Chaeronea, the Granicus, Issus, Gaugamela, were battles in which the pike phalanx was crucial for engaging the bulk of the enemy's heavy troops, but in which the heavy cavalry shattered the enemy's morale by getting behind him. When a pike phalanx lacked the help of this strong, mobile offensive arm, a nimbler opponent was able to seize and exploit advantages more quickly than it could. If the phalanx's support troops could be driven off, its inherent vulnerability to flank and rear attacks doomed it.

And a nimbler opponent was waiting for it, not far away in the Italian peninsula.

Notes

1. Plutarch, *Life of Cleomenes*: 4.5
2. Plutarch, *Life of Cleomenes*: 12.
3. Polybios, *Histories*: 2.65.
4. Plutarch, *Life of Cleomenes*: 23.
5. Polybios, *Histories*: 2.69.
6. Proposed battlefield location: 37.188089, 22.449847. The left wing contingents did not deploy one behind the other as is commonly supposed, but one 'after' (*epi* and *katopin*) the other, i.e. after each other in the same

line. Polybios affirms the Spartan light troops were able to attack the rear of this line as there were no reserves behind it – *Histories*: 2.67. The Illyrians were not deployed in alternate blocks with the Macedonian phalangites as they would then have been clearly visible, and Plutarch mentions that Cleomenes could not see them nor the Arcananians – *Cleomenes*: 28. Antigonus most likely intercalated the files of the Illyrians between those of the phalangites – an arrangement known as interjection (*parembole*) – to conceal them whilst hiding the Arcananians behind the Epirotes. At the commencement of the battle the Illyrians probably countermarched to the rear of the phalangites, formed column and marched around to the flank of the hoplites on Euas, followed by the Arcananians. The Boeotians are placed in the left wing in the diagram although neither Polybios nor Plutarch mention them in their accounts of the battle as their addition gives the right-wing Macedonian infantry a width that matches that of the Spartans.

7. Polybios, *Histories*: 2.68.
8. Demosthenes, *Second Olynthiac*: 2.17.
9. S. English, *The Army of Alexander the Great*: 4; Matthew, *An Invincible Beast*: 1.
10. http://soa.org.uk/sm/index.php?topic=3385.15
11. Thucydides, *History of the Peloponnesian War*: 2.100.
12. Thucydides, *History of the Peloponnesian War*: 1.62.
13. 'Armes, Armement et Contexte Funéraire dans la Macédoine Hellénistique: Avec un appendice sur les trouvailles d'armes relatives à l'archaïsme et aux débuts de l'époque classique en Macédoine & sur ses confins', (*Akanthina*, Gdańsk, 2017); cited by Duncan Head, 'Origins of the Macedonian Infantry', *Slingshot* 319.
14. Thucydides, *History of the Peloponnesian War*: 4.123.
15. The Argive One Thousand, the Syracusan Six Hundred, the 300-man Sacred Band of Thebes, the Arcadian *Eparitoi*, and the Three Hundred and the Four Hundred at Elis.
16. Xenophon, *Cyropaedia*: 6.2.10; 7.1.33.
17. Xenophon, *Anabasis*: 4.7.16.
18. Didymus: *Demosthenes*: 11.22. col, 13.3–7 'The third wound he took in the invasion of the Triballians, one of the pursuers thrusting the sarissa through his right thigh and laming him.' This same injury also killed his horse according to Justin (11.3.2), hence it is probable that Philip's pursuer was mounted. Duncan Head (Slingshot 214) affirms it unlikely that a cavalryman would strike another cavalryman in the thigh rather than the torso or head, whereas an infantryman's long lance would be aimed at the lower part of the body. The thigh however is the largest unprotected part of a mounted rider and hence the easiest to target. When Alexander fights the Triballians later there is no mention of their infantry having sarissas (Arrian, *Anabasis*: 1.2).

19. Matthew, *An Invincible Beast*: 1.
20. Tarn, *Military and Naval Developments*: 43; Matthew, *An Invincible Beast*: 1.
21. The Alexander Mosaic from the Casa del Fauno in Pompeii is commonly cited as depicting Macedonian sarissas, but this is highly unlikely. The long spears are intermingled with the Persian cavalry (the Persian standard-bearer is behind two spears). They are wielded against Alexander and the advancing Companions, and they are in disorder. They are probably the spears of mercenary hoplites of which one can be seen fallen behind his *aspis* before Darius' chariot. These hoplites had most likely been armed with long spears – Diodorus affirms that Darius 'had fashioned swords and lances [ξυστὰ – *xysta*] much longer than his earlier types because it was thought that Alexander had had a great advantage in this respect in the battle in Cilicia [i.e. at Issus]'. – *Library*, 17.53.1. *Xysta* is a term that can apply to infantry as well as cavalry weapons (though Diodorus does not use it elsewhere explicitly for infantry). In this case infantry seem indicated as Darius would have known after Issus that hoplites armed with traditional spears stood little chance against phalangites. There is no mention anywhere of Persian cavalry being equipped with long lances and Alexander's Companions appear to outrange them with their lances: '…the Macedonian cavalry, commanded by Alexander himself, pressed on vigorously, thrusting themselves against the Persians and striking their faces with their spears'. – Arrian, *Anabasis*: 3.14. At Gaugamela the mercenaries were stationed in the centre of the Persian line, near Darius (Arrian, *Anabasis*: 3.11).
22. *Thebaid*: 7.269.
23. *Anabasis*: 1.15.
24. Matthew, *An Invincible Beast*: 2.
25. D.W. Engels, *Alexander the Great and the Logistics of the Macedonian Army*: 157.
26. *Ibid.*
27. https://www.wood-database.com/european-ash/
28. To calculate its area multiply the area of the cross section at its midpoint by its length. Area = $1{,}132cm^3$. Weight = 0.68g x $1{,}132cm.^3$ = 769.76g
29. To calculate point of balance of a tapered shaft, first calculate weight of an untapered shaft with a diameter of 28mm. Weight = $\pi 14^2$ x 251.8 x 0.68g = 1054.45g. Point of balance of tapered shaft = point of balance of untapered shaft x weight of tapered shaft / weight of untapered shaft = 125.9 x 770g / 1054.45g = 92 cm from the wider end.
30. Matthew, *An Invincible Beast*: 2.
31. Minor M. Markle, *A Shield Monument from Veria and the Chronology of Macedonian Shield Types*.
32. K. Liampi, *Der makedonische Schild*.
33. Pierre Juhel, 'Fragments de 'Boucliers macédoniens' au nom du roi Démétrios trouvés à Staro Bonce', *Zeitschrift für Papyrologie und Epigraphik*,

Bd. 162 (2007), pp. 165–180; Nicholas Sekunda, *Macedonian Armies after Alexander 323–168 bc*.

34. http://soa.org.uk/sm/index.php?topic=3777.105
35. Pausanias 5.26.3; Strabo 14.2.27; Herodotus 2.141.5; Lucian, *Anacharsis*. 27; Lucian, *Herodotus and Aetion*, 5; Procopius, *De Bellis*, 1.1.13.
36. Pierre Juhel, 'The Regulation Helmet of the Phalanx and the Introduction of the Concept of Uniform in the Macedonian Army at the End of the Reign of Alexander the Great', *Klio* 91(2), 2009.
37. Matthew, *An Invincible Beast*: 3.
38. *Ibid.*
39. Siculus, *Library*: 16.8.
40. Polyaenus, *Stratagems*: 4.2.6.
41. Arrian, *Anabasis*: 7.9.6.
42. Asklepiodotus: 2.1–2; Aelian: 4, 5; Arrian: 5, 6.
43. Diodorus Siculus: 17.17.3. Diodorus states there were 12,000 Macedonian heavy infantry of which it is generally assumed 3,000 were hypaspists. In any case all were armed and fought as phalangites, at least at Issus where there is no mention of hypaspists fighting differently from the main body of the phalanx.
44. Quintus Curtius Rufus, *History of Alexander*: 3.9.12.
45. Asklepiodotus: 2.2; Aelian: 5; Arrian: 6.
46. The manuals do not expressly describe this method of doubling files, but it can be inferred from their description of even-numbered files countermarching behind odd-numbered files to double the depth of a phalanx – the inverse process for doubling the number of files. See Chapter 1: 3. *Heavy Infantry – Manoeuvres*.
47. Asklepiodotus: 2.8–10; Aelian: 9.
48. Asklepiodotus: 2.10; Aelian: 9.
49. Sheppard, *Alexander the Great at War*: 79; Connolly, *Greece and Rome*: 69; M.G. Carey, *Operational Art in Classical Warfare: The Campaigns of Alexander the Great* 14; M. Thompson, *Granicus 334 bc: Alexander's First Persian Victory* (Osprey, Oxford, 2007) 24; Daniel, 'The Taxeis of Alexander', 43; W. Heckel and R. Jones, *Macedonian Warrior: Alexander's Elite Infantryman*: 30; R.D. Milns, 'Arrian's Accuracy in Troop Details: A Note', *Historia*: 27:2 375; Nicholas Sekunda, *Army of Alexander*: 28; Nicholas Sekunda, *Macedonian Armies after Alexander 323–168 bc*: 21; J.F.C. Fuller, *The Generalship of Alexander the Great*: 50; W. Heckel, *The Conquests of Alexander the Great*: 26; and others.
50. There is another example of this non-agreement between a relative pronoun and its antecedent in Arrian, *Anabasis*: 2.8: 'First, upon the right wing near the mountain he placed the agema and the hypaspists, under the command of Nicanor, son of Parmenio; next to these the *taxis* of Coenus, and close to them that of Perdiccas'. The *taxis* of Perdiccas is close to the *taxis* of Coenus, '*taxis*' being in the singular, whilst 'close to them' – ἐπὶ δὲ τούτοις – is in the plural.

51. Arrian describes this same ordering during Alexander's attack against Sagalassus: 'But Alexander drew up the phalanx of Macedonians in the following way: on the right wing, where he had himself taken up his position, he held the hypaspists, and next to these he extended the *pezhetairoi* as far as the left wing, in the order that each of the generals had precedence in the array that day'. – *Anabasis*: 1.28. Note that in this case the hypaspists take precedence over the pezhetairoi (i.e. the agema).

52. *Anabasis*: 5.13.

53. *Anabasis*: 5.13.

54. *Anabasis*: 5.14.

55. Arrian: 4.24. The two *chiliarchia* of the archers represent the entire force of archers as Arrian makes clear at the beginning of the chapter.

56. Arrian: 4.26.6.

57. *Slingshot*: Issue 297.

58. Arrian, *Anabasis*: 1.6.

59. Diodorus Siculus, *Library*: 17.17.

60. Diodorus Siculus, *Library*: 17.17.

61. Asklepiodotus: 10.4; Aelian: 24.

62. Arrian, *Anabasis*: 1.14.

63. Arrian, *Anabasis*: 1.29.

64. Arrian, *Anabasis*: 1.24.

65. Arrian, *Anabasis*: 1.29.

66. Arrian, *Anabasis*: 5.11.

67. Arrian, *Anabasis*: 5.12. R.D. Milnes, *Alexander's Seventh Phalanx Battalion*, affirms that there were seven pike units (not including the agema and hypaspists) by the time of the Hydaspes. This rests on the assumption that the three commanders mentioned for the detachment situated between Alexander and the Macedonian camp each commanded a 'battalion'. Arrian however does not say what each of them commanded, merely that the troops under their command comprised the 'Grecian mercenaries, cavalry and infantry' – *Anabasis*: 5.12.1. A completely separate force would need a single commander, hence it is reasonable to suppose that Meleager (the first of the named commanders) was responsible for the entire detachment whilst taking personal charge of the cavalry – as was the case with Craterus at the camp – whilst the other two commanders had a *telos* each. The commander of the Grecian mercenaries is not named.

68. Asklepiodotus: 2.9; Aelian: 9.

69. Asklepiodotus: 11.3; Aelian: 35.

70. Asklepiodotus: 11.3.

71. Asklepiodotus: 4.1; Aelian: 11.

72. Polybios, *Histories*: 18.25 .

73. Asklepiodotus: 4.3.

74. Polybios, *Histories*: 2.69.

75. Livy: *History of Rome*: 37.42. For arguments identifying the scene on the plaque with the Battle of Magnesia, see Michael J. Taylor: 'The Attalid victory at Magnesia on a lost plaque from Pergamon', *Anatolian Studies*, 66 (2016).

76. *Journal of Roman Military Equipment Studies II*, 2000.

77. The needs of warfare have brought forth three systems of intervals: the most open order, in which the men are spaced both in length and depth four cubits apart, the most compact, in which with locked shields [συνησπικὼς] each man is a cubit distant on all sides from his comrades, and the intermediate, also called a 'compact formation', in which they are distant two cubits from one another on all sides. – Asklepiodotus: 4.1.

   Interlocking of shields [συνασπισμὸς] occurs whenever you densify the phalanx to the extent that the formation no longer allows a continuous slant in either direction. – Arrian: 11.4.

   The interlocking of shields [συνασπισμος], or the close order, is effected when the entire phalanx is further reduced by width and depth to the point that the men stand almost shoulder to shoulder. – Aelian:11.

78. Mathews, *An Invincible Beast*, 4: Bearing the Phalangite Panoply.

79. *Anatomy of Battle*.

80. Plutarch, *Aemilius Paulus*: 20.

81. Sellasia: Polybios, *Histories*: 2.69:
    Cynoscephalae: Polybios, *Histories*: 18.26:
    Pydna: Plutarch, *Life of Aemilius*: 2.

82. See Richard Taylor: 'Pushing in Greek Infantry Formations', *Slingshot* 311.

83. http://www.polevaultpower.com/forum/viewtopic.php?t=7544

84. Alexander's elite hypaspists and agema execute this wheel around the Greek mercenary left, but only when certain there is no-one else able to engage them: 'Hereupon the regiments on the right wing, perceiving that the Persians opposed to them had already been put to rout, wheeled round towards the Grecian mercenaries of Darius and their own hard-pressed detachment'. – Arrian, *Anabasis*: 2.11. It is also possible that the hypaspists and agema were not equipped like phalangites but more like hoplites, precisely to enable them to execute the classical flank envelopment manoeuvre of the hoplite phalanx's right wing whilst keeping spears lowered against an enemy attack.

Chapter 4

The Triplex Acies

1. The Battle of Vesuvius, 340 BC

In 340 BC the Roman Republic faced perhaps the gravest threat in its 170-year history. Its Latin allies, who had supplied half the infantry and most of the cavalry in its armies, rebelled against their senior partner, demanding a Latin consul, half the seats in the senate and Roman citizenship. The senate replied with a declaration of war. The consuls Titus Manlius Torquatus and Publius Decius Mus raised two Consular armies. A consular army normally had two Roman and two Latin legions, but with the Latins in revolt the Consuls now created a combined army of four Roman legions. They marched southeast into the territory of the Marsi and Paeligni where they were joined by a force of allied Samnites. From there they headed south to Capua where the Latin army along with their Campanian, Volscian, Sidicinian and Auruncian allies was waiting for them.[1] The Roman army pitched camp near Capua but did not fight the Latins there. Instead it marched south in the direction of Vesuvius, about 32km away, followed by the Latin coalition.[2]

Titus Manlius was a consummate general and chose his position well, placing himself between the rocky spurs of Vesuvius and the sea. The narrow space negated the Latin superiority in cavalry and the uneven ground on the slopes of the volcano was perfect terrain for the lightly-equipped Samnites. His flanks were secure.[3]

The legions deployed in six lines, the first three known as the *antepilani*. In front were the leves, lightly armed skirmishers. Behind them stood the hastati, heavy infantry armed with pila, shields and swords. Then the principes, similarly armed. Behind the *antepilani* were the triarii, veteran troops armed with shields, swords and spears. Just behind the triarii were the rorarii, charged with increasing the depth of hard-pressed sections of the line, and finally the accensi, lower-grade troops who were equipped like the triarii.[4]

The Latins had fought alongside the Romans for generations and their military system was identical. The two consuls knew they were in for a very hard battle and each agreed to practise the *devotio* – a personal sacrifice of their lives to encourage their men – if their half of the combined army showed signs of buckling.

As the battle commenced the hastati on the Roman left gave way before their numerically superior opponents and fell back through the principes. Decius Mus recited the words of his *devotio* and charged on horseback into the enemy lines, where he was killed after a bout of fierce fighting. The principes, heartened by this sacrifice, held against the Latins, who were obliged to commit their own second line. The rorarii moved up to support the principes on the left and hastati on the right.[5]

It eventually became clear to the surviving consul, Manlius, that the triarii would have to be committed. Knowing that the Latins would expect this and commit their own triarii, he played a trick, sending in the accensi instead. The Latins mistook them for triarii and moved up their own triarii. The accensi were lower calibre troops but in this case they fought with exceptional courage, wearing down the enemy triarii sent against them until the moment when Manlius, like a magician pulling a rabbit from his hat, ordered back all the front line troops and sent in

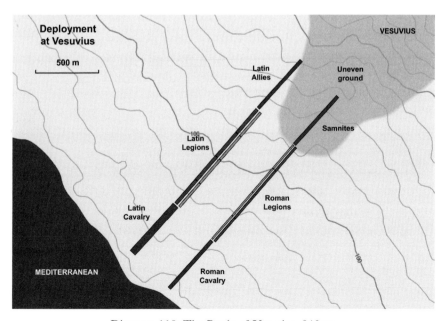

Diagram 115: The Battle of Vesuvius, 340 BC.

his triarii. Faced with this fresh and unexpected reserve, the Latin triarii crumbled, followed in rapid succession by the other demoralised lines of Latin infantry. According to Livy[6] three quarters of the Latin army was killed or captured, the survivors fleeing north to Menturnae.

The Roman infantry had fought with obduracy under generals who were prepared to sacrifice their own lives in order to shame their men into doing the same, but the multi-line system meant that fresh and resolute troops could constantly be thrown into the fray until the enemy finally had enough. Unlike hoplite battles, the outcome was not decided in a single stroke. Twice the Roman army nearly lost the battle and twice it was able to redeem the situation and go on to win. It was this tactical tenacity, combined with the tenacity of the individual soldier, that eventually made the legion the dominant military force of Antiquity.

2. The Development of the Triplex Acies

The Early Roman Hoplite Phalanx

The descriptions of the Roman army in its earliest form come from Livy[7] and Dionysius of Halicarnassus.[8] Both accounts give a similar description of how the army of the Roman kingdom was organised but are sufficiently different in detail to argue against a single common source. Servius Tullius, king of Rome from about 575–535 BC, reorganised the army. Roman citizens were expected to supply their own arms and armour and hence were divided into classes depending on their income and the equipment they could afford. These classes are summarised in Diagrams 116–118.

Class	Income (livy) in minae	Income (Dionysius) in 1000 lbs. weight of copper	Equipment (Livy)	Equipment (Dionysius)	Centuries in Army (junior/ under 45)	Centuries in City (senior/ over 45)
I	+100	+100	Helmet, aspis, greaves, breast-plate, spear, sword	Helmet, aspis, greaves, breast-plate, spear, sword	40	40
II	75 - 100	75 - 100	Helmet, oblong shield, greaves, spear, sword	Helmet, oblong shield, greaves, spear, sword	10	10
III	50 - 75	50 - 75	Helmet, oblong shield, spear, sword	Helmet, oblong shield, spear, sword	10	10
IV	25 - 50	25 - 50	Spear, javelin	Oblong shield, spear, sword	10	10
V	11 - 25	12.5 - 25	Slings	Javelins, slings	15	15
TOTAL					85	85

Diagram 116: Infantry.

Support Personel (Livy)	Support Personel (Dionysius)	Centuries
Mechanics (Class I)	Armourers & Carpenters (Class II)	2
Hornblowers & trumpeters (Class V)	Hornblowers & trumpeters (Class IV)	2

Diagram 117: Support personnel.

Cavalry (Livy)	Centuries	Cavalry (Dionysius)	Centuries
Foremost citizens - *Primes*	12 + 6	Of the highest rating and distinguished birth	18

Diagram 118: Cavalry.

How large was a century at that time? According to Dionysius centuries were not fixed military units but rather administrative subdivisions, and each century furnished more or less men according to the needs of the state at that moment.

> For instance, whenever he had occasion to raise ten thousand men, or, if it should so happen, twenty thousand, he would divide that number among the hundred and ninety-three centuries and then order each century to furnish the number of men that fell to its share – *Antiquities*: 4.19.

An army numbering 20,000 men would require that each of the centuries furnish about 100 men: 193 centuries (actually 192 centuries) x 100 men = 19,300 men which is a close approximation. But centuries might furnish only half that number, or possibly even more than 100 men as Dionysius does not affirm that 20,000 men was the upper limit of the Roman kingdom's military manpower, although his passage does suggest that musters of 10,000 and 20,000 men were the norm. Dionysius affirms that in its war with the Latins in 495 BC, the Roman field army numbered 23,700 foot and 1,000 horse,[9] which probably represents the greater part of available Roman manpower since many disillusioned Latins had defected to the Romans and supplied troops for guard forces near Rome and its outlying fortresses:

> These the Romans received, and such of them as came with their wives and children they employed in military services inside the walls, incorporating them in the centuries of citizens, and the rest

they sent out to the fortresses near the city or distributed among their colonies, keeping them under guard, so that they should create no disturbance. – *Antiquities*: 6.2.2.

Presuming that each century supplied an upper limit of about 100 men, Rome could field an army of 4,000 hoplites and an additional 2,000 or 3,000 heavy infantry and 1,000 or 2,000 skirmisher troops, with 1,800 cavalry, and a reserve army of older men at Rome with the same number of infantry as the field army. Could Rome have raised an army this size?

The Roman kingdom of Servius Tullius was not as small as many think, and compares in size with the major Greek poleis of the era. Athens had a land area of about 2,600km^2, whilst Boeotia covered an area of about 2,700km^2 and Sparta an area of about 5,000km^2. Most of this land was mountainous, unfit for cultivation. The Roman kingdom in c.550 BC covered an area of about 1,500km^2, the greater part of it flatter ground suitable for farming. Agriculturally, Rome was able to support a population comparable to that of Athens, Boeotia or Sparta (see Diagram 119).

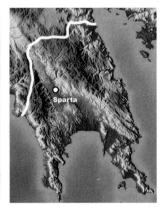

Diagram 119: A comparison of Rome with contemporary Greek Poleis.

Athens could field an army of 13,000 hoplites,[10] 16,000 older garrison troops,[11] 1,200 cavalry and 1,600 archers. At the Battle of Delium Boeotia fielded an army of 7,000 hoplites, 500 peltasts, 10,000 psiloi and 1,000 cavalry.[12] At Leuctra Boeotia fielded 6,000–7,000 hoplites and 1,500 cavalry.[13] Sparta fielded 10,000 hoplites and 35,000 helots at Plataea.[14] These numbers make the size of the Roman army described by Livy and Dionysius quite reasonable.

The Roman infantry line of Servius Tullius was hoplite, but not in the style of the hoplite phalanx of classical Greece. The early Roman infantry were modelled on the Etruscan phalanx, which was a somewhat different animal. The Etruscans had arisen as a loose commonality of city states after the 9th century BC. From their homeland in Tuscany they spread north into the Po valley and south into Latium and Campania. From its foundation Rome fell under their sphere of influence and three Roman kings – Lucius Tarquinius Priscus, Servius Tullius and Lucius Tarquinius Superbus – were Etruscans.

The Etruscan military was affected by a variety of cultural influences. Archaeological evidence shows that they adopted the Greek hoplite panoply – Greek aspis, cuirass, greaves and various forms of Greek helmet – in the middle of the 7th century BC and used the phalanx formation. However it is probable that they adopted a phalanx that corresponded more to the Homeric than the classical model (the latter being invented only later). Their other melee weapons, such as the long sword from 44–70cm in length and long and heavy single-bladed axe (up to the 5th century BC), would have been unsuitable in the confines of an othismos crush. They also used large knives with curved blades (machaira).

Besides hoplite panoply, Etruscan warriors are depicted with oblong and rectangular shields.[15] In some cases the warriors are armed with a single spear[15] and in others with a pair of spears.[16] The Etruscan spear is always depicted short, never in excess of six feet, and would have been suitable for throwing as well as thrusting. Etruscans in hoplite gear are sometimes depicted with throwing spears.[17]

A variety of helmets were used. The commonest was the pot helmet, some with cheek pieces and many crested in the Greek style. Less common was the conical, pointed helmet. Corinthian and other Greek-style helmets were also used (see Diagram 123).

Diagram 120: Etruscan situla, 600–550 BC from the Certosa
necropolis showing warriors with aspides, rectangular shields
and pot helmets. Wikimedia Commons licence.

Diagram 121: Same situla showing warriors with oblong shields and
pointed conical helmets. Wikimedia Commons licence.

Diagram 122: Detail from Situla of the Panier (7th century BC) showing
hoplite-equipped Etruscan warriors. Wikimedia Commons licence.

Diagram 123: Etruscan helmets. Wikimedia Commons licence.

Etruscan society lacked a substantial middle class, and consisted of a few rich families ruling over clients and slaves who formed the rest of the population. The depiction of hoplite-equipped warriors in Etruscan tombs is proof that the rich could afford hoplite gear but not that everyone else could. Only the front ranks of an Etruscan infantry line hence could have been made up of hoplites, the remainder being kitted out in various panoplies.

Although there is no explicit mention of the Etruscans ever employing a second line in the manner of the Italic armies of Latium, Volscium and other Italian polities, they did sometimes keep back an infantry reserve.

> At the same time the enemies' line was now weakened, for, trusting to their superiority in numbers, they had detached their reserves [*subsidia*] and sent them to storm the camp. – Livy: 2.47.4

This reserve was clearly meant to replace the first line or parts of the first line should it be losing the fight, which meant withdrawing the first line through the reserves in the heat of battle. This argues in favour of a formation that was not as packed as a typical Greek phalanx. Greeks never employed reserves or second lines, probably because their files were close enough together so that shields overlapped, which would make it impossible for the hoplites of the front line to retire between the files of a second line as the second line's shields would prevent them (whether a 3-foot wide *aspides* or a 2½-foot wide oblong *thureos*).

Even supposing the second line deployed in open order, with one file conforming to two 60cm-70cm wide files of the front line – necessary if the front ranks of the second line was to double to intermediate order after the first line had passed through and present the same overlapping shieldwall – there would still be insufficient space between the shields of each file to easily permit the hoplites in front to retire between the files at the back (see Diagram 124).

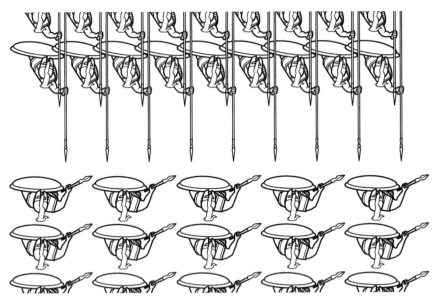

Diagram 124: Diagram showing how a front line of hoplites would be unable to pass through a rear line, even if the latter was in open order.

A typical Etruscan phalanx therefore was probably a looser affair than the classical phalanx of 5th century Greece, relying on a missile exchange followed by close-quarter melee combat to win a battle. Since not all, and possibly not even most, of the infantry had bowl-shaped *aspis* shields, the standard Etruscan infantry line as a whole could not have practised othismos, the diversity of shields making it impracticable as only bowl-shaped *aspides* allowed the hoplite to breathe during the pressure of othismos.

There is at least one instance however where Etruscan infantry did make use of othismos. After the destruction of the Fabii clan at the

Cremora river in 477 BC, the Etruscan army, composed of Veientian troops plus reinforcements from most of the other cities of Etruria, attacked the two-legion army of the consul Menenius not far away. Gaining possession of a hill adjacent to the Roman army, the Etruscan infantry, outnumbering the Romans two to one, formed up deep and advanced downhill driving the Roman foot back.

> When they engaged, there was a great slaughter of the Romans, who were unable to keep their ranks. For they were forced back by the Tyrrhenians, who not only had the terrain as an ally, but were also helped by the vigorous pressure of those who stood behind them, their army being drawn up with deep files. – Dionysius: 9.23.7.

How did the Etruscan infantry apply 'vigorous pressure' without asphyxiating themselves into the bargain? Possibly because the Etruscan cities had sent their best men – i.e. with a large proportion armed as hoplites – to the aid of the Veientes, and when deployed deep they had enough ranks of infantry equipped with aspides to make othismos practical. This successful use of othismos however seems to have been rare, requiring the right circumstances (and/or a canny general) to work. The same army that drove Menenius back was unable to drive back another Roman army outside Rome. At the battle of Sutrium in 311 BC the Etruscan infantry, though again outnumbering the Roman foot, were unable to push them back, even though they fought only half the Roman infantry at a time, i.e. the Roman first line followed by the second line.

> The Etruscans had the advantage in numbers, the Romans in courage. The contest was equally maintained and cost many lives, including the bravest on both sides, nor did either army show any signs of giving way until the second Roman line came up fresh into the place of the first, who were wearied and exhausted. The Etruscans had no reserves to support their first line, and all fell in front of their standards or around them. – Livy: 9.32.

The diversity of the Etruscan panoply is reflected in the infantry of Servius Tullius. Of the 85 infantry centuries, 40 were hoplites, the remainder being divided between skirmishers and non-hoplite heavy infantry armed with oblong shields. The heavy foot were preceded by 15 centuries of slingers and javelinmen (Dionysius), or 25 centuries of skirmishers armed with throwing spears, javelins and slings (Livy).

How did the classes deploy? Infantry battle lines in Antiquity were rarely less than 8 ranks deep (to cope with cavalry charges among other reasons), hence the most logical deployment of the infantry would be 8 ranks of class I hoplites, followed by 2 ranks of class II infantry, 2 ranks of class III infantry, then possibly, according to Dionysius, a final 2 ranks of class IV infantry, forming a line 12–14 ranks deep if the centuries were at full strength.

Taking the larger muster of Dionysius where each century numbered about 100 men, a 12-rank deep line of which class I was 8 ranks deep and class II and III each 2 ranks deep would make the class I century 12 ranks wide with a few files having 9 men rather than 8. The total width of the line then comes out at about 12 x 40 = 480 men. If each file occupied a standard breadth of a yard, that creates a line about 480 yards wide.

A century 12 men wide is convenient as it permits the centuries of the second, third and fourth lines to deploy exactly (or nearly exactly) 48 men wide, allowing these lines to match the width of the first line whilst maintaining a near-constant depth. Each of the 15 centuries of the fifth class would be 32 men wide and generally 3 men deep with a few files 4 men deep (see Diagram 125).

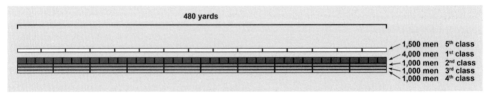

Diagram 125: The deployment of the early Roman infantry.

The infantry could also at the limit have deployed at half this depth and double the width, creating 4 ranks of class I hoplites followed by one rank each of class II, III and possibly IV infantry, for a line

6–7 ranks deep and about 960 yards wide at the most, again presuming the centuries were at full strength or near it. The fifth class, theoretically 1½ ranks deep, would have to deploy more loosely in files of one or two men. This broader deployment is the optimal maximum width for infantry but rather less than the optimal depth making it a less likely configuration.

For Dionysius' smaller muster the centuries would each number about 50 men. If they maintained the same depths the centuries would be half as wide, creating an infantry line 240 yards wide or, if they deployed at half the depth, 480 yards wide.

In 508 BC Rome deposed Tarquinius Superbus and established a Republic. Shortly afterwards, Tarquinius with a combined army from the Etruscan cities of Tarchuna (Tarquinii) and Veii tried to retake Rome. He was met by an army commanded by the newly-minted consuls Lucius Junius Brutus and Lucius Tarquinius Collatinus. The ensuing battle followed the course of a typical hoplite phalanx engagement, with each right wing routing the enemy's left.

> The engagement between the rest of the horse commenced at the same time, and soon after the foot came up. There they fought with doubtful success, and as it were with equal advantage, and the victory doubtful. The right wings of both armies were victorious and the left worsted. – Livy: 2.6.

This account is interesting as it is the *only* instance in the sources that gives any indication of the Roman infantry fighting as a hoplite phalanx. A careful examination of those sources shows that the Romans in fact abandoned the phalanx soon after this battle.

Abandonment of the Hoplite Aspis for the Oblong Scutum
Dionysius mentions that in addition to furnishing their own equipment, the soldiers had to provide their own supplies and other necessities whilst on campaign.

> As to the expenditures that would be needed for the provisioning of soldiers while on duty and for the various warlike supplies, he

would first calculate how much money would be sufficient, and having in like manner divided that sum among the hundred and ninety-three centuries, he would order every man to pay his share towards it in proportion to his rating. – *Antiquities*: 4.19.

According to Livy, the Romans abandoned the round shield (clipeus) in favour of the oblong shield (scutum) when they became *stipendiarii*.

The Romans had formerly used round shields [*clipeis*]; then, after they began to serve for pay [*postquam stipendiarii facti sunt*], they made oblong shields [*scuta*] instead of round ones. – *History*: 8.8.3.

Postquam stipendiarii facti sunt is commonly translated as 'serving for pay', but the phrase literally means: 'after they became stipendiarii'. In every other instance in which Livy uses this word it is in the sense of *paying* a sum of money, rather than being paid one:

That the other states of Asia, which had been tributary [*stipendiarii*] to Attalus, should likewise pay tribute to Eumenes; and such as had been tributary [*vectigales* – synonym for *stipendarius*, with the meaning of payers of tribute/tax] to Antiochus, should be free and independent. – *History*: 37.55.6.

Those which had been tributaries [*stipendiariae*] to King Antiochus but had sided with the Roman people were granted freedom from taxation; those which had been partisans of Antiochus or tributaries [*stipendiariae*] to King Attalus were all ordered to pay tribute to Eumenes. – *History*: 38.39.6.

For the present he resolved to persist in the lenient line of conduct with which he had begun, and sending collectors round to the tributary states [*stipendiarias civitates*], to give the soldiers hopes of soon receiving their pay. – *History*: 28.25.9.

When did the Roman soldiers become stipendiarii? According to Livy they did so during the reign of Servius Tullius, however they were still equipped with *aspides* under that king. With the accession of Tarqinius

Superbus many of Tullius' reforms were abolished[18] and the Roman army was completely reorganised, being made up largely of non-Roman allies whom Tarquinius trusted.[19] After Tarquinius' deposition the Roman army was again composed entirely of Roman citizens, each of whom paid his share towards the army's requirements as before.[20] Hence it is probable that the round shield was abandoned in favour of the oblong soon after the inception of the Republic.

Introduction of the Double Line

Another change was introduced around this time. In 496 BC Tarquinius made another attempt to regain his throne with the support of an army of the Latin League under the Etruscan general Octavius Mamilius. The Roman army was led by the consuls Postumius and Aebutius. The two armies met in battle at Lake Regillus, and for the first time there is mention of a second support line of infantry arrayed behind the first line. Both armies adopted this arrangement.

> As Postumius was drawing up his men and encouraging them in the **first line** [*prima in acie*], Tarquinius Superbus, though now enfeebled by age, spurred on his horse with great fury to attack him; but being wounded in the side, he was carried off by a party of his own men to a place of safety. In the other wing also, Æbutius, master of the horse, had charged Octavius Mamilius; nor was his approach unobserved by the Tusculan general, who also briskly spurred on his horse to encounter him. And such was their impetuosity as they advanced with hostile spears, that Æbutius was run through the arm and Mamilius struck on the breast. The Latins received the latter into **their second line** [*in secundam aciem*]. – Livy: 2.19.

Note that the Romans fought a Latin army serving under Etruscan command. The Etruscans' own infantry may on occasion have had a reserve but they did not habitually deploy in two lines, as can be seen from Livy's description of the battle between Rome and Etruria at Sutrium in 311 BC:

The battle being doubtful, carries off great numbers on both sides, particularly the men of greatest courage; nor did victory declare itself, until the **second line** [*secunda acies*] of the Romans came up fresh to the front, in the place of the first, who were much fatigued. The Etrurians, because their **front line** [*prima acies*] was not supported by any fresh reserves, fell all before and round the standards – Livy: 9.32.

The double line can be seen nine years after the battle against Tarquinius when the consul Gaius Aquilius fights the Hernicii near Praeneste in 487 BC. After initial skirmishing and a cavalry vs. cavalry contest the infantry close for battle. Here, the second line actively supports the first. The fighting is furious but after a time the Roman first line begins to weaken. Aquilius commits the second line piecemeal to the sections of the first line that are giving way.

Aquilius, observing this, ordered that the troops which were still fresh and were being reserved for this very purpose should come up to reinforce the parts of the line that were in distress and that the men who were wounded and exhausted should retire to the rear. – Dionysius: 8.65.3.

The double line appears again five years later when the Roman army fights a Volscian army under the defector Coriolanus, who had trained the Volscians in Roman methods of warfare. Both sides' infantry fight furiously and the battle looks like a draw. Then the Volscians retire in order, tempting the Romans to pursue in disorder and lay themselves open to a counterattack. The ruse works and the second Roman line does not keep pace with the first, but falls to plundering the battlefield and surrounding area.

The Romans, supposing that they were beginning flight, kept pace with them as they slowly withdrew, they too maintaining good order as they followed, but when they saw them running toward their camp, they also pursued swiftly and in disorder; and the **maniples which were last and guarded the rear** fell to stripping the dead, as if they had already conquered the enemy, and turned to plundering the country. – Dionysius: 8.85.1.

Two lines appear yet again in 468 BC, when the consul Quintus Servilius fights the Volscians in 468 BC.

> When day dawned, the Romans, invigorated and refreshed with sleep, on being marched out to battle, at the first onset overpowered the Volscians, wearied from standing and want of rest; though the enemy rather retired than were routed, because in the rear there were hills to which there was a secure retreat, **the ranks behind the first** [Volscian] **line** being unbroken….The [Roman] cavalry, crowding around the general, proceed more violently: they cry out that they would proceed before **the first** [Roman] **line**. – Livy: 2.65.

The Triarii

Triarii were an old institution, as old, according to Dionysius, as the Roman Republic itself. During Rome's first battle as a Republic against Tarquinius in 509 BC – when it still used the hoplite phalanx – the triarii were older veterans who guarded the camp.

> … the sons of King Tarquinius put the left wing of the Romans to flight, and advancing close to their camp, did not fail to attempt to take it by storm; but after receiving many wounds, since those inside stood their ground, they desisted. These guards were the triarii, as they are called; they are veteran troops, experienced in many wars, and are always the last employed in the most critical fighting, when every other hope is lost. – Dionysius: 5.15.4.

During the battle between the Romans and the Volscians in 482 BC quoted earlier, the triarii again appear as camp guards. After defeating the army of Lucius Aemilius, the Volscians attempted to storm their camp.

> But when, after attacking the hill and surrounding the camp, they endeavoured to pull down the palisades, first the Roman horse,

obliged, from the nature of the ground, to fight on foot, sallied out against them, and, behind the horse, those they call the triarii, with their ranks closed. These are the oldest soldiers, to whom they commit the guarding of the camp when they go out to give battle, and they fall back of necessity upon these as their last hope when there has been a general slaughter of the younger men and they lack other reinforcements. – Dionysius: 8.86.4.

They are still camp guards in 480 BC when the consuls Gnaeus Manlius and Marcus Fabius gained a hard-fought victory against the Etruscans. After driving back the Roman right wing, the Etruscan infantry take the first and then the second camp of the Romans.

In the meantime the Tyrrhenians who had possessed themselves of the camp abandoned by Manlius, as soon as the signal for battle was given at headquarters, ran with great haste and alacrity to the other camp of the Romans, suspecting that it was not guarded by a sufficient force. And their belief was correct. For, apart from the triarii and a few younger troops, the rest of the crowd then in the camp consisted of merchants, servants and artificers. – Dionysius: 9.12.1 (see also Livy: 2.47.4).

This battle is also interesting as it shows how the second line could be used to counter an envelopment of a wing.

When Marcus Fabius, the other consul, who commanded in the centre, was informed of this [the envelopment of the Roman left wing], he took with him the best of the maniples, and summoning Caeso Fabius, his other brother, he passed beyond his own line, and advancing a long way, till he had got beyond the enemy's right wing, he turned upon those who were encircling his men, and charging them, caused great slaughter among all whom he encountered . – Dionysius: 9.11.3.

The 'best of the maniples' were evidently not those of the first line already locked in combat with the Etruscan centre, but were part of the uncommitted maniples of the second line.

The last time triarii are mentioned as camp guards is in 437 BC when they are used to repel an attack by the Veientian troops of Lars Tolumnus at Fidenae.[21]

In 350 BC they have a more active role, constructing field works near a Gallic army in Latium whilst the two infantry lines stand guard. The Gauls attack the lines – now called hastati and principes by Livy – who repel them whilst the triarii continue working.

> On the side of the Romans neither the works were interrupted, (it was the triarii who were employed at them) but the battle was commenced by the hastati and the principes, who stood in front of the workmen armed and prepared for the fight. – Livy: 7.23.7.

It is possible the triarii were engaged in this same occupation 40 years earlier in 394 BC, when Camillus entrenched the high ground above a Faliscan army, but the crucial word in Livy (*History*: 5.26.7) is rendered as either *triarii* (Weissenborn, Müller) or *trifariam* (three places/sides: Foster, Conway, Walters).

The Legion of the Latin War

In 340 BC the Latin League, of which Rome had been the senior and increasingly dominant partner, demanded to be treated by Rome on terms of equality, with a Latin consul at Rome and an equal representation in the Senate. This provoked a declaration of war by Rome. In describing the similarity between the two military systems of the Latins and Romans Livy details the organisation of the Roman army, an army very different from the Etruscan-style hoplite phalanx of the 6th century.

At this time Rome habitually fielded 4 legions, each numbering about 5,000 men, with an equal number of legions furnished by her Latin allies.[22] Facing an earlier rebellion from her Latin allies, Livy mentions that Rome had raised ten legions from her own citizens, each with 4,200 men (*History*: 7.25.8) but without implying that these were normal-strength formations. Polybios[23] affirms a standard legionary strength of 4,200 men at the time of the Battle of Cannae in 216 BC but adds that a legion could be brought up to 5,000 men in an emergency, and in fact legions during the Second Punic War and afterwards generally tended to be in the 5,000-man range. Since Livy's 5,000 man legion included lower calibre elements of the Roman population (see below) one can reasonably conclude that the normal legion of 340 BC corresponded to a large extent to the emergency (but pretty much standard) legion of a century later.

Livy describes how each legion was organised.

Romans formerly used the round shield [*clipeus*], then, after they became stipendiarii, they replaced the round shield with the oblong shield [*scutum*], and whereas they had formerly been in a phalanx like the Macedonians, afterwards their lines were organised in a manipular fashion [*manipulatim*] – the lines in the rear into a greater number [*plures*] of units [*ordines*]. A unit [*ordo*] had sixty soldiers, two centurions and one standard-bearer.

The first line, or hastati, comprised fifteen maniples, with short distances in the midst of [*inter*] them; the maniple had twenty light-armed soldiers, the rest of their number carried oblong shields [*scuta*]; moreover those were called 'light' [*veles*] who carried only a spear [*hasta*] and javelins [*gaesum*]. This front line in the battle contained the flower of the young men who were growing ripe for service.

Behind these came a line of the same number of maniples, made up of men of a more stalwart age; these were called the principes; they all carried oblong shields [*scuta*] and were the best-armed.

This body of thirty maniples they called antepilani, because behind the standards there were again stationed another fifteen units [*ordines*], each of which had three sections [*partes*], the first being known as the *primus pilus*.

The unit [*ordo*] consisted of three banners [*vexilla*]; a single banner had sixty soldiers, two centurions, one standard-bearer; they numbered a hundred and eighty-six men.

The first banner led the triarii, veteran soldiers of proven valour; the second banner the rorarii, younger and less distinguished men; the third banner the accensi, who were the least dependable, and were, for that reason, assigned to the rearmost line.

> When an army had been marshalled in these units [*his ordinibus*],
> the hastati were the first of all to engage. – *History*: 8.8.

The legion consists of five lines: hastati, principes, triarii, rorarii, and accensi. The first two lines are divided each into 15 *manipuli*, the last three into 15 *ordines* each. *Manipulum* (literally 'handful') is the term for a small company of soldiers. *Ordo* (literally 'spinning' or 'weaving' from which an 'arrangement' or 'order') refers to a company of indeterminate size and can also refer to a rank or file of soldiers. The term is vague, hence when Livy affirms that an *ordo* has 60 soldiers, 2 centurions and a standard bearer, and then later affirms that the *ordo* of the troops behind the antepilani numbered 186 men, he is using *ordo* in the sense of 'unit', applying it to different levels of the army's hierarchy.

The three *partes* behind the antepilani do not exactly total three *ordines* – 63 x 3 = 189 men. The discrepancy can be resolved by accepting that Livy got the maths slightly wrong. It is also possible that the standard-bearer was one of the 60 soldiers, making an ordo 62 men in all.

A maniple was probably the same size as Livy's *ordo* of 63/62 men. Notice that the rear lines are organised into more, or greater number of (*plures ordines*), implying that the maniples of the first two lines are also similarly *ordines*. Notice also that at the end Livy says the entire army, including hastati and principes, are marshalled 'into these units' – *his ordinibus* – which implies that maniples are to be considered units like the other *ordines*. And again the 15 **other** (*alii*) ordines behind the hastati and principes, implying the hastati and principes are also *ordines*. Thus the number and composition that Livy gives for an *ordo* also applies to a maniple, which is why Livy does not describe the maniple's size and makeup separately.

The only difference indicated between *ordo* and *manipulum* in this passage is the fact that the three rearward lines are organised into composite units each with three subunits, whereas the maniples of the two front lines are independent units. It is uncertain whether the size of a maniple of hastati included the 20 leves (which means there were 43 hastati) or whether the 20 leves are a separate subunit. Making the leves a separate subunit and the hastati a maniple of 63 men gives the legion

5,025 men in total, which accords with Livy's estimate of the legion's size.[24]

Two centurions for a unit of only 60 men originated from Tarquinius Superbus splitting Roman and Latin maniples into halves and then recombining one Roman half with one Latin half, with a centurion for each half, in an attempt to dilute the doubtful loyalty of the Romans.

> In compliance with the order contingents assembled from all the thirty towns, and with a view to depriving them of their own general or a separate command, or distinctive standards, he mingled the Latin and Roman maniples that from both he might make one and from one, both; and he placed centurions over these paired maniples. – Livy: 1.52.6.

In front of each maniple of the first line are 20 lightly-armed *leves*, equipped with a throwing spear (hasta) and a heavy javelin (gaesa). The legion is divided into two halves: the first half is composed of the leves, hastati and principes and are called the *antipilani*; the second half of the triarii, rorarii and accensi which form up behind them.

If each maniple/ordo deployed in an approximate 8x8 square (with three files having 9 men to accommodate the centurions and standard-bearer), then the legion would be about 120 yards wide. Four legions would be about 480 yards wide. Alternatively, the maniples/ordines could each deploy 4 ranks deep and 15 files wide (with three files having an extra man), creating a formation 240 yards wide, which corresponds more closely to the width of the later legion described by Polybios.[25] A 4-rank line is shallow, but if the principes deploy immediately behind the hastati (see the section on line relief below) the composite line will be an optimal 8 ranks deep.

Diagram 126 does not depict the maniples or *ordines* spaced out in the conventional chequerboard formation for reasons which will be seen later. The triarii, rorarii and accensi are put together as they would normally have functioned on the battlefield as a single unit.

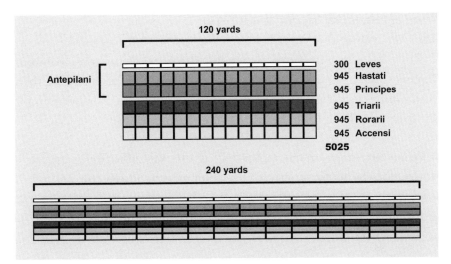

Diagram 126: The early Republican legion.

Livy, after describing the legion's structure, adds that 'there were generally [*fere*] four legions enrolled, consisting each of 5,000 men, and 300 cavalry were assigned to each legion'.[26] *Fere* in this context has the sense of 'generally', 'usually', 'commonly', i.e. that four legions of 5,000 men each was the **normal** strength of the army at this time, not the emergency strength mentioned by Polybios, which matches almost perfectly the numbers he gives when breaking the legion down (if one accepts that an *ordo* was the same size as a maniple).

A legion of the subsequent era was often reinforced to make up 5,200 men which Livy describes as being 'according to ancient precedent' (see below). How was it done? This is speculative, but the simplest way – assuming the reinforcements are drawn from the poorer elements of Roman society (the wealthier elements being already mobilised) – would be to increase the number of leves. At 20 men per hastati maniple they are spread rather thin. If the hastati deploy 8 wide the leves will be 2–3 ranks deep, whilst if the hastati deploy 16 wide the leves will be about 1 rank deep. Adding 12 men to each leves unit to bring it up to 32 men enables it to deploy either 4 or 2 ranks deep, which makes its missile impact more effective. With an additional 12 extra men per leves unit, the entire legion now numbers 5,205 men.

The Legion of the Second Punic War

After describing the Second Punic War up to the Battle of Cannae and parallel events in Greece and the Hellenistic kingdoms, Polybios digresses on the political and military institutions of the Roman Republic at that time, i.e. 218–216 BC. This digression includes a description of the structure of the legion. Here are the relevant extracts:

> When they arrive on the appointed day, they first select the youngest and poorest to form the velites, then next to them the hastati, while those who are in the prime of life they select as principes, and the oldest of all as triarii. For in the Roman army these divisions [διαφορά – *diaphora*], distinct not only as to their ages and nomenclature, but also as to the manner in which they are armed, exist in each legion. The division is made in such proportions that the senior men, called triarii, should number six hundred, the principes twelve hundred, the hastati twelve hundred, and that all the rest as the youngest should be reckoned among the velites. And if the whole number of the legion is more than four thousand, they vary the numbers of these divisions proportionally, except those of the triarii, which is always the same. – *Histories*: 6.21.

> The principes, hastati, and triarii, each elect ten centurions [ταξίαρχος – *taxiarchos*] according to merit, and then a second ten each. All these sixty have the title of centurion alike, of whom the first man chosen is a member of the council of war. And they in their turn select a rear-rank officer each who is called optio [οὐραγός – *ouragos*]. Next, in conjunction with the centurions, they divide the several divisions into ten companies [μέρος – *meros*] each, and appoint to each company two centurions and two optiones; the velites are divided equally among all the companies; these companies are called tagmata [τάγμα – *tagma* = cohort in this context] or maniples [σπεῖρα – *speira* = maniple] or vexilla [σημεία – *semeia* = century in this context], and their officers are called centurions [κεντυρίον – *kenturion*] or tribunes [ταξίαρχος – *taxiarchos*]. – *Histories*: 6.24.

The maniples have been doubled in size whilst their number in each line has been reduced from 15 to 10. The rorarii and accensi have disappeared, and the velites when combined are equal in number to the hastati or principes.

Polybios also describes the equipment of each line of the legion,[27] which are summarised in the table in Diagram 127.

Line	Number of men	Number of ordines/ maniples	Equipment
Velites	1,200	Split among Hastati, Principes and Triarii	Sword, javelins, parma (round shield)
Hastati	1,200	10	Helmet, oblong shield (scutum), two pila, sword, greaves
Principes	1,200	10	Helmet, oblong shield (scutum), spear (hasta), sword, greaves
Triarii	600	10	Helmet, oblong shield (scutum), spear (hasta), sword, greaves
TOTAL	4,200		

Diagram 127: Legionary equipment according to Polybios.

What is interesting here are the velites. They form the front line of skirmishers but are also equipped for melee combat. They are not organised into their own maniples but are co-opted to the maniples of the hastati, principes and triarii. This suggests that after initial skirmishing they withdrew, one-third to each of the lines, to augment them, probably forming the rear ranks. This dual role was originally performed separately by the 900 rorarii and 300 leves of the earlier legion, the leves skirmishing and the rorarii augmenting the lines, which suggests these two lines were combined into one – the beginning of a process of simplification of the legion's troop types that eventually culminated in the all-purpose Marian legionary.

Each maniple of the hastati and principes consists of 120 men whilst that of the triarii has 60 men. Deploying the hastati and principes 20 men wide and 6 deep and the triarii 3 deep enables the velites to deploy 20 wide and 6 deep, and subsequently reinforce each maniple of the hastati, principes and triarii with an additional two ranks, making the hastati and principes lines an optimal 8 ranks deep and the triarii

5 ranks deep. The legion will be about 200 yards wide and the 4-legion infantry of a manipular army about 800 yards wide (see Diagram 128).

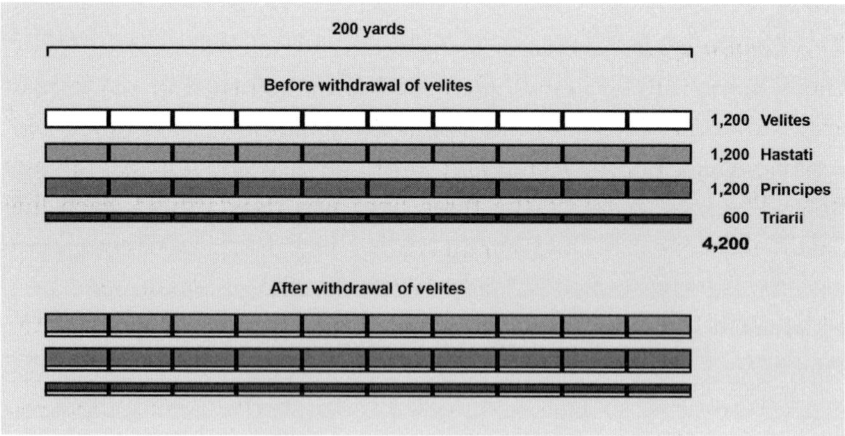

Diagram 128: The Polybian legion.

These numbers represent the legion's book strength in normal times. Like the earlier legion, the legion of Polybios could vary in size, being boosted to 5,000 men in times of national emergency.[28] During the era of the Second Punic War and afterwards 5,000–5,200 was in fact the commonest size for the legion. Livy mentions legions at a strength of 4,000 twice (*History*: 21.17; 28.28), 5,000 four times (23.34; 26.28; 39.38; 41.21), 5,200 five times (40.18; 40.36; 41.9; 42.31; 43.12), 6,000 twice (42.31; 43.12), and 6,200 once (24.34). In the two passages on the 6,000 man legion, 5,200 is given as the size 'according to ancient precedent', whilst 6,000 is the legion at inflated strength.

How were the additional men inserted into the legion? Polybios affirms that 'if the whole number of the legion is more than four thousand, they vary the numbers of these divisions proportionally, except those of the triarii'. In the case of the 5,000 man legion, the simplest arrangement would be to split the extra 800 men between the hastati and principes, increasing their centuries by 20 men each to 83 men. The hastati and principes would now deploy 8 deep, 10 deep once the velites were withdrawn (which makes them square, ideal as units of manoeuvre). For the 5,200 man legion, adding another 200 men to the velites would enable them to reinforce the triarii with an addition 3 ranks rather than 2 once they were withdrawn. A similar arrangement would apply to a 6,000 and 6,200 man legion.

The Legion after Marius

Gaius Marius (157–86 BC) is often cited as the reformer of the Roman army, around 107 BC. The former property qualifications were abolished. Anyone could join the legion and would be paid and equipped by the state. The equipment of the three lines was standardised, each line having the same arms and armour. The velites disappeared completely and the maniple structure was replaced by the 480-man cohort, of which each legion had ten, the first cohort being twice the size of the others.

With the exception of the removal of the property qualification, there is no clear evidence in the primary sources that Marius implemented any of these reforms. Unlike earlier versions of the legion, there is no reliable description of the size, organisation and equipment of the post-Marian legion from any writer who did not live centuries after the period. The only writer in fact who attempts such a description is Vegetius, whose *De Re Militari* (written some time in the later-4th or early-5th century AD) contains a legion that is a mix of units, organisational structure and equipment from the republican, early imperial and late imperial periods. The individual elements of his legion may be historical, but the composite formation is a fantasy, or more likely Vegetius' ideal of the kind of legion he wanted to see restored.

The best single source we have is *De Munitionibus Castrorum* (attributed to Hyginus Gromaticus), which describes the layout of an early 2nd century AD field army camp, giving information on the size and organisation of the legion's units insofar as necessary to calculate the camp's dimensions and tenting arrangements. The technical nature of the work suggest the author was a military surveyor who would have had first-hand knowledge of the legion and is hence reliable in what he affirms about it.

The earliest mention of the post-Marian legion is from Lucius Cincius Alimentus (fl. 200 BC), or more likely another Cincius who was a grammarian in the time of Augustus. He is quoted by Aulus Gellius: 'In a legion there are sixty centuries, thirty maniples, and ten cohorts'.[29]

This is repeated by Maurus Servius Honoratus, a late-4th century, early-5th century AD grammarian: 'By maniple is meant that entity of which according to the ancient manner there were thirty in a legion: a legion had ten cohorts, sixty centuries'.[30]

These sources are confirmed by Hyginus, who gives additional details. *De Munitionibus Castrorum* describes a camp for an army of 3 legions with a number of additional units. He begins with the century.

> We will now explain the way in which the cohorts described above pitch their tents. One tent occupies ten feet; this length is increased by two feet for the pitching, and it shelters eight men. A complete century has 80 soldiers, so there will be ten tents which will run in a line 120 feet long …. Since 4 men per watch from each century are on guard duty, they do not pitch more than eight tents per century. In this way their centurion has a place to pitch his tent on the same area as those tents would have been. Otherwise it would have been necessary to allocate more space. – *De Munitionibus Castrorum*: 1.

The century then has 80 men, which would normally require ten 8-man tents, but since four men are assigned to each watch during the night the number that actually sleep that night is reduced to 64 men, requiring 8 tents. There were four watches in the night, so 16 men in total would be on guard duty. The centurion's tent occupies the space vacated by two legionary tents.

Notice that Hyginus does not explicitly state that each tent caters for a 10-man unit (8 men sleeping and 2 men on watch). It is Vegetius who affirms that each tent housed a 10-man unit under the command of a *decanus*:

> The centuries were also subdivided into messes of ten men each who lay in the same tent and were under orders and inspection of a decanus or head of the mess [*caput contubernii*]. – *De Re Militari*: 2.8.

Since the file was always the fundamental building block of an infantry line it is probable the *contubernium* was a file unit with the *decanus* acting as file leader.

Hyginus is clear that 6 centuries make up a cohort of 480 men, as a cohort occupies six times the area of a century.[31] His camp holds three complete legions[32] with 30 cohorts[33] hence each legion has 10 cohorts. The first cohort of each legion is double sized. He appears to contradict himself as he goes on to give the size of a cohort as 600 men.[34] However this apparent inconsistency can be resolved: the passage in Latin reads: *sescentenos homines* – 600 men, 'men' understood in the sense of 'people', whereas the century has *milites LXXX* – '80 soldiers'. The best source for the missing 120 men appears to be military slaves (*calo* or *servus castrensis*), who were not soldiers but were probably attached to the legion and were trained, armed, and expected to defend the camp in the absence of the regular troops.[35] They did not sleep in the same tents as the legionaries.

The doubled size of the first cohort is confirmed by Vegetius[36] and by archaeology: two excavated camps at Caerleon and Inchtuthil show space for a double sized first cohort. Discharge inscriptions show about twice as many men discharged from the first cohort as from the others. This enlarged cohort seems however to have been a temporary innovation introduced in the 1st century AD that was ultimately abandoned: most excavated legionary camps show that the space for cohorts varied and there is no evidence the first cohort was larger than the rest. A larger first cohort seems to have applied only to legions on campaign, whilst legions in quieter areas could be well understrength. The legion in the late-Republican and Imperial period, like that of the mid-Republican period, varied considerably in size.[37]

An ideal legion including its military slaves numbered 9 x 600 men plus 1 x 1,200 men (for the doubled first cohort) = 6,600 men of which 5,280 were legionaries. If its ten cohorts were all the same size it numbered 4,800 legionaries. Using this latter figure, how did it deploy? The post-Marian legion was not a completely new invention but a development of the earlier legion of the Punic war. It generally formed up in three lines of which the third line was thinner than the first two. Which suggests the arrangement shown in Diagram 129: each 'C' represents a century.

The *contubernia* are the right size for file units, hence the first two lines probably deployed with the *contubernia* as files, creating a line about 10 ranks deep. Each cohort thus deployed about 48 yards wide and the

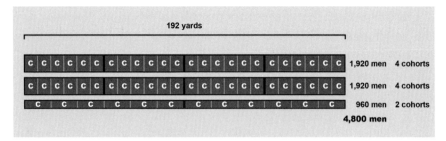

Diagram 129: The Marian legion.

entire legion occupies a frontage of 192 yards. The third line, deploying 5 ranks deep in half-*contubernia* would not have found its lack of depth a problem since after the retirement of the first two lines it would have been reinforced by an additional 20 ranks. Frontinus[38] affirms that Pompey deployed his three lines each ten men deep at Pharsalus see Diagram 130). This is possible if Pompey deployed three cohorts in each line and split the tenth cohort between the three lines, the greater depth presumably to narrow the frontage of his more numerous legions to match that of Caesar.

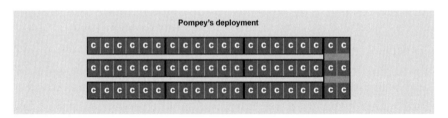

Diagram 130: Pompey's deployment.

This incidentally is the only reference in the sources to the depth of a *triplex acies* Roman line in regular battle order. Arrian's mention of a legionary battle line 8 ranks deep in his *Array Against the Alans* describes an experimental formation used in 135 AD that was to become the single line anti-cavalry arrangement of the late-Roman army, in which heavy infantry in the front ranks, armed with a large pilum and later a spear, employed the *foulkon* to repel cavalry whilst missile armed infantry in the rear ranks with archers at the back shot overhead.

Against the above model it is generally assumed that there were four cohorts in the first line, three in the second and three in the third, following Caesar's description of his deployment against Afranius in Spain. A careful reading of the passage however indicates that this deployment was unusual.

> *Acies erat Afraniana duplex legionum v, tertium in subsidiis locum alariae cohortes obtinebant; Caesaris triplex;* **sed** *primam aciem quaternae cohortes ex v legionibus tenebant, has subsidiariae ternae et rursus aliae totidem suae cuiusque legionis subsequebantur.*
>
> Afranius' five legions were in two lines. The third line was in reserve with the cohorts occupying the place of the wings. Caesar had three lines, **but** the first line had four cohorts from each of the five legions, behind it the reserve had three and the following line the same number, each from their own legion. – *Commentaries on the Civil War*: 1.18.

Notice the 'but'. This means that Caesar deployed in the standard three-line arrangement, however the distribution of his cohorts in each of the three lines was not standard, and he goes into some detail describing it. It is possible that Caesar's novel deployment was a clever means of countering Afranius' concentration of his third line on his flanks. This was meant as a guard against Caesar's superior cavalry, but could also have been used to envelope Caesar's infantry *a la Cannae* whilst Afranius' cavalry kept Caesar's horse busy. If Caesar's second and third line deployed about 5 men deep, that would free up five cohorts per line to counter Afranius' reserve, but without Afranius being aware of the fact.

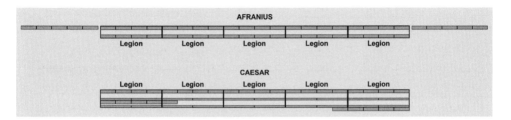

Diagram 131: Caesar deployed against Afranius.

How would a legion with the first cohort doubled in size deploy? It not actually possible to neatly fit what is effectively an additional cohort-strength unit into the ten-cohort three-line arrangement without splitting the *contubernia* into irregular fractions – which goes against the universal military practice of keeping units together with their officers. This suggests that the double-strength cohort may have freed up one of the other nine regular cohorts as a tactical reserve able to function separately on the battlefield. Vegetius mentions this use of reserves.[39] Employing cohorts in this manner was not uncommon, as can be seen above and elsewhere.[40] It does not make sense to simply deploy the oversized first cohort at double depth: the additional ranks would add nothing to the fighting efficacy of the cohort since the legion did not practise othismos.

The maniple worked in conjunction with the cohort and later survived, at least for a time, as a residual administrative unit, but without any importance on the battlefield, where the century, being roughly square in shape (like the Spartan *pentekosty* and the Macedonian *syntagma*), was the unit of manoeuvre. The cohort, corresponding in function to the Spartan *mora* or Macedonian *chiliarchia*, was useful as an independently-operating detachment for undertakings smaller than a full-scale battle.

When was the cohort introduced? Livy mentions cohorts as existing at the foundation of the Roman republic.[41] They appear frequently afterwards in the period of the early Republic as Roman and Latin units.[42] However Livy appears to be using 'cohort' as a generic term for a sizeable body of men, either of cavalry or infantry, rather than a fixed infantry formation, though on one occasion he describes Hernician cohorts in 362 BC – their elite troops – as having 400 men each.[43]

The cohort understood as the specific unit of foot that became the building block of the legion appears for the first time in Spain. Polybios affirms its existence at the Battle of Ilipa (206 BC):

> Scipio with the three leading squadrons of cavalry from the right wing, preceded by the usual number of velites and three *speiras* [σπείρας] – a contingent of infantry which the Romans call a cohort [κοόρτις] – *Histories*: 11.23. See also 11.33.

Cohorts are used in the Jugurthine War in Africa[44] but the maniple remains in existence.[45] The final recorded instance of the velites is during the Jugurthine war.[46] Marius was the last Roman general to fight Jugurtha, eventually defeating him by persuading Jugurtha's father-in-law Bocchus to hand Jugurtha over. After Marius the cohortal system became standard in the Roman army and the maniple no longer played any distinct role on the battlefield.

3. The Roman Soldier's Panoply

For the sake of brevity, this section will look at the armament only from the mid-Republic to the early-Empire, i.e. the period of the *triplex acies*. This armament consisted of the pilum, the lighter javelin or verutum, the gladius, the oval and later rectangular scutum, the helmet, greaves and body armour.

The Pilum

Polybios describes two pila carried by soldiers at the time of the Second Punic War:

> In addition to these they have two pila, a brass helmet, and greaves. Some of the pila are thick, some fine. Of the thicker, some are round with the diameter of a palm's length, others are a palm [74mm] square. The fine pila are like moderate sized hunting spears, and they are carried along with the former sort. The wooden haft of them all is about three cubits long; and the iron head fixed to each half is barbed, and of the same length as the haft. They take extraordinary pains to attach the head to the haft firmly; they make the fastening of the one to the other so secure for use by binding it half way up the wood, and riveting it with a series of clasps, that the iron breaks sooner than this fastening comes loose, although its thickness at the socket and where it is fastened to the wood is a finger and a half's breadth [28mm]. – *Histories*: 6.23.

Of Etrusco-Italic origin, the pilum was the characteristic weapon of the Roman soldier. It consisted of a long metallic shank fastened to a wooden shaft. The main purpose behind this design was a weapon heavy enough to penetrate an enemy shield and wound the man bearing it. Once the narrow point had passed through the shield, the thin metal ferrule behind it would slide easily through the hole, enabling the point to reach the enemy's body. If the enemy was not wounded it was still impossible for him to remove the pilum from the shield which was now a serious encumbrance. A useful side-effect of the thin ferrule was its propensity to bend, making it unusable by the enemy, though in some cases pila kept their shape enabling the Gauls to throw them back.[47]

There were two kinds of pila at the time of the Second Punic War, a large and small one. Archaeological samples show that both large and small pila varied in size, but neither were the length of 3 cubits (144cm) for the haft and the same length for the ferrule as affirmed by Polybios. Dionysius[48] gives a correct length of three feet for the ferrule. The average length of four specimens of heavy pila iron shanks recovered at La Caridad is about 100cm, whilst the average length of four light pila iron shanks is 39.3mm.[49]

The small pilum was probably thrown first, followed by the large pilum as the enemy drew nearer. After throwing the pila, the Roman soldiers drew their swords and charged the enemy.

By the time of Caesar it appears the soldiers had only one pilum each,[50] of which the iron ferrule was not hardened in order to bend more easily on impact: 'The spears were not like javelins, but what the Romans called *pila*, four-sided, part wood and part iron, and not hard except at the pointed end'. – Appian, *Gallic History*: 1.

The velites used the smaller verutum.

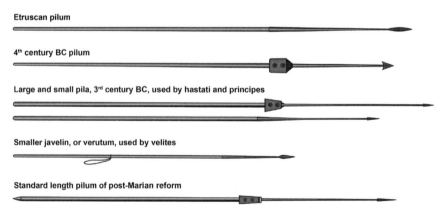

Etruscan pilum

4th century BC pilum

Large and small pila, 3rd century BC, used by hastati and principes

Smaller javelin, or verutum, used by velites

Standard length pilum of post-Marian reform

Diagram 132: The evolution of the *pilum*.

The Hasta

The large spear or hasta was used by the Roman army from the foundation of the republic and the archaeological record shows it remained in use all the way through the republican into the imperial periods.[51] Spearheads are generally leaf shaped and varied in size, with examples showing a very large leaf-shaped point 34cm long and socket 9.5cm long, and others with leaf-shaped points about 10cm long. Sockets could be as long as 17cm.[52]

The Gladius

The short sword was the standard weapon of the Roman infantryman from the mid-Republican era until the 2nd century AD. It was composed of a hilt (*capulus*), a handguard (*mora*), a blade (*lamna*) with a point (*mucro*) and was sheathed in a scabbard (*vagina*).[53] The original Iberian version, the *gladius hispaniensis*, was in use from the 3rd century BC.[54] It was pattern-welded from several hard layers of steel.[55] The sword evolved, with the blade becoming broader, into the *gladius mainz* of the imperial era, though many other versions of the sword exist in the archaeological record (see Diagram 133).

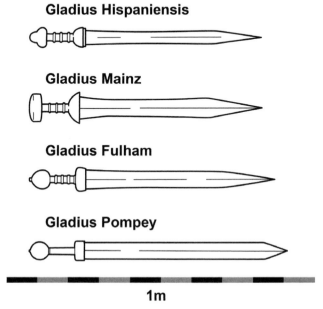

Diagram 133: The evolution of the *gladius*.

The hilt was not made of metal but of bone, wood or even ivory. It was generally fluted to improve grip and had a large pommel at the end to prevent the sword from being pulled from its wielder's hand, necessary if the sword point was wedged in the enemy's shield or body armour.

The sword was usually slung from the military belt on the right side of the body (left side for officers) though this was not an absolute rule. Wearing the sword on the right side made it easier for the soldier to draw his sword in battle whilst keeping his shield in front of him.

The gladius was primarily a thrusting weapon and legionaries were trained to use it this way[56] but it was also effective for slashing strokes in looser order combat, as in the case of a cavalry vs cavalry fight between Romans and Macedonians, after which the Macedonians were horrified by the extent of the slash wounds inflicted by the *gladius hispaniensis*.[57]

The Shield

According to Sallust the Senate adopted all weaponry used by the Romans (which would necessarily include the shield) from the Samnites.

> Our ancestors, Fathers of the Senate, were never lacking either in wisdom or courage, and yet pride did not keep them from adopting foreign institutions, provided they were honourable. They took all their armament (*arma atque tela militaria*) from the Samnites, the badges of their magistrates for the most part from the Etruscans. – *The War With Catiline*: 51.37.

Plutarch[58] affirms that the Romans got the shield from the Sabines. This is repeated by the *Ineditum Vaticanum*. Diodorus[59] refers to the Romans adopting their shield from 'other people'. It is possible to reconcile the accounts. The Samnites are generally considered to be an offshoot of the Sabines. Their own name for themselves – *Safineis* – is a variant of the Sabine name. Sabines and Samnites were originally part of a single linguistic and cultural group that occupied central Italy and spoke Oscan. The Samnites appear as a distinct entity in the historical record only in 354 BC, when they made a treaty with Rome, shortly after which they went to war with the Romans for the first time. According to Livy however, Rome had been at war with the Sabines from the time of the kings. So in affirming that the Samnites gave Rome the oval shield, Sallust is probably confusing them with their parent people. This interpretation is reinforced by the fact that he implies the acquisition of weaponry from the Samnites happened before or at about the same time the Fathers acquired the badges of office from the Etruscans, which is long before the Romans had contact with the Samnites proper.

This also may explain why Diodorus does not specify from which people the Romans took their shield. He may have been aware of the confusion and did not commit himself.

Polybios describes the *scutum* (or *thureos*) at the time of the Second Punic War.

> The second rank, the Hastati, are ordered to have the complete panoply. This to a Roman means, first, a large shield [θυρεός – *thureos*], the surface of which is curved outwards, its breadth two and a half feet, its length four feet, – though there is also an extra-sized shield in which these measures are increased by a palm's breadth [74mm]. It consists of two layers of wood fastened together with bull's-hide glue; the outer surface of which is first covered with canvas, then with calf's skin, on the upper and lower edges it is bound with iron to resist the downward strokes of the sword, and the wear of resting upon the ground. Upon it also is fixed an iron boss to resist the more formidable blows of stones and pikes, and of heavy missiles generally. – *Histories*: 6.23.

The 3rd century AD Dura-Europas shield, a complete imperial Roman shield (minus the boss), is similar in construction to Polybios' description. It is 105.5cm high, 41cm across and 30cm deep due to its semicylindrical shape. It is composed of three layers of wood, two with the grain running vertically and one horizontally, glued together, with an outer covering of leather. It is 5–6mm thick. A circle is cut out of the middle of the shield, across which a horizontal handbar grip is placed, and which would have been covered on the outer edge by a round metal boss. The shield weighed about 5.8kg.[60]

Diagram 134: Left: reconstruction of a Republican Shield. Roman shield (scutum).
Archaelogical Site of Kelin. Paraje los Villares, Caudete de las Fuentes, Valencia.
Right: Dura Europas scutum, Yale University Art Gallery. One can see the horizontal
handgrip which would have been covered by the metal boss.

The altar of Ahenobarbus, constructed towards the end of the 2nd
century BC, has the oldest images of Roman shields, corresponding to
the description of Polybios (see Diagram 135). From the metal boss a rib
ran up and down the centre of the shield, supplying additional stiffening
and protection against weapon-thrusts.

Some shields had a double grip, as can be seen on the *metopae* of the
Plancus monument and on the Aquileia reliefs dated to the Caesarian
period.[61]

Diagram 135: Details from Altar of Ahenobarbus.

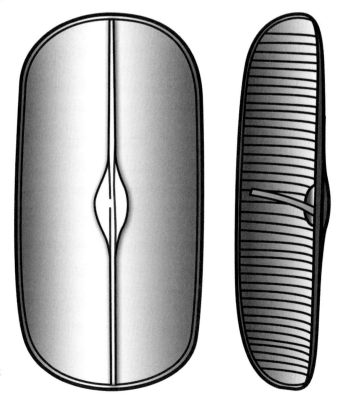

Diagram 136:
The Kasr El-Harit
shield.

The shields had a pronounced curvature as shown by the only fully-intact Roman or imitation Ptolemaic example from the Republican era uncovered at Kasr El-Harit, Egypt (see Diagram 136). This shield consists of three layers of birch glued together, the outer and inner layers of horizontal strips and the middle layer of vertical strips. The wood was covered with lamb wool felt. There was no metal reinforcing of the top or bottom edges or of the central boss. The shield is 128cm tall and about 68.3cm wide.[62]

The Helmet

The Romans wore a variety of helmets in the era of the *triplex acies*. Some types evolved from others, but in an age without mass production a helmet could remain in use for a century or more and be used alongside later types.

By the time of the Second Punic War the commonest infantry helmet was the Montefortino, developed from a Gallic helmet type in the 4th century BC. Cast in bronze, it consisted of a bowl tapering up to knob, probably to protect against strikes from above. A neck guard protruded from the back. Bronze cheekguards were attached by two rivets. It remained in use until the 1st century AD.

The Coolus helmet, developed in the first half of the 1st century BC, was originally a simplification of the Montefortino type. The knob at the top was gone, and in some cases there were no cheek guards, just holes on the sides for the chin strap. The later Hagenau version, developed during the Caesarean period, had a more pronounced neck guard and a brow piece to protect against strikes against the front of the helmet. The helmet type remained in use until the second half of the 1st century AD.

The Imperial Gallic helmet was a further development of the previous two types, appearing in the late 1st century BC. The neck guard became even more pronounced and tended to slope downwards. Ear openings protected by turned-out flanges enabled the soldier to better hear what was going on around him. Stylised eyebrows were embossed on the front. This type remained in use until the 2nd century AD. A derivative, the Imperial Italic helmet, had two cross-bracing reinforcing bars on the helmet bowl to protect against the Dacian falx. The neck guard grew in size, offering protection to the shoulders.

Alongside these common types a variety of helmets influenced by Hellenistic design were used, though only by officers and elite units as their elaborate design made them too expensive for common soldiers. These types include the Attic and Apulian–Corinthian designs.

Diagram 137: Left: Montefortino helmet; middle: Coolus helmet (Hagenau); right: Gallic Imperial helmet.

Body Armour

Roman infantry and cavalry wore every conceivable kind of body armour in the last three centuries BC but for the ordinary soldier in the time of Hannibal it consisted largely of a simple brass plate, cheap and easy to manufacture. At this time only wealthier soldiers, largely belonging to the cavalry, used chainmail.

> The common soldiers also receive a brass plate, a span [24cm] square, which they put upon their breast and call a breastpiece [καρδιοφύλαξ – *kardiophylax*], and so complete their panoply. Those who are rated above a hundred thousand asses, instead of these breastpieces wear, with the rest of their armour, coats of mail [θώραξ – *thorax*]. – Polybios, *Histories*: 6.23.

By 120 BC most soldiers wore a chainmail vest, the *lorica hamata*, as can be seen in the Ahenobarbus monument. It was usually made of iron. The Republic was now large and wealthy enough to equip its infantry with chainmail vests each composed of several thousand rings. They protected the torso and upper thighs, sometimes the torso only. Some had short sleeves that covered the upper arms. The shoulders were sometimes covered with mail *humeralia* lined with leather, imitating the *epomides* of the Greek linothorax. The mail was worn over a padded corselet and sometimes had pteryges. In other words, the Roman chainmail vest came in a variety of styles.

The *lorica segmentata* were not commonly used in this period, appearing only towards the end of the 1st century BC. Officers sometimes wore iron breastplates and higher ranking officers were often equipped with elaborately muscled cuirasses.

The linen linothorax was also used, as can be seen on coins depicting the rebellion of slaves in Sicily and on the Glanum reliefs.[63] Leather body armour was used as well. Not all soldiers had body armour as can be seen from many other monuments of that time.[64]

According to Polybios a single greave (προκνημίς – *proknemis* in the singular) was worn by the hastati, principes and triarii.[65] Arrian[66] affirms that one greave was worn on the left shin. For Vegetius the greave was worn on the right shin.[67] The Adamclisi reliefs from the time of Hadrian show soldiers sometimes with a greave on one leg and sometimes with greaves on both legs. Soldiers are often depicted without greaves, as on the Arc d'Orange.[68] So it is probable that soldiers in the Republican era generally wore one greave if they wore a greave at all, but later on more heavily armed legionaries, especially those who fought the falx-armed Dacians, wore two. Centurions and higher-ranking officers are always depicted with two greaves.

4. The Roman Soldier

The Roman Republic at its inception had no standing army. Citizens were organised into five classes of centuries depending on their income and were expected to serve for a campaign season that did not last more than a few months from spring to autumn. They provided their own equipment and supplies for the army. The early Republic however was embroiled in numerous wars that required frequent absences of its soldiers from their livelihood.

As the Roman Republic grew in size its theatre of military operations became ever wider and it was necessary to keep the legions in the field for longer periods. It was this that probably led to soldiers receiving pay for the first time during the siege of Veii in 396 BC.[69] Livy recounts that before the declaration of war against Veii the men liable for military service had complained that there was too much fighting, with a war being conducted every year.[70] After Veii they were supported by the state whilst under arms, so they could afford to stay away from their farms and trades more frequently. Nonetheless they were not yet professional soldiers, being disbanded after a campaign was concluded.

With the advent of the Punic Wars soldiers could remain in service for years at a time. The survivors of Cannae were obliged to remain under arms until the conclusion of the Second Punic war 14 years later. They joined the army raised by Scipio Africanus that campaigned in Spain and North Africa for nine years before finally defeating Hannibal at Zama in 202 BC. By the 2nd century BC these 'conscript professionals' were becoming the norm. Livy relates a speech by Spurius Ligustinus, a farmer with a *iugerum* (¼ hectare) of land and a cottage, who spent more than twenty years in the army. The occasion was the raising of an army in 171 BC against Macedonia.

I became a soldier in the consulship of P. Sulpicius and C. Aurelius. For two years I was a common soldier in the army, fighting against Philip in Macedonia; in the third year T. Quinctius Flamininus gave me in consideration of my courage the command of the tenth maniple of the hastati.

After Philip and the Macedonians were vanquished and we were brought back to Italy and disbanded, I at once volunteered to go with the consul M. Porcius to Spain. Men who during a long service have had experience of him and of other generals know that of all living commanders not one has shown himself a keener observer or more accurate judge of military valour. It was this commander who thought me worthy of being appointed first centurion in the hastati.

Again I served, for the third time, as a volunteer in the army which was sent against Antiochus and the Aetolians. I was made first centurion of the principes by Manius Acilius. After Antiochus was expelled and the Aetolians subjugated we were brought back to Italy.

After that I twice took service for a year at home. Then I served
in Spain, once under Q. Fulvius Flaccus and again under Ti.
Sempronius Gracchus. I was brought home by Flaccus amongst
those whom, as a reward for their courage, he was bringing home
to grace his triumph. I joined Tiberius Gracchus at his request.
Four times, within a few years, have I been first centurion in the
triarii; four-and-thirty times have I been rewarded for my courage
by my commanders; I have received six civic crowns. I have served
for twenty-two years in the army and I am more than fifty years
old. – *History*: 42.34.5–11.

Ligustinus was an exceptional case, but he showed the trend of the
times. By the end of the 2nd century BC Roman soldiers were full-
time professionals. The official minimum property qualification which
had been steadily reduced in the course of the 2nd century (and often
ignored before that) was finally dropped to zero by Marius in 107 BC.[71]
It was not until Augustus however that the mandatory length of service
for infantrymen was fixed at first 16 then 20 years.[72] But before this date
soldiers could and did serve for as long as that and longer.

Through the period of the *triplex acies* the Roman infantryman was an
experienced soldier who became increasingly competent as the periods
of service grew longer, and with a training that was equal to that of
full-time professionals. Being well-trained and battle-hardened he could
not be easily panicked and was often able, even in the heat of battle, to
adopt formations and execute manoeuvres usually performed only by
career soldiers. From the time of Pyrrhus he was a match for the best
that the standing armies of Carthage and the Successor States had to
offer, and more than a match, at least in open battle, for the numerically
superior seasonal levies of Gaul and Spain.

5. Fighting Techniques

The Roman soldier, initially either a skirmisher or a heavy infantryman,
eventually became an amalgam of the two. The fundamental fighting
techniques of the legion however remained unchanged. An initial volley
of javelins and pila (later just pila) was followed by a charge and hand-
to-hand combat with swords. The initial volley was intended to pierce

the shields of the enemy troops in the front rank and wound or even kill them, or at least make their shields unusable. But it was the melee fight with swords that gave the knockout blow.

Roman soldiers did not indulge in elaborate swordfighting. Their technique was simple and brutal: shelter behind their shields and give lightning jabs with their gladius past the top or side of the shield at unprotected areas of the enemy's bodies. Vegetius describes the method.

> They were likewise taught not to cut but to thrust with their swords. For the Romans not only made a jest of those who fought with the edge of that weapon, but always found them an easy conquest. A stroke with the edges, though made with ever so much force, seldom kills, as the vital parts of the body are defended both by the bones and armour. On the contrary, a stab, though it penetrates but two inches, is generally fatal. Besides in the attitude of striking, it is impossible to avoid exposing the right arm and side; but on the other hand, the body is covered while a thrust is given, and the adversary receives the point before he sees the sword. This was the method of fighting principally used by the Romans, and their reason for exercising recruits with arms of such a weight at first was, that when they came to carry the common ones so much lighter, the greater difference might enable them to act with greater security and alacrity in time of action. – *De Re Militari*: 1.

The recruits used training shields and wooden swords twice the weight of their real counterparts in order to build up the necessary muscle to strike with speed and strength. They practised striking at narrow posts six feet high, the aim being to be able to thrust accurately from high, middle and low positions. The swords could also be used to slash, but with the same thrusting motion used to drive their points into the enemy's body.

> We are informed by the writings of the ancients that, among their other exercises, they had that of the post. They gave their recruits round bucklers woven with willows, twice as heavy as those used on real service, and wooden swords double the weight of the common

ones. They exercised them with these at the post both morning and afternoon.

… Every soldier, therefore, fixed a post firmly in the ground, about the height of six feet. Against this, as against a real enemy, the recruit was exercised with the above mentioned arms, as it were with the common shield and sword, sometimes aiming at the head or face, sometimes at the sides, at others endeavouring to strike at the thighs or legs. He was instructed in what manner to advance and retire, and in short how to take every advantage of his adversary; but was thus above all particularly cautioned not to lay himself open to his antagonist while aiming his stroke at him. – *De Re Militari*: 1.

As for any kind of close-contact fighting, the soldier would need space behind him to recoil when necessary (See Chapter 1: 2. *Heavy Infantry – Organisation*). Recoiling in fact was an expected part of his fighting technique – 'what manner to advance and retire' – and unlike the hoplite he was quite prepared to give ground, handing over the fight to the line behind him if necessary. In other words, the Roman soldier did not see the retreat of his line as a precursor to defeat. If his own line could not manage the enemy then the line behind him would. This made it difficult to panic him.

Reenactment groups using the procedures of Vegetius confirm that they are very effective.[73] The shield completely protects the soldier at all times and hides his sword from the enemy, making it impossible to predict where the strike will come from. They also reveal that the Roman soldier required very little lateral space beyond the width of his shield to fight, disproving the notion that infantry files needed to be six feet wide for the infantry to properly wield their weapons.

6. The Legion on the March

When passing through safe territory the army typically marched in a single column with scouts in front, cavalry at the front and rear and possibly also on the flanks, and the legions and baggage in the centre.[74]

When in close proximity to the enemy a Roman army marched in one of two formations: the square (*agmen quadratum*) and the triple line.

Onasander (1st century AD) recommends the square as the most effective way of countering a surprise attack from any side whilst stipulating that the marching lines must be sufficiently deep so as not to be pierced by enemy.[75] Varro, quoted by Servius,[76] affirms the square protected the baggage and could set up camp anywhere.

The square was used by Roman commanders from the inception of the Republic. Livy mentions the formation twelve times, from the Republic's first battle against Tarquin the Proud[77] to Popilius during the war against Perseus.[78] Marius is recorded using it in north Africa[79] and Caesar used it during his war against the Bellovaci.[80]

The second formation, the triple line, was in effect the army deployed for battle but with its lines marching in parallel columns as described by the tacticians.[81] Polybios describes this formation for the legion at the time of the Second Punic War.

> The order of march, however, is different at times of unusual danger, if they have open ground enough. For in that case they advance in three parallel columns, consisting of the hastati, principes, and triarii: the beasts of burden belonging to the maniples in the van are placed in front of all, those belonging to the second behind the leading maniples, and those belonging to the third behind the second maniples, thus having the baggage and the maniples in alternate lines. With this order of march, on an alarm being given, the columns face to the right or left according to the quarter on which the enemy appears, and get clear of the baggage. So that in a short space of time, and by one movement, the whole of the hoplites are in line of battle – except that sometimes it is necessary to countermarch up [προσεξελίσσω – *prosexelisso*] the hastati also – and the baggage and the rest of the army are in their proper place for safety, namely, in the rear of the line of combatants. – *Histories*: 6.40.

Following the tacticians' principle that parallel columns march by rank, Polybios' triple line column probably looked as in Diagram 138, with the velites joined to their respective maniples of hastati, principes and triarii.

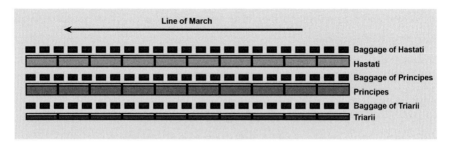

Diagram 138: The legion on the march.

When faced by a threat on either flank the individual soldiers turned left or right, instantly forming lines, and then advanced beyond the baggage. If the threat came from the flank bordered by the triarii, the hastati would countermarch through the principes and triarii to face it, presumably followed by the principes, which suggests the three columns were marching in open order, allowing the files of one line to countermarch between the files of the others (see Chapter 1: 3. *Heavy Infantry – Manoeuvres*).

Caesar used the triple line order of march at least once when campaigning against the Usipetes and Tencteri[82] and Tacitus implies that Germanicus used it against Arminius.[83]

7. Line Relief

The Problem of the Quincunx

Readers will have noticed that I have made no reference to the quincunx or chequerboard formation when describing the structure of the legion. This is deliberate. The mechanism of line relief, by which each line of the three-line legion successively handed over the fight to the line behind it, is the most misunderstood feature of the Roman army. An in-depth analysis of the primary sources, paying especial attention to the meaning of some crucial Latin and Greek terms, shows that line relief in fact employs continuous lines whilst making use of a mechanism described by the tacticians to permit one line to withdraw through another.

It is widely accepted that the three lines of a Republican legion deployed in a chequerboard formation, as shown in Diagram 139, with maniple-wide gaps between one maniple and the next (version A). One variant of this idea is that one century of a maniple deployed in front of the other (version B).

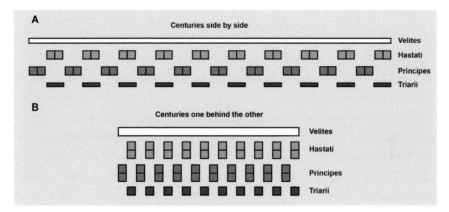

Diagram 139: The two common variants of the *Quincunx*.

The velites, after initial skirmishing, fall back through the gaps between maniples to the rear of the legion. In version A, the maniples of the hastati, initially deployed with each file having a width of 3 feet, then spread out, closing the gaps between them until each file now has a width of 6 feet. The idea that each Roman soldier occupies 6 feet of frontage when engaged in combat originates from a misunderstanding of Polybios, 18.30 (see Chapter 1: 2. *Heavy Infantry – Organisation*). If the hastati are worsted, they retire through the gaps between the maniples of the principes – though it is not explained how the hastati deployed in front of the principes would reach those gaps – after which the principes themselves widen out to close the gaps and present a solid line with six-foot wide files. The principes themselves if necessary retire through the gaps between the triarii who likewise widen out their files to fight the enemy.

In version B the velites retire through the gaps to the rear after which the rearmost centuries of the hastati march to the left or right and then advance to close the gaps. If the hastati are outfought they retire through the gaps between the principes' centuries, though again it is not explained how the hastati centuries deployed in front of the principes centuries actually reach those gaps, and so on until the fight reaches the triarii, who presumably march the rear halves of their centuries to fill the gaps between the front halves.

These two mechanisms pose several problems. In both versions a line – the principes for example – will not be able to close its gaps before the enemy, following on after the retreating line in front – hastati in this case – has reached those gaps and is now able to attack the exposed flanks of the principes' own maniples. The retreating hastati can offer no help as they have been outfought (which is why they are retreating) and the triarii behind them are not in a position to help either as they are obstructed by the retreating hastati. The isolated principes maniples in front will be attacked on three sides and rapidly cut to pieces.

This needs to be emphasised: a body of infantry that is attacked on its flanks as well as its front is soon destroyed. It is for this reason that infantry lines were continuous and protecting the flanks was so important – and getting around those flanks often decided a battle.

Myke Cole proposes that the enemy would not exploit the exposed maniples as the second line would then catch them in a vulnerable position: 'You charge through the gap and attack the exposed flank of a maniple of *hastati*. You have just turned your own flank to a maniple of *principes*, men in their prime with more experience and better equipment than the *hastati*. Who would be crazy enough to risk that?'[84]

The weakness of this argument is the assumption that the individual soldier's battle awareness extended along the battle line of which he is part. This is not the case. In the dust and noise of battle the individual soldier has little knowledge of events beyond his immediate vicinity. If his opponents are retreating he will advance, smelling victory. Infantry lines would often fragment in this way as parts of the line advanced against a retreating foe whilst other parts were held up. Infantry in retreat signalled that they were losing, and the infantry opposing them would most certainly follow up, allowing the infantry adjacent to the flanks of the exposed maniples to attack those flanks.

If it is the velites that are retiring then the hastati might have enough time to close their gaps before the enemy, advancing from a couple of dozen yards away, reach them. But in the case of hastati retiring past the principes there is a problem. The hastati are engaged in combat with the enemy and hence will fall straight back, this being the natural response to a superior opponent (see Chapter 1: 2. *Heavy Infantry – Organisation*). After filtering back between the principes' maniples, the hastati still have to get past the triarii which means being obliged to split and move left and right. Besides the unlikelihood of the front-rank hastati being able to move sideways whilst facing enemy troops, this will immediately expose the individual hastati at the edges of the split line to flank attacks by the advancing enemy and they will be killed before the triarii can move up to cover the gap. The hastati could try doing it rank by rank: the rear rank splits and moves left and right around the triarii, then the hastati fall back a little and the next rank splits and moves left and right, then the hastati fall back a little more, and so on, until the front rank finally splits and, covered by the triarii just behind it, works around the triarii left and right. The whole process would take time. Meanwhile the isolated principes maniples in front have been annihilated.

The problem is worse in the case of the principes retiring past the triarii. In this case there is no second line to cover the gaps between the isolated triarii maniples and their demise will be swift.

The second problem with both these models is the ability of the maniples to close the gaps between them whilst engaging the enemy. The first model requires that a maniple spreads its files out sideways with its front ranks locked in combat. The second model requires that the posterior century march sideways then up alongside the prior century without having to engage the enemy, and quickly enough so that the prior century is not cut to pieces (bearing in mind that the posterior centuries still have to wait whilst the retreating troops of the line in front filter past the maniples of the line behind them).

The simple fact is that when infantry are engaged in hand-to-hand combat they do not manoeuvre. They stand where they are and fight. It is only unengaged infantry that can execute complex manoeuvres of this kind. Which obliges the proponents of both models to suppose that the enemy make line relief possible by breaking off long enough for the relief manoeuvres to take place. But if the enemy are winning the fight – hence making line relief necessary – why would they stop? And if they knew that a successful line relief manoeuvre would bring up a fresh Roman line against them then, again, why would they stop? Much better to press their already successful attack, disrupt the line relief mechanism, throw the maniples into chaos, and win the battle.

An Alternative Mechanism of Line Relief

So how did line relief actually work? To answer the question we need examine exactly how the lines were deployed, which means taking a closer look at Livy's description of the legion in *History*: 8.8.

This may sound like presumption on the part of someone who is not a professional historian, but it has been my experience, again and again, that translations cannot be trusted. To be a competent translator of primary sources it is not enough to have a good grasp of the original language; one also has to be thoroughly familiar with the period. Ancient writers often allude to or assume things familiar to their contemporaries but unknown to us. Context is everything. Translation is not transliteration: the sense of a language must be accurately transposed, sometimes using different words or even phrases. To do this the translator must know what the writer is getting at. The text does not always spell it out.

Get even one key word wrong and the understanding of a whole passage can be substantially skewed. There is a classic example here, the word *inter*.

Every translation of Livy's description of the hastati's maniples translates '*inter*' in the sense of 'between':

The first line, or hastati, comprised fifteen maniples, with short distances between [*inter*] them. – *History*: 8.8.5.

Inter however must be obligatorily translated as 'between' only if referring to two objects: *Inter Padum atque Alpes* – 'Between the Po and the Alpes'.

If referring to a group of objects it has the sense of 'between the individual objects of the group', which is better translated by 'among': *inter multos saucios spe incertae vitae relictus* – 'among many cares left with the hope of an uncertain life'.

If referring to a collectivity – a group of objects designated by a single noun – it also has the sense of 'between the individual objects of the collectivity', and must be translated by 'among': *tibicines inter exercitum positi* – 'musicians placed among the army'; *inter multitudinem* – 'among the crowd'.

Taking a closer look at Livy's Latin:

Prima acies hastati erant, manipuli quindecim, distantes inter se modicum spatium.

A word-for-word transliteration gives:

First line hastati were, maniples fifteen, standing-apart between/ among themselves small space.

Question: what was 'standing apart'? The hastati or the maniples? In the first case we are talking about a group, in the second a collectivity, so a Latin reader would naturally take *inter* in the sense of 'among.' If *distantes* refers to the hastati (more likely since the hastati are the subject of the sentence), then the sense that emerges is of small spaces between the individual hastati, i.e. the hastati files are in **open order**. If *distantes* refers to the maniples (less likely), then it can be translated either as 'among' – the maniples are in open order with small spaces between one file and the next – or 'between', with gaps between one maniple and the next.

At the limit the text can be given an ambiguous meaning, but the sense leans towards a continuous line with narrow spaces between the files, rather than large maniple-wide gaps between one maniple and the next. The text does say 'small space,' which would hardly apply to intervals as wide as the maniples themselves.

This interpretation – spaces within the maniples rather than between them – is reinforced elsewhere in the passage:

Si hastati profligare hostem non possent, pede presso eos retro cedentes in intervalla ordinum principes recipiebant.

If the hastati could not prevail against the enemy, they were received, as they fell back under pressure, into the intervals of the principes' units [*ordines*]. – *History*: 8.8.9.

Here the Latin is clearer. The hastati are received into the intervals **of** the principes' units, not the intervals between them.

Triarii consurgentes, ubi in intervalla ordinum suorum principes et hastatos recepissent.

The triarii, rising up after they had received the principes and hastati into the intervals of their units – *Ibid*: 8.8.12.

The triarii likewise receive the hastati and principes into the intervals **of** their units.

It is just about possible to stretch the sense of these extracts to mean gaps between one maniple and the next, but that goes against the primary and most obvious meaning of the Latin.

Taking Livy's text in its natural sense, what are the implications? What we now have is a legion deployed in continuous, open order lines. Instead of the customary 3-foot width, each file occupies an area 6 feet wide, leaving a 4-foot gap between the shoulders of the men in adjacent files.

After initial skirmishing the light troops withdraw through the file spaces of the hastati who then close up from open to intermediate order by doubling files as explained by the tacticians.[85] A similar process is described by Onasander in a military treatise destined for Quintus Veranius Nepos, consul in 49 AD and Legate of Britain. It applies to Hellenistic-style skirmishers like slingers and archers withdrawing through a phalanx of heavy foot, but the mechanism would be familiar (and relevant) to a Roman general like Nepos.

> There should be intervals [διαστήματα – *diastemata*, which means 'gaps' in this context] within the ranks [κατὰ τὰς τάξεις – *kata tas taxeis*; in this context *kata* means 'throughout'; *taxeis* in the plural applied to a single phalanx line means 'ranks'], so that, when the light-armed troops have discharged their weapons while the enemy is still advancing, before the two armies come to close quarters, they may about-face, pass in good order through the centre of the phalanx, and come without confusion to the rear. For it is not safe for them to go around the whole army, encircling the flanks – since the enemy would quickly anticipate them in this manoeuvre, coming to close quarters and intercepting them on the way – nor is it safe for them to force their way through the closed ranks, where they would fall over the weapons and cause confusion in the lines, one man stumbling against another. – *Strategikos*: 19.1.

After the velites are withdrawn, the hastati engage the enemy (see Diagram 140).

> Where the army was formed up in these units, the hastati were the first to engage in battle. – *History*: 8.8.9.

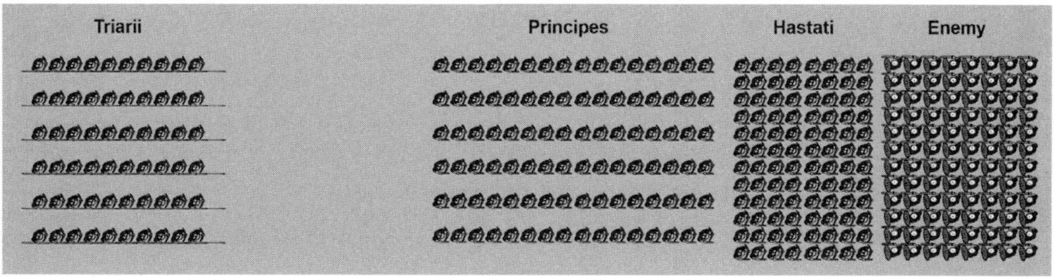

Diagram 140: The *hastati* engage.

If the hastati could not prevail against the enemy, they were received, as they fell back under pressure, into the intervals of the principes' units. – *Ibid*: 8.8.9.

No complicated manoeuvres are required. The rear ranks of the hastati simply fall straight back through the gaps between the principes' files whilst the front ranks continue to engage the enemy (see Diagram 141).

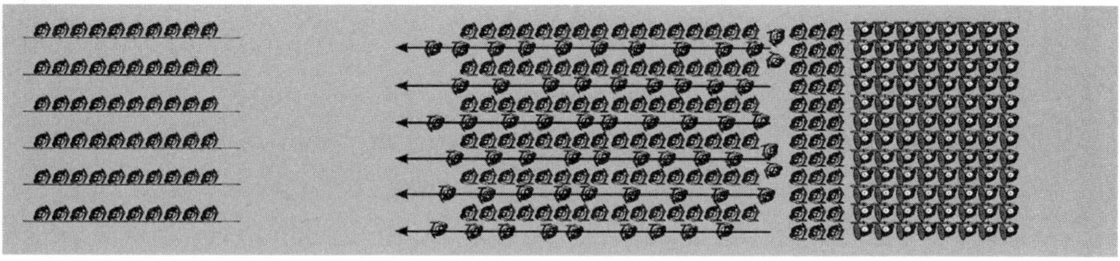

Diagram 141: The *hastati* retire through the *principes*.

When the last hastati have passed through, the principes quickly double files to plug the gaps, giving the enemy no time to exploit them (see Diagram 142).

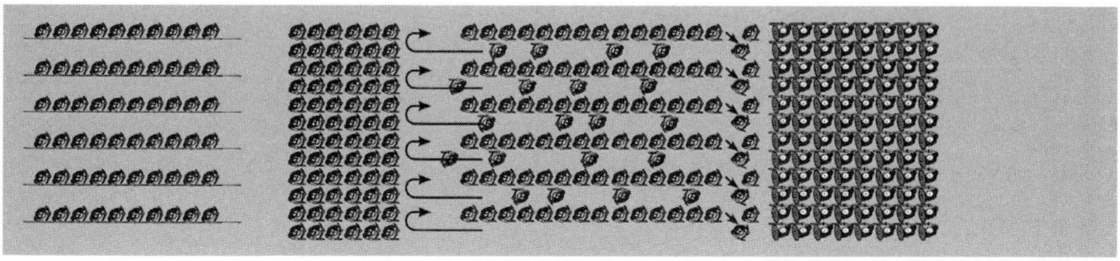

Diagram 142: The *principes* double files.

The hastati followed the principes as they took up the fight. – *Ibid*: 8.8.9.

The principes complete their transition from open to intermediate order whilst engaging the enemy, and the hastati move up behind them (see Diagram 143).

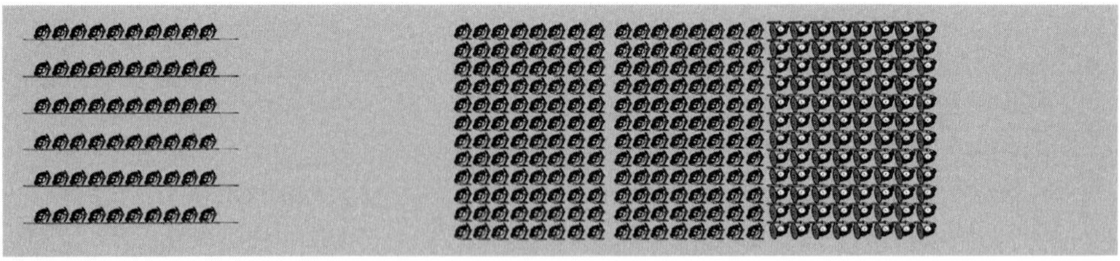

Diagram 143: The *principes* engage the enemy.

If the principes also did not make a sufficient impression on the enemy, they retreated slowly from the front to the triarii. Hence, when a difficulty is felt, 'Matters have come to the triarii', became a usual proverb. – *Ibid*: 8.8.11.

The principes fall back, preceded by the hastati. Notice that there is a small distance between the principes/hastati and the triarii, which was there to enable the hastati to regroup behind the principes earlier (see Diagram 144).

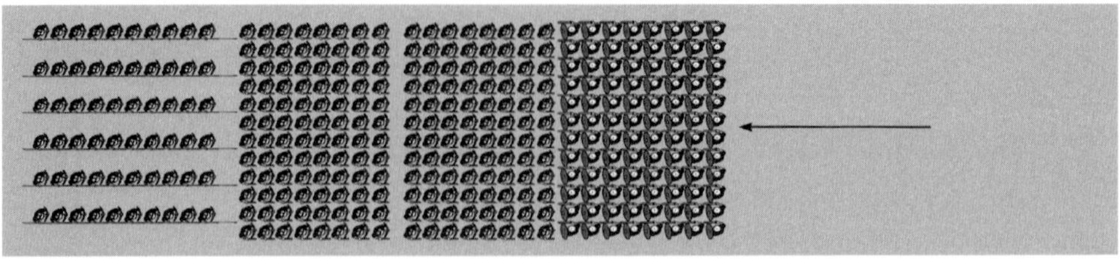

Diagram 144: The *principes* and *hastati* fall back.

The principes fall back through the triarii file gaps, preceded by the hastati. Notice that line relief is carried out whilst under enemy pressure. Livy does not mention any pauses in the fighting (see Diagram 145).

Diagram 145: The *principes* and *hastati* retire through the *triarii*.

The triarii, rising up after they had received the principes and hastati into the intervals of their units, would at once draw their units together and close the lanes, as it were; then, with no more reserves behind to count on, they would charge the enemy in one compact array as the last hope of the army. – *Ibid*: 8.8.12–13.

Notice how this mechanism of line relief readily fits the text. Once the last of the principes are through, the triarii immediately double files to close the gaps, rapidly converting from open to intermediate order. They then take up the fight, either winning the day or covering the retreat of the rest of the legion (see Diagram 146).

Diagram 146: The *triarii* close formation and prepare to continue the fight.

Interpreting the *intervalla inter ordines* as file spaces within a unit rather than between one unit and the next finds echoes elsewhere in Livy.

In a war between the Etruscans and the Romans led by M. Valerius Maximus, the Roman cavalry had been ambushed and beaten. Once Maximus returned from Rome the Romans unmasked another ambush attempt, obliging the Etruscans to fight an open battle. They initially attack the Roman outposts whilst Maximus assembled his main army and marched down against them. He then prepared a trick of his own.

The standard bearers were to march in front to convince the Etruscans all his forces are committed. In the meantime his infantry advanced with intervals wide enough to permit the passage of cavalry:

> The standards of the legions were in front, to prevent the enemy from suspecting any sudden or secret manoeuvre, but the Dictator had left intervals amongst [*inter*] the units of foot through which the cavalry could pass. The legions raised the battle-shout, and at the same moment the cavalry charged down upon the enemy, who were unprepared for such a hurricane, and a sudden panic set in.- Livy, *History*: 10.5.

The precise phrase is *intervalla inter ordines peditum*. Since these intervals were meant to be hidden from the enemy it would hardly make sense to have large gaps between one unit and the next, gaps that would be immediately detected by the enemy, spoiling the surprise. And a four-foot wide gap between files in open order is sufficient to let a horse and rider pass, the horse itself being about two feet wide.

The Roman Consul, Papirius was locked in battle with a Samnite army when he was heartened by the arrival of Roman reinforcements, and urged his men to greater efforts before the new arrivals should claim victory for themselves.

> He rode along while saying this, and commanded the tribunes and centurions to open their ranks to allow passage for the cavalry. He had previously told Trebonius and Caedicius that when they saw him brandish his spear aloft they should launch the cavalry against the enemy with all the force they could. His orders were carried out to the letter; paths were opened amongst the units [*panduntur inter ordines viae*], the cavalry galloped through and with levelled spears charged the enemy's centre. – Livy, *History*: 10.41.

Note that the opening of the paths was done in the heat of battle. This is feasible if conceived as close order troops moving back to create open order files whilst covered by the front ranks, but not if conceived as sizeable gaps opened between one unit and the next. The enemy would exploit these gaps before the process was complete, catching the exposed units on their flanks.

Objection to the Alternative Mechanism – The Battle of Zama

Polybios' description of the Roman deployment at Zama is often cited as proof that the quincunx, with gaps between the maniples, was the standard legion battle formation, adapted in this case to particular circumstances: Here is a standard translation of Polybios, *Histories*: 15, 9:

> The hastati first, with an interval between their maniples; behind them the principes, their maniples not arranged to cover the intervals between those of the hastati as the Roman custom is, but immediately behind them at some distance, because the enemy was so strong in elephants.

But what exactly does the Greek say?

> πρῶτον μὲν τοὺς ἀστάτους καὶ τὰς τούτων σημαίας ἐν **διαστήμασιν**, ἐπὶ δὲ τούτοις τοὺς πρίγκιπας, τιθεὶς τὰς σπείρας οὐ κατὰ τὸ τῶν πρώτων σημαιῶν **διάστημα**, καθάπερ ἔθος ἐστὶ τοῖς Ῥωμαίοις, ἀλλὰ καταλλήλους ἐν ἀποστάσει διὰ τὸ πλῆθος τῶν παρὰ τοῖς ἐναντίοις ἐλεφάντων.
>
> proton men tous hastatous kai tas touton semaias en **diastemasin**, epi de toutois tous prinkipas, titheis tas speiras ou kata to ton proton semaion **diastema**, kathaper ethos esti tois Romaiois, alla katallelous en apostasei dia to plethos ton para tois enantiois elephanton.

There is one crucial word in this passage: *diastema* – 'interval'. It has several other meanings: 'radius', 'aperture', 'difference', 'ratio', 'extension' and 'dimension'. Its overarching meaning is a distinct and separate extension in space which may or may not be occupied by an object. It comes from διίστημι – *diistemi* – meaning to set apart, to place separately, to separate.

In its first use in the paragraph it is plural:

'First the hastati and their maniples in intervals [*en diastemasin*]' – or more accurately, 'in separate entities.' The word here does not mean 'gap' – the maniples are not transformed into a row of empty spaces.

In its second use it is singular. Here it cannot mean the hastati's 'intervals' as there are several of them (and in any case the prior use of *diastemata* in this passage does not mean 'interval'). The principes' maniples do not all cover a single gap between the hastati's maniples. With 'interval' ruled out the only other possible meaning is 'extension' or 'dimension', i.e. the space of ground covered by the entire hastati line, or the whole hastati line considered as a 'separate entity':

Behind them the principes, their maniples not matching the extension/dimension [*diastema*] of the first maniples as the Roman custom is.

Using *diastema* in this sense is not a rarity in Greek:

Now it [place] has three dimensions [*diastemata*], length, breadth, depth, by which all body also is bounded. But the place cannot be body; for if it were there would be two bodies in the same place. – Aristotle, *Physics*: 4.1.

To finish the analysis of this passage: first, the standard translation.

But immediately behind them at some distance, because the enemy was so strong in elephants.

This part is perhaps better rendered as:

But corresponding to them [i.e. the principes' maniples are deployed in the same manner as the hastati maniples] from a certain distance away, due to the great number of opposing elephants.

Why do the principes keep a 'certain distance' from the hastati? This may have something to do with the way the hastati and principes closed their lines once the elephants had passed through, but we can only speculate on how that was achieved.

The point to note is that Polybios takes the trouble to describe two peculiarities about Scipio's deployment: first that he arranges his hastati with gaps between one maniple and the next; second that his principes, rather than cover the width of the line formed by the hastati – habitual Roman practice – instead conform their maniples exactly to the dispositions of the hastati, leaving gaps between one maniple and the next. This is not a variation of a standard Roman deployment but an entirely new formation, designed for a specific purpose: to funnel Hannibal's elephants straight through the Roman infantry and into the rear.

The fact that Scipio's deployment at Zama was anything but the norm for a Roman army is confirmed by Livy. There are not normally gaps between maniples.

> However, he did not form cohorts in **close contact** [*confertas*], each in advance of its standards, but rather maniples at a considerable distance from each other, so that there should be an interval where the enemy's elephants might be driven through without breaking up the ranks. – *History*: 30.33.

Notice the 'considerable distance' – *aliquantulum inter se distantes* – between the maniples, which does not correspond to the 'short distance' – *modicum spatium* – of *History*: 8.8.5. *Aliquantulum*, with the meanings of 'somewhat', 'some', 'moderate', 'tolerable', 'considerable', 'not a little', designates the medium between 'much' and 'little'.

The fact that there were not normally gaps between cohorts or maniples is repeated by Frontinus.

> Against this formation Scipio drew up the flower of his legions in three successive front lines, arranged according to hastati, principes, and triarii, **not making the cohorts touch** [*nec continuas construxit cohortes*], but leaving a space between the detached maniples through which the elephants driven by the enemy might easily be allowed to pass without throwing the ranks into confusion. – *Stratagems*: 2.3.16.

In other words the default deployment of the cohorts (and their constituent maniples) was a **solid line**, with the units packed one next to the other. At Zama Scipio did something exceptional: separate the maniples with sizeable gaps – 'considerable distance' – between them to let the elephants through. This was highly unusual and Livy, Polybios and Frontinus go to some lengths to describe it.

8. Conclusion: the Effectiveness of the Triplex Acies

The classical hoplite phalanx dominated the battlefields of Greece from Marathon to Chaeronea, a period of 152 years. Its successor, the Macedonian phalanx, ruled the eastern Mediterranean from Chaeronea to Cynoscephalae, a further 141 years. The *triplex acies* successfully expanded and defended the Roman state from before the Latin War to well into the 3rd century AD, some 600 years, or over half a millennium. A tactical system must be extremely effective to last this long, but why was it so good?

Battles in Antiquity were primarily a question of morale. If a foot soldier perceived that his formation was being outfought by the enemy and was no longer able to secure his flanks and rear he would usually panic and flee. The Roman soldier, knowing there were one or more support lines behind him, was not unduly concerned by the performance of his own unit. Furthermore, lines were graded according to seniority: the youngest troops were in the first line, more experienced troops in the second, and the veterans in the third (with perhaps inferior last-ditch reserves behind them). The troops of the line in front were fighting under the eyes of their superiors and the motivation to excel in combat would have been very potent. Finally, the Roman soldier's morale was not tied to the survival in battle of his general, at least not until Scipio Africanus.

But it goes further than that. The legion did not always win its battles – in fact it often lost them. Nonetheless during the era of the Republic at least, a defeat, even a major defeat, did not signal the end of a war. This was a peculiarity of Rome – a refusal to seeks terms with an enemy until that enemy was beaten. This political inflexibility was never more evident than during Hannibal's invasion of Italy. After defeating two

Consular armies at the Trebia and Trasimene Hannibal annihilated the largest army Rome had ever raised, killing about 50,000 infantry and nearly 6,000 cavalry at Cannae, roughly one fifth of Rome's military manpower. Any other state would immediately have sued for peace. Rome did not.

It is not clear exactly where this martial stubbornness came from, perhaps from the Republic fighting so many wars and coming close to extinction several times, against the Etruscans (who reached the walls of Rome), the Latin league, the Gauls (who sacked Rome), the Sabines, and others. An enemy in the field was perceived as a mortal threat to Rome's existence, not simply another state one could negotiate with.

This stubbornness went hand-in-hand with an astonishing ability to raise army after army to replace those destroyed in battle. This was possible for several reasons. First, every Roman male citizen of military age who possessed some property was expected to fight. In Greece only those citizens who could afford hoplite equipment – the middle class – were called up for military service, bringing their servants along who acted as light troops. Carthage relied largely on mercenaries, with a core of professional *Poeni* infantry, whilst the rest of her citizens got on with the business of making money. Macedonian and the Successor armies were formed around a core of full-time professionals supplemented by mercenaries and the mobilisation of ethnic Macedonian citizens, which, outside of Macedonia, was limited in numbers compared to their Italian equivalents. Only the tribes of Gaul, Spain, Germany and Britain used all their capable males in a war, but they were not trained or equipped as well as Roman troops.

Secondly, the Roman infantryman's kit cost relatively little to manufacture. A hastatus or princeps was the equivalent of a class II or class III soldier of Servius Tullius' roster. His shield was easier to make than a hoplite *aspis* or phalangite shield. His body armour, a simple rectangular brass plate, was a fraction of the cost of a breastplate or linen corselet. His helmet was simple. His pila were cheap, his sword perhaps rather more expensive, but his opponents also used swords. And yet, though cheaply equipped, he was able to fight as heavy infantry, on a par with most of the better-equipped heavy infantry he faced in battle.

Thirdly, due to the frequency of her wars, Rome's citizenry were for a large part experienced in warfare. Romans who were called up as reserves had often fought many times before and required little training or adjustment to military life. Added to this was the fact that the *triplex acies* was a fairly simple formation. Soldiers had to learn to form up in files and double from open to intermediate order when executing line relief. More complex manoeuvres were usually not required and if so were performed by experienced units.

The Republic then, no matter how badly hammered, could always bounce back.

When the Republican hastatus and princeps turned into the full-time professional legionary of the Empire, things changed. Joining the army was voluntary; the ordinary Roman citizens were no longer expected to fight and lost their martial *élan*. Legionaries became better and more expensively equipped. An army destroyed in battle could not be easily replaced. This however was not a serious problem as the Empire from Trajan to Theodosius was able to afford an enormous military establishment of around half a million men. The loss of several legions did not compromise the Empire's ability to defend itself. The fall of the Western Empire was not due to military defeats, but to a paralysis in the higher echelons of political and military command. But that is a subject for another book.

Notes

1. Livy: 8.5.7.
2. Livy: 8.9.1.
3. This proposed site for the battle is based on the statement by Livy that the battle took place at the foot of Vesuvius where the road led to Veseris. Veseris seems best identified as a river that formerly ran through Herculaneum (cf. Romanelli, *Topographica Antiqua*: III, p543).
4. Livy: 8.8.
5. Livy: 8.9.14.
6. *History*: 8.10.6.
7. *History*: 1.43.
8. *Antiquities*: 4.16–18.
9. *Antiquities*: 6.5.5.
10. Thucydides, *History of the Peloponnesian War*: 2.31.

11. Thucydides, *History of the Peloponnesian War*: 2.13.
12. Thucydides, *History of the Peloponnesian War*: 4.93.
13. Diodorus: 15.52–3. The army consists initially of six Boeotarchs (commanders of 1,000 men) who are joined by a seventh. According to the *Hellenica Oxyrhynchia* (16.3–4) each Boeotarch supplied 100 cavalry along with his infantry.
14. Herodotus: 9.29.
15. Certosa situla, ca. 500 BC, shows warriors with rectangular, oblong and round shields armed with a single spear.
16. Arnoaldi situla, fifth century BC, shows six warriors with rectangular shields and one warrior with a round shield carrying two spears, and one warrior with a rectangular shield carrying one spear.
17. Bronze cista from Praeneste (Palestrina) ca. 325–275 BC; Apulian volute krater from Basilicata, made in Puglia ca. 340–320 BC.
18. Dionysius: 4.41.1.
19. Dionysius: 4.50.1.
20. Dionysius: 5.47.1.
21. Livy: 4.17.8.
22. Livy, *History*: 8.8.14–15.
23. *Histories*: 6.20.
24. *History*: 8.8.14.
25. *Histories*: 6.21.
26. *History*: 8.8.14.
27. *Histories*: 6.22–23.
28. *Histories*: 6.20.
29. *Attic Nights*: 16.4.6.
30. *Commentary on the Aeneid of Vergil*: 11.463.
31. *De Munitionibus Castrorum*: 2.
32. *De Munitionibus Castrorum*: 30.
33. *De Munitionibus Castrorum*: 44.
34. *De Munitionibus Castrorum*: 5.
35. Jonathan Roth: 'The Size and Organisation of the Imperial Roman Legion', *Historia: Zeitschrift für Alte Geschichte* Bd. 43, H. 3 (3rd Qtr., 1994), pp. 346–362.
36. *De Re Militari*: 2.8.
37. Catherine M. Gilliver: *The Roman Art of War: Theory and Practice*: 3.
38. *Stratagems*: 2.3.22.
39. *De Re Militari*: 3.18.
40. Caesar, *African War*: 81; *Civil War*: 3.89.
41. *History*: 2.11.
42. *History*: 2.14; 2.20; 2.64; 3.5; 3.43; 3.69; 4.39, etc.
43. *History*: 7.7.
44. Sallust, *The Jugurthine War*: 51; 56; 77; 88; 93; 94; 99; 100.

45. Sallust, *The Jugurthine War*: 49; 100.
46. Sallust, *The Jugurthine War*: 42.
47. Caesar, *Gallic War*: 2.27.
48. *Antiquities*: 5.46.2.
49. Raffaele d'Amato, *Arms and Armor of the Imperial Roman Soldier*: I.
50. Caesar: *Gallic War*: 1.25.
51. Raffaele d'Amato, *Arms and Armor of the Imperial Roman Soldier*: I.
52. Raffaele d'Amato, *Arms and Armor of the Imperial Roman Soldier*: I.
53. Raffaele d'Amato, *Arms and Armor of the Imperial Roman Soldier*: I.
54. Polybios, *Histories*: 6.23; Livy, *History*: 31.34.
55. Raffaele d'Amato, *Arms and Armor of the Imperial Roman Soldier*: I.
56. Vegetius, *De Re Militari*: 1.
57. Livy: 31.34.
58. *Life of Romulus*: 21.1.
59. *Library*: 23.2.
60. Simon Timothy James: *The Arms and Armour from Dura-Europos, Syria : Weaponry Recovered from the Roman Garrison Town and the Sassanid Siegeworks during the Excavations, 1922–37.*
61. Raffaele d'Amato, *Arms and Armor of the Imperial Roman Soldier*: I.
62. http://www.roman-reenactor.com/scutum el fayum.html
63. Raffaele d'Amato, *Arms and Armor of the Imperial Roman Soldier*: I.
64. Raffaele d'Amato, *Arms and Armor of the Imperial Roman Soldier*: I.
65. *Histories*: 6.23.
66. *Tactica*: 3.5.
67. *De Re Militari*: 1.
68. Raffaele d'Amato, *Arms and Armor of the Imperial Roman Soldier*: II.
69. Livy: 3.59.11; Diodorus, *Library*: 14.16.5.
70. *History*: 4.58.8–10.
71. Plutarch, *Marius*: 9.1; Sallust, *The War with Jugurtha*: 86.2.
72. Paul Erdkamp, *A Companion to the Roman Army*: 24.
73. https://www.youtube.com/watch?v=GIUQAtdz2i8; https://www.youtube.com/watch?v=jnoiTX0xZ0Y
74. Polybios, *Histories*: 6.40–41; Vegetius, *De Re Militari*: 3.5.
75. *Strategikos*: 6.
76. *Commentary on the Aeneid of Virgil*: 12.121.
77. *History*: 2.6.
78. *History*: 44.9.
79. Sallust, *The Jugurthine War*: 100.
80. *Gallic War*: 8.8. See also Tacitus, *Annals*: 1.51.
81. Asklepiodotus: 11.3; Aelian: 37.2,3,53.
82. *Gallic War*: 4.14.
83. *Annals*: 2.16.
84. *Legion versus Phalanx*: III.
85. See Chapter 1: 3. *Heavy Infantry – Manoeuvres*.

Chapter 5

The Golden Age of Heavy Infantry

T he Achaemenid army was the culmination of 2,000 years'
development of weaponry and tactics in the Fertile Crescent.
The first recorded instance of infantry being organised in
regular files and ranks is probably depicted on the Sumerian Stele of the
Vultures (2600–2350 BC) that probably shows, not a pike phalanx, but a
stylised representation of spearmen in files 6–7 men deep, with 6 men
holding spears and – possibly – one man holding a large pavise in front
(it would be anatomically impossible for the hands of all 6 men to project
together just beyond the shields of the front rank: see Diagram 147).

Diagram 147: Stele of the Vultures. Eric Gaba –
Wikimedia Commons licence.

Infantry forces grew in size and were subdivided into archers and heavy or medium melee troops. The Sumerian battle cart evolved into the chariot. Cavalry as a significant military arm appeared for the first time under the Assyrians. Siege warfare developed. Logistics became a science, with food dumps prepared sometimes years in advance to allow a large army to travel great distances. In the end the military genius of Babylon, Media, Assyria, Egypt and Anatolia was absorbed by one vast empire that conquered them all.

The Achaemenid army however, that had campaigned successfully from the Balkans to the Indus valley, could make no impression on the Greek phalanx. Two crushing defeats at Marathon and Plataea and a humiliating failure at Thermopylae (until the Spartans were outflanked) confirmed the supremacy of the hoplite, and the Persian kings would thereafter use hoplite mercenaries as their choice infantry.

Even less could the Achaemenids deal with the Macedonian phalanx, attempting unsuccessfully to stop it at Issus using hoplite mercenaries positioned along a steep riverbank and at Gaugamela using scythed chariots and hoplite mercenaries armed with long spears. Cavalry, once the arm of decision in Middle Eastern armies, played a secondary role in Greece and in the Successor States after Alexander. In Italy, Roman cavalry devolved from battle winners that could charge through enemy infantry,[1] to guarding the flanks whilst the infantry won the battles.

It was the apogee of the heavy infantryman. Other troop types did not disappear, as any effective army in this era to some extent used diverse arms. But in this era battles were won primarily by the infantry.

The Parthians seem to be the exception to the rule. In 53 BC a Roman army of 7 legions, 8,000 auxiliaries, 4,000 cavalry and 4,000 light infantry was annihilated by a smaller Parthian force of cataphracts and horse archers. This however was due largely to the incompetent generalship of the Roman commander. Ignoring the recommendation of his Armenian ally Artavasdes, Crassus marched through flat terrain ideally suited to Parthian cavalry where he was met by the Parthian army under Surena.

Initially following the advice of Cassius, his second-in-command, Crassus deployed in a long line flanked by cavalry to avoid encirclement, but then changed his mind and rearranged his infantry into a square with twelve cohorts on each side and his cavalry in the middle.[2] Twelve cohorts have a frontage of about 576 metres, short enough to allow Surena to co-ordinate and control an encirclement of the Romans, something that would not have been possible if all the cohorts had deployed in a long line. A square is a defensive formation and by adopting it Crassus surrendered the initiative to the Parthians who, plentifully equipped with arrows, took full advantage of it, showering the legionaries with arrow fire all day. The Romans' Gallic cavalry were insufficient to break the Parthian stranglehold and after their destruction Crassus had no choice but to try and sue for peace. He was killed during the negotiations and the remainder of his army was destroyed.

When a Roman army was led by a general who knew his business it was a different story. Fourteen years later in 39 BC an invading Parthian army was met in the Taurus mountains by Publius Ventidius, a skilled general who had served under Caesar. Ventidius deployed his infantry, reinforced with slingers, in a line on rugged slopes and kept back his cavalry on the flanks. The Parthian horse archers surged up the slopes to engage the Roman infantry who launched a surprise charge against them, catching them before they could execute a retirement. The horse archers were butchered in numbers and the remainder panicked and fled.[3] Ventidius followed up this victory with a second victory over the Parthians at the Amanus Pass,[4] after which the Parthian army withdrew from Roman territory.

Next year the Parthians returned with a larger army under the command of Pacorus, son of king Orodes. After crossing the Euphrates they met Ventidius at the town of Gindarus. Repeating his earlier tactic, Ventidius deployed his legions on the slope of a small hill. The Parthian horse archers moved up to shoot them and Ventidius charged the Parthians with his infantry, catching them before they could retire and then going on to rout the cataphracts deployed behind them, killing Pacorus in the process. This time, having beforehand placed infantry and cavalry along their line of retreat, he succeeded in destroying a large part of the Parthian army.[5] Thereafter Parthia would still win victories against Roman armies, but none as shattering as Carrhae. Roman legionaries would frequently defeat the Parthian cavalry, on several occasions going on to sack the Parthian capital Ctesiphon. Parthia was not an exception to the rule.

A far better candidate for rule-exception is the Macedonian cavalry wedge. In 338 BC a Macedonian army of about 30,000 infantry and 2,000 cavalry faced off against an allied Greek army of about 35,000 men. The Greeks had chosen a good position. Their left flank lay across the foothills of Mount Thurion and the right flank rested against the Kephisos River, near a projecting spur of Mount Aktion. Hence both their flanks were secure. Philip on the right commanded the pike phalanx whilst Alexander led the cavalry on the left. The place of honour at the right of the Greek phalanx was occupied by the crack Theban Sacred Band, the best hoplites of the coalition. Diodorus describes what happened next.

> Then Alexander, his heart set on showing his father his prowess and yielding to none in will to win, was the first of a number of good men who fought with him to break through the continuity of the enemy's battle line, and striking them down, he crushed the numbers of those drawn up in order near him. His comrades with him achieving the same thing, the continuity of the battle line kept being broken. With many corpses piled up, those round about Alexander, having first been overpowered like the others, turned and fled. – Diodorus: 16.86.1–3.

Diodorus does not explicitly affirm that Alexander led cavalry, but this is clearly cavalry work. Unlike Philip, who 'first forced back the troops stationed before him and then by compelling them to flee became the man responsible for the victory',[6] Alexander punched right through the Thebans in the same way the Republican Roman cavalry punched through enemy infantry. In the case of Alexander however, his cavalry slaughtered the Thebans as they passed through them.

> It is said, moreover, that the Band was never beaten until the battle of Chaeronea; and when, after the battle, Philip was surveying the dead, and stopped at the place where the three hundred were lying, all where they had faced the sarisai, with their armour, and mingled one with another, he was amazed… – *Life of Pelopidas*: 18.5.

'Sarisai' might suggest that Alexander's troops were phalangites, however Philip had equipped his cavalry as well as his infantry with long pikes. One cavalry unit was even called the *sarissaphoroi* – 'sarisa bearers'.[7] In every one of his subsequent battles Alexander led lance-armed cavalry, using them to pierce the enemy line. Chaeronea was no exception.

How Alexander's cavalry managed to slice through Greece's best hoplites at Chaeronea and Persia's finest infantry later at Issus is a topic beyond the scope of this book. In any case the lance-armed heavy cavalry of the Successor armies never attempted a frontal charge against the pike phalanx. Nor did Pyrrhus' heavy cavalry ever frontally charge a legion. After Alexander heavy infantry resumed their dominant role on the battlefield.

This dominance began to decline from the 3rd century AD onwards when the eastern Roman armies increasingly adopted the armament and methods of the cavalry-heavy Sassanians, even though they had generally managed to cope with the largely mounted armies of Parthia during the three preceding centuries. The Sassanians appear to have introduced the multi-purpose armoured lancer-archer and successfully integrated it into a combined arms force of horse and foot archers, elephants and spearmen that gave increasing trouble to the Roman infantry. The Romans adopted the cataphract and subsequently created their own version of the lancer-archer which grew in importance until it became the principal arm of the Roman army by the time of Belisarius. At the battle of Dara Belisarius placed his unreliable infantry behind a ditch well back from the cavalry on either wing and near the city walls where they could receive missile support from the wall defenders. They played little part in the ensuing battle, won by Roman, Hunnic and Herule cavalry that successfully absorbed Sassanian attacks before counterattacking in their turn.[8]

In the western Empire heavy infantry maintained its importance for longer, but it is significant that a general like Aetius largely relied on Hunnic cavalry and had recourse to infantry only after the Huns turned against him. The battle of Chalons in 451 AD was the final moment of glory for Roman legions that succeeded in driving back the Huns.

The battlefield was a plain rising by a sharp slope to a ridge, which both armies sought to gain; for advantage of position is a great help. The Huns with their forces seized the right side, the Romans, the Visigoths and the Auxiliaries the left, and then began a struggle for the yet untaken crest....

So then the struggle began for the advantage of position we have mentioned. Attila sent his men to take the summit of the mountain, but was outstripped by Thorismud and Aetius, who in their effort to gain the top of the hill reached higher ground and through this advantage of position easily routed the Huns as they came up. – Jordanes, *History of the Goths*: 38.

That the 'Romans' were in fact Roman troops is clear from Attila's subsequent speech, given to hearten his men after their initial failure.

You know of how little consequence the weapons of the Romans are. They are weighed down, I will not say even by the first wound, but by the dust itself while they are still gathering in formation and joining up their battle lines and tortoises. – *Ibid*: 39.

Attila tries to convince his men, not that the Romans are easy to beat – the Huns had just been beaten by them – but that they are slow, being heavily-equipped. Notice the 'tortoises'. The tortoise formation was used during the late Republic and early Empire but was obsolete from the late Empire onwards. It had been replaced by the *foulkon*, an anti-missile and anti-cavalry formation in which the men of the first three ranks held their shields one above the other and sloping back to protect against arrow fire, whilst bracing closely together against a cavalry charge.[9] The formation was used only by Roman regulars, not by barbarian *foederati*. Before Maurice the formation was not known as a *foulkon* and 'tortoise' would have been an equivalent term.

After the fall of the western Empire the role of cavalry became increasingly important in Europe and the eastern Mediterranean though heavy infantry continued to be a large component of armies. The Muslim army that defeated the Byzantines at Yarmuk in 636 AD had 36 infantry regiments for 4 cavalry regiments and one elite cavalry reserve under its brilliant general Khalid ibn al-Walid. But despite the preponderance of Arab infantry, it was the Arab cavalry that contributed all the decisive action during the 5-day battle, eventually dispersing the Byzantine cavalry and outflanking the Byzantine infantry line.

At the pivotal Battle of Guadalete in 711 AD the Berber cavalry played a decisive role in annihilating the Visigoths. The Franks under Charles Martel were able to defeat the Moslem army twenty years later only because they deployed in a square on a hill, with trees to impede the Umayyad cavalry charges, and though in a defensive and hence passive formation, were prepared to outwait the Moslem commander Abd-al-Raḥmân who had no choice but to attack them or retreat. Even then it was a close battle: the Umayyad cavalry penetrated the Frankish square several times, only finally breaking off when rumours of a Frankish attack on their camp caused them to run back to secure their loot, the run turning into a rout.

The Franks got the message. By the time of Charlemagne cavalry was the principal component of the Frankish army.

It would be another 700 years before heavy infantry regained its former ascendency in the form of the Swiss pike block that was imitated and eventually became universal in western Europe. It held that ascendency for two centuries, not losing it until the perfection of the flintlock musket in the late 17th century changed the nature of infantry warfare forever.

Notes

1. *Histories*: 3.70.4–10; 8.30.6–7.
2. Plutarch, *Life of Crassus*: 23.
3. Cassius Dio, *Roman History*: 48.40.
4. Cassius Dio, *Roman History*: 48.41.
5. Cassius Dio, *Roman History*: 49.19.
6. *Ibid*: 16.86.4.
7. Arrian, *Anabasis*: 1.14.1; 4.4.6.
8. Procopius, *History of the Wars*: 1.13.
9. Maurice, *Strategikon*: 12.A.7.49–60.

Bibliography

Primary Sources

Aelian: *Tactics*
Appian: *Gallic History*
Aristotle: *Physics*
Arrian: *The Anabasis of Alexander*
Arrian: *Array Against the Alans*
Arrian: *Tactics*
Asklepiodotus: *Tactics*
Aulus Gellius: *Attic Nights*
Caesar: *African War*
Caesar: *Civil War*
Caesar: *Gallic War*
Cassius Dio: *Roman History*
Charles the Bold: *1473 Burgundian Ordnance*
Cornelius Nepos: *Lives of Eminent Commanders*
Curtius: *History of Alexander*
Demosthenes: *Second Olynthiac*
Didymus: *Demosthenes*
Diodorus Siculus: *Library*
Dionysius: *Antiquities*
Frontinus: *Stratagems*
Grattius: *Cynegeticon*
Harpocration: *Lexicon*
Herodotus: *The Histories*
Homer: *Iliad*
Hyginus Gromaticus: *De Munitionibus Castrorum*
Ineditum Vaticanum
Jordanes: *History of the Goths*
Julius Africanus: *Kestoi*
Justin: *Epitome of the Philippic History of Pompeius Trogus*
Kauṭilya: *Arthaśāstra*
Livy: *The History of Rome*
Lucian: *Anacharsis*
Lucian: *Herodotus and Aetion*

Maurice: *Strategikon*
Maurus Servius Honoratus: *Commentary on the Aeneid of Vergil*
Onasander: *Strategikos*
Pausanias
Plutarch: *Lives*
Plutarch: *Moralia*
Polyaenus: *Strategems*
Polybios: *Histories*
Procopius: *De Bellis*
Quintus Curtius Rufus: *History of Alexander*
Sallust: *The Jugurthine War*
Sallust: *The War with Catiline*
Strabo: *Geography*
Tacitus: *Annals*
Theophrastes: *Causes of Plants*
Theopompus: *History of Philip II* (cited in *Die Fragmente der griechischen Historiker*
   by Felix Jacoby)
Thucydides: *The History of the Peloponnesian War*
Vegetius: *De Re Militari*
Xenophon: *Agesilaus*
Xenophon: *Anabasis*
Xenophon: *Constitution of the Lacedaemonians*
Xenophon: *Cyropaedia*
Xenophon: *Hellenica*

Secondary Sources

d'Amato, R.: *Arms and Armor of the Imperial Roman Soldier*
Bardunias, P: *Hoplites at War, A Comprehensive Analysis of Heavy Infantry Combat in
   the Greek World, 750–100 BCE*
Brueggeman, G.: *The Roman Army* – http://www.romanarmy.info/
Carey, M.G.: *Operational Art in Classical Warfare: The Campaigns of Alexander the
   Great*
Cole, M.: *Legion versus Phalanx*
Connolly, P.: *Greece and Rome*
Edmonds, J.M: *Elegy and Iambus, Volume I*
Engels, D.W.: *Alexander the Great and the Logistics of the Macedonian Army*
English, S: *The Army of Alexander the Great*
Erdkamp, P: *A Companion to the Roman Army*
Fuller, J.F.C.: *The Generalship of Alexander the Great*
Gilliver, C. M.: *The Roman Art of War: Theory and Practice*
Head, D: *Origins of the Macedonian Infantry, Slingshot 319*

Heckel, W. and Jones, R: *Macedonian Warrior: Alexander's Elite Infantryman*

Heckel, W.: *The Conquests of Alexander the Great*

Lazenby, J.F.: *The Spartan Army*

Liampi, K.: *Der makedonische Schild*

Markle, M.M.: *A Shield Monument from Veria and the Chronology of Macedonian Shield Types*

Matthew, C.: *An Invincible Beast, Understanding the Hellenistic Pike Phalanx at War*

Matthew, C.: *A Storm of Spears, Understanding the Greek Hoplite at War*

Romanelli: *Topographica Antiqua: III*

Roth, J.: 'The Size and Organisation of the Imperial Roman Legion', *Historia: Zeitschrift für Alte Geschichte Bd. 43*

Sekunda, N.: *Army of Alexander*

Sekunda, N.: *Macedonian Armies after Alexander 323–168 BC*

Sheppard, R.: *Alexander the Great at War*

Simon Timothy James: *The Arms and Armour from Dura-Europos, Syria : Weaponry Recovered from the Roman Garrison Town and the Sassanid Siegeworks during the Excavations, 1922–37*

Tarn, W.W.: *Military and Naval Developments*

Taylor, M.J.: 'The Attalid victory at Magnesia on a lost plaque from Pergamon,' *Anatolian Studies*, 66

Taylor, R.: 'Pushing in Greek Infantry Formations', *Slingshot 311*

Thegn Thrand: https://www.youtube.com/watch?v=U5E1vKsDUBo

Thompson, M.: *Granicus 334 BC: Alexander's First Persian Victory*

Index

Accensi, 214, 215, 232–4, 237

Achaemenid army, xviii, 1, 12, 35, 73–4, 84–5, 91, 101, 120, 124, 131, 134, 141–2, 177–9, 185, 188, 191–3, 210, 280

Achilles Painter amphora, 89, 91

Aelian, ix, 1, 2, 5, 10, 14, 21, 31–2, 35, 45, 49, 50, 62–3, 73, 82, 97, 152–4, 156, 185, 192, 203–205, 211–13, 278

Aetius, 283–4

Agema, 169, 172–5, 177–9, 183–4, 211–13

Agesilaus, xvii, 105–106, 127–9, 134–5

Alexander I, 141, 143

Alexander II, 140–1, 143, 149

Alexander III the Great, ix, xix, 3, 75, 82–3, 120, 124, 140, 151–4, 160, 162–4, 168–72, 174–86, 188, 191, 193, 209–13, 280, 282–3

Alexander mosaic, 151–2, 210

Amyntas, father of Philip II, 149

Anaximenes of Lampsacus, 140

Ankyle, 63, 86

Antelabe, 95, 157, 159

Antepilani, 214, 232–3

Antigonus III Doson, 137, 139, 209

Archaeology, ix, xi, 143, 241

Archers, xiii, 22, 63–5, 70–1, 79, 120, 131, 168, 170–1, 174–5, 212, 218, 242, 266, 280

Argyraspides, 169–70, 207

Aristotle, 106
 Physics, 272
 Scholia on Euripides' Rhesus, 148

Armoured heavy cavalry, *see* Cataphracts

Arrian, ix, 1–2, 154
 Array Against the Alans, 242
 Anabasis of Alexander, 75, 83, 135, 151–2, 154, 164, 169, 174–9, 182–3, 186, 191, 209–13, 285
 Tactics, 6, 35, 40, 53, 57, 82–3, 187, 203–204, 254

Artaxerxes, 73, 74

Arthaśāstra of Kauṭilya, 1, 78, 79

Ash wood, 90, 152, 155–6, 210

Asklepiodotus, ix, 1–2, 5–7, 10, 21–2, 24, 35–7, 42, 45, 57, 62, 71, 73, 82, 104, 133, 135, 152–4, 156, 163, 184, 192, 203–204, 211–13, 278, 285

Aspis, *see* Hoplite shield

Athens, xvii, 104, 106, 144, 154, 170, 218
 Athenian taxiarch, 106
 Athenian taxis, 106

Attila, 284

Baggage, 9–13, 163, 180, 258–60

Balkan tribes, 131, 162

Bardunias, Paul, 96, 111, 113, 121, 124–6, 133–5

Belisarius, 283

Boeotarch, 106, 277

Boeotia, 13, 105–106, 209, 218

Brasidas, 144–5

Breastplate, 131, 157, 206, 253–4, 275

Caesar, 242–3, 246, 259–60, 277–8, 281